T0321499

INSIDE THE BLOODY CHAMBER

Christopher Frayling

INSIDE THE BLOODY CHAMBER

ON ANGELA CARTER, THE GOTHIC
AND OTHER WEIRD TALES

OBERON BOOKS
LONDON

WWW.OBERONBOOKS.COM

First published in 2015 by Oberon Books Ltd
521 Caledonian Road, London N7 9RH
Tel: +44 (0) 20 7607 3637 / Fax: +44 (0) 20 7607 3629
e-mail: info@oberonbooks.com
www.oberonbooks.com

A catalogue record for this book is available from the British Library.

PB ISBN: 9781783198214
E ISBN: 9781783198207

Cover and book illustrations © Andrzej Klimowski

For Edward and the Saturday morning circle

Contents

1

Introduction

THE NOVELIST ANGELA CARTER died of lung cancer in February 1992 at the age of 51 – so we are approaching the 25th anniversary of her shockingly early passing. Since 1992, her reputation – as writer and thinker – has soared, to the point where her collection of re-imagined folk and fairytales for the modern age, *The Bloody Chamber and other stories* – re-imagined with sympathy, wonder, excess and filtered through a sharp critical mind – is now a school set text in England, and is taught on many university-level literature courses worldwide. There are M.A. programmes entirely devoted to her writings: Carter Studies. Her complete works have been printed and reprinted over the last quarter-century, and films – *The Company of Wolves* (1984), *The Magic Toyshop* (1987) – and plays – such as *Nights at the Circus* (Kneehigh, 2006) – have been derived from them. Her influence on 'the contemporary Gothic', on current readings of fairytales, and on feminist literature of the magical realist kind has been both wide-ranging and profound, even though she was – as Marina Warner has rightly pointed out – 'more independent-minded than the traditional feminists of her time'.

I knew Angela very well, when she lived in Bath in the 1970s, and when her key works – *Fireworks*, *The Bloody Chamber*, *The Sadeian Woman*, *The Passion of New Eve*, her *New Society* essays on contemporary culture – were being written. I was researching and writing my study of *The Vampyre* in literature at this time, as well as completing a doctorate on eighteenth-century French literature including the novels of Rousseau, Laclos and Sade. And so we shared a lot of conversations, ideas and inspirations, often at the very witching hour. In fact, one of the stories in *The Bloody Chamber – The Lady of the House of Love*, the first to be written – is loosely based on a research visit I made to Transylvania at that time; I became 'Hero', a fine upstanding public school chap ('a hero out of the *Boys' Own Paper* circa 1914') who encounters all sorts of erotic surprises as he travels...and who in the end destroys the vampire countess 'by the innocence of his kiss'. Angela published *New Eve* on the same day as *The Vampyre*, both with Victor Gollancz or 'Gollys' as she liked to call them. Our perspectives were different, but the subject-matter was shared territory.

Starting with a long essay, a memoir of 'Angela and me', this collection gathers, reprints and updates some of the various articles and public lectures I have written since the 1970s on aspects of the Gothic and fantasy – several in hard-to-find places, some never published before. The subjects loosely match Angela's interests – mirrored in the stories within the collection *The Bloody Chamber* – and they also mesh with my memories of the 1970s in Bath: experiences of opera and art exhibitions, of films and performances, discussions about folklore and fairytale today, readings of critically neglected texts and questions about the accepted hierarchies of high and low. These essays – and the stories – include a wolf, a vampire, a spectral beast, a retelling of *Beauty and the Beast*, an erotic-horrific painting, and a piece of music by the composer of *Faust* which tells of the death of a marionette. The memories, and the cast of characters, are why I have called this collection *Inside the Bloody Chamber*. Angela's stories are about wolves and lambs, leopards and kids, carnivores and herbivores, latent desire and anxiety, romance and bawdy humour – and they are variations on the theme of the lion and the lamb reaching some kind of mutual understanding rather than the one always tearing the other to pieces. On the whole, the lamb is expected to join the lion's side, but sometimes vice versa. They are also a challenge to traditional consolatory myths about the role of women – embodied in traditional interpretations of fairytales: women who seem to connive in their own servitude. At their heart – as several critics have pointed out – is latent desire reinterpreted from a young woman's point of view, and the search for a workable sense of self.

So in 'The Tiger's Bride', one of the stories, the virginal heroine discovers that she, too, is an animal and all the better for that. In the three wolf stories – 'The Werewolf', 'The Company of Wolves' and 'Wolf-Alice' – the little girl discovers, in different ways, that she is 'meat for no one', she takes control by refusing to be frightened, and she learns that there is much more to life than 'eat or be eaten'; also, that being a victim is not much fun. She comes in the process to a particularly useful realisation: that some wolves are hairy on the inside. 'I'm nobody's meat, not I!'

In the title story, Bluebeard meets his match in the form of the heroine's formidable mother, who has spent time shooting man-eating tigers in Indochina. And in 'The Courtship of Mr Lyon', the beast is transformed into a herbivorous human being by the power of mutual love, which conquers stereotyping and aggression.

So the stories include three wolves, three cats and a vampire – as Margaret Attwood has wittily pointed out, they are organised by categories of meat-eater, from cats ('sleepily cruel by nature') across the bloody spectrum to wolves ('fearful of gift rather than plunder'). Angela evidently enjoyed provoking the vegans and vegetarians of alternative Bath, just down the road from her house...

Angela and me is expanded from a lecture given at the Watershed in Bristol (May 2012) based partly on Angela's notebooks kept in the British Library manuscripts department, mainly on personal reminiscences. In the audience for the lecture were several of Angela's acquaintances from her Bristol days – and some graduates of her creative writing classes. There was a lively discussion.

Freud's Nightmare is a scholarly article about Henry Fuseli's famous painting of 1781 – a reproduction of which hung in Sigmund Freud's waiting room in Vienna. I went with Angela to the Tate's big *Fuseli* exhibition in April 1975, and often discussed with her Freud, the uncanny and fairytales (especially Bruno Bettelheim's study of the uses of enchantment). Also Fuseli's various versions of Titania awakening from her dream, surrounded by sinister fairies. I subsequently, in February to May 2006, co-curated *Gothic Nightmares – Fuseli, Blake and the Romantic Imagination* at Tate Britain. *Freud's Nightmare* has been adapted from a presentation to an interdisciplinary conference on *Fear*, at Trinity College Dublin, originally given on 19 May 2006. The proceedings were published by Four Courts Press, Dublin (eds. Kate Hebblethwaite and Elizabeth McCarthy) the following year and the article is reproduced with the permission of Four Courts Press.

The Funeral March of a Marionette started life as an article in an Italian catalogue for an exhibition (July to September 2002) in Madonna di Campiglio about the life and work of Alfred Hitchcock: *Hitchcock – Brividi di Carta* (ed. Roberto Festi, Stampalith, 2002). The essay refers to the music of Charles Gounod, puppets, the music-hall, short stories and the macabre – all of them, as it happens, at the heart of either *The Bloody Chamber* or *Wise Children*. The article has been expanded and revised for this collection.

The House That Jack Built was originally a chapter in (ed.) Sylvana Tomaselli and Roy Porter: *Rape: an historical and social enquiry* (Blackwell, Oxford, 1986), a collection which was selected as one of the 1987 notable books of the year by the *New York Times Book Review*. It then turned into my television documentary *Shadow of the Ripper* (1988). Angela Carter's interest in the Whitechapel murders arose from her admiration for the film *Pandora's Box* and the two Wedekind plays on which it was based. In some ways, her story *The Bloody Chamber* fuses Perrault's tale with the fin de siècle world of *Lulu*. The article is reproduced with the permission of Blackwell.

Home Counties Transylvania – an essay centred on Terence Fisher's seminal film version of *Dracula* (1957) – locates Hammer-land in a late-1950s cultural context and questions some of the recent, anachronistic claims made about it by over-enthusiastic critics. It explores how and why the reputation of 'the Gothic' has so radically changed over the last quarter-century – and how, ironically, it is now firmly lodged within 'the heritage'. *Home Counties Transylvania* began as a paper for the conference *It Came From the 1950s – popular culture, popular anxieties*, held at Trinity College Dublin in May 2008. The proceedings were published by Palgrave Macmillan (eds. Darryl Jones, Elizabeth McCarthy and Bernice Murphy) in 2011. The essay was originally called 'Hammer's Dracula', and is reproduced with the permission of Palgrave Macmillan.

Disney and the Beast is adapted from an article in *The Sunday Times Culture* magazine, published a year after the release of the Walt Disney film, on 11 October 1992. The Disney version owes a lot to Jean Cocteau's film of 1946, which was one of Angela's all-time favourites – and the image of the heroine has noticeably moved with the times, a whole world away from *Snow White*, *Cinderella* and *The Sleeping Beauty*. As Angela once put it, in response to a question on radio's *Woman's Hour* about the role of females in traditional fairytales: 'you couldn't say that the Sleeping Beauty was a figure full of get up and go,' could you...?

Nothing But a Hound Dog was originally delivered as one of the annual 'Baker Street Irregulars Distinguished Lectures', in New York, January 2008, given to the Sherlock Holmes Society in London, October 2009, and subsequently published in *The Baker Street Journal*. It is based on Arthur Conan Doyle's unpublished pocket diary for 1901, which includes the time spent writing *The Hound of the Baskervilles* and Doyle's whistle-stop visit to Dartmoor, discoveries which postdate my *Introduction* to the Penguin Classics edition. In the mid-1970s, before *The Bloody Chamber* was published, Angela Carter – a Bristol graduate whose first novels were set in the city – was considered by several critics to be 'a West Country author': and she liked writing about furry, carnivorous creatures with blazing eyes...

Peter and the Wolf began as an introduction to live performances with orchestra of Suzie Templeton's now-classic animated film (2006-7). It was then adapted to become a BBC Radio 4 *Archive Hour*

(Christmas 2014), about how this 'symphonic fairytale' has radically changed its meaning over time since the première in Stalin's Moscow, April 1936. Angela wrote her own distinctive version of *Peter*, included in the collection of stories *Black Venus* (1985) – where the focus is as much on the she-wolf as on the young goatherd who finds her. Angela's draft version of the screenplay for *The Company of Wolves* (July 1983) includes *Peter and the Wolf* as one of its many tributary stories – which did not survive to the final version. It is told to the resourceful Rosaleen, by the handsome hunter, in the forest: in his version of the tale, it is an old woman rather than Peter who discovers the she-wolf and her secret.

We Live in Gothic Times, in an earlier version, was part of my *Introduction* to *The Gothic Reader – a critical anthology* (ed. Martin Myrone, consultant editor Christopher Frayling, Tate Publishing, 2006), which accompanied the Tate's *Gothic Nightmares* exhibition. It included a wide range of extracts from Gothic texts and commentaries from the publication of Horace Walpole's *The Castle of Otranto* through to modern times. The essay is reproduced with the permission of Tate Publishing.

Since the 1970s, when Angela Carter was preparing *The Bloody Chamber*, attitudes towards the Gothic – in academe, wider commentary and popular culture – have changed utterly, and a terrible beauty has been born. The horror movie – and the superhero comic – have taken over from the Western as the bread-and-butter of Hollywood production. Interviewed by Kim Evans for the BBC television documentary 'Angela Carter's Curious Room' in the last months of her life – it was her final piece of work – she recalled that some critics had questioned her continuing obsession with metaphor, masks, magic and hyperbole, challenging the clichés by exaggerating them beyond the real. Her reply was:

> I would really like to have had the guts and the energy and so on to be able to write about people having battles with the DHSS. But I haven't. I've done other things. I mean, I'm an

arty person. Okay, I write overblown, purple, self-indulgent prose. So fucking what…

It was important for her to react against 'the tyranny of good taste', against the modern tendency to treat fairytales as nothing more than 'consolatory nonsense', and against the dominance within the literary establishment of a conventional realist aesthetic. Also to find a point of contact with 'the imagination of the ordinary men and women whose labour created our world'. Today, she has posthumously entered the literary mainstream – although whether that would have made her feel less embattled is a moot point. 'Alienated is the only way to be, after all.'

As she also liked to observe, 'we are living in Gothic times'.

We certainly are…

2

Angela and me: a literary friendship

THE CITY OF BATH is chock-full of monuments to the great British tradition of literature, theatre and the visual arts in the eighteenth and nineteenth centuries: little bronze plaques with scrolls, put up in late Victorian and Edwardian times, attached to the fronts of Georgian dwellings like solid theatre programmes announcing the names above the title. Writers, artists, actors and beautiful people of the day. Jane Austen at number 4, Sydney Place; Henry and Sarah Fielding at Widcombe Lodge; Charles Dickens at 35, St. James's Square; Walter Scott at 6, South Parade; and where painting is concerned Thomas Gainsborough at 17, The Circus – a couple of doors away from Clive of India. Plus, of course, the impresario and style guru Beau Nash – the character of whom Angela Carter wrote: he was 'surely one of the most boring men who ever lived – boring and totalitarian – a veritable Stalin of good taste'. His plaque is next to the Theatre Royal.

These weathered metal monuments are distributed, like cultural armour plating, protecting the citadel in the valley. Early in 1975, I had a long conversation with my good friend Angela Carter about the assumptions which were buried behind the plaques. We had both been reading Roland Barthes' *Mythologies* and John Berger's recently published *Ways of Seeing*; the visual language of signs was in the ether. Angela was, as she put it, busy 'looking at things very, very carefully and writing about them' – and I had just been reading, at her suggestion, Virginia Woolf's *A Room of One's Own* with its famous comments on the catalogue of the British Museum's old Reading Room – under the heading 'W for Women': 'Shakespeare's opinion of...'; 'Dean Inge's opinion of...'; 'Dr. Johnson's opinion of...'; 'Pope's opinion of...'; and so on. Not to mention 'small size of brain of...' and 'physical inferiority of...'. 'Why,' wrote Virginia Woolf with feigned surprise, 'are women, judging from this catalogue, so much more interesting to men than men are to women?' Her point, some forty years before Michel Foucault, was about how archives and classifications reflect the times in which they are compiled; about the worldliness of the arts, and structures of power. As Angela wrote in her notebook at around this time: 'everything is a signifier, everything is a sign, everything is an evocation of another reality'.

In the case of Bath, the reality of the late 1890s and the Edwardian era, when many of the metal plaques went up. The first 45 plaques were installed in 1898, part of the rebranding of Bath as a tasteful heritage city.

Why, we asked that afternoon, was Thomas De Quincey not considered worthy of a plaque, when he lived most of his childhood at 6, Green Park? Was it because he wrote *The Confessions of an English Opium-Eater*, and Bath never forgave him for it? Or why not the radical journalist John Wilkes, for that matter, who stayed six doors away from Walter Scott's dwelling in South Parade – though not at the same time. Why were there so many plaques dedicated to people who had just dropped in for the weekend? And why was there a plaque at what used to be 18, Brock Street – just off Royal Crescent – to one John Christopher Smith: 'Here dwelt John Christopher Smith, Handel's friend and secretary'.

What it should *really* have said, observed Angela, was 'Here dwelt John Christopher Smith, sycophantic arse-licker'. Or rather, as she preferred to call it, practitioner of 'anal lavage'. But above all, where on earth was the plaque to Mary Shelley, author of *Frankenstein* – who didn't just drop in, or eat the occasional Bath Bun at Sally Lunn's; she actually *wrote* the bulk of her novel in the centre of the city.

For although the creation scene of *Frankenstein* had first been told by Mary Godwin (as she then was) on the night of 17 or 18 June 1816 – as part of the famous ghost story session in a holiday villa overlooking Lake Geneva which also involved Lord Byron, Percy Shelley, Clare

Clairmont and Dr. John Polidori – she turned the story into a full-length novel between October 1816 and February 1817 in Bath. While Mary Godwin elaborated on her fireside idea of a young scientist who engages in spare-parts surgery – by adding Victor Frankenstein's education at Ingolstadt, explorer Robert Walton's letters on his expedition to the North Pole and the creature's autobiography – she was simultaneously being given tuition in drawing and painting (by a 'Mr. West'), developing her interest in popular science by attending talks by Dr. Wilkinson in the lecture rooms on Kingston Parade, and experiencing intense pressure from her father William Godwin to get married to Percy Shelley – which she did at the end of 1816.

It seemed to us, therefore, that the Bath environment might well have had a profound influence on the final shape of *Frankenstein*.

So I wrote a letter, on Bath university-headed paper, to Bath City Council, with Angela's blessing, suggesting that they commission and install a metal plaque 'Frankenstein was created here by Mary Shelley, 1816-1817' on the site of what used to be 5, Abbey Churchyard, just above the Roman Baths, which also housed a circulating library at the time.

In the event, the City Council remained unconvinced. They wrote back saying that there had been several requests in the past to put up a plaque on that same site to *Percy* Shelley – which they had turned down – and Mary Shelley to their mind had less of a claim than her husband. In any case, they added with an exclamation mark, hadn't *Frankenstein* become more to do with Hollywood than Bath – 'the book of the film, as it were!' The plaque would surely lower the tone in the City of Beau Nash and Jane Austen. 'We get many requests of that nature', etc. etc. The answer was no. 'We are sure you will understand. Yours sincerely.'

Looking back, the exchange of letters was about much more than just a bronze plaque: it was about the critical respectability of Jane Austen and Henry Fielding and Walter Scott and – in the mid-1970s – the continuing unrespectability of gothic novels and the many guilty pleasures to be had from them. Gothic novels were not quite pukka –

they were too stagy, used too many adjectives, were not to be taken seriously. They held up a curious, haunted mirror to the true-to-life mainstream of English literature – F.R. Leavis's 'great tradition' – and as for their authors, they certainly did not qualify for entry into Eng. Lit.'s almost all-male cricket eleven. Mary Shelley? – forget it. One of Angela's favourite lines at the time was from the Marquis de Sade: 'Art is the perfect immoral subversion of the established order'. Of *Frankenstein*, she wrote at Christmas 1976 that it was 'as much philosophic science fiction as horror story – in which the monster, far from being a figure of fun [as in the movies], is a tragic hero…'

At the time, in 1975, Angela encouraged me to write the letter for various reasons: because there were too many plaques devoted to 'the chaps' (as she liked to call them); because science fiction and fantasy literature were looked down upon, patronised, and put in a separate box marked 'cult' by the literary establishment – 'left out of conventional rankings and listings', when writers such as J.G. Ballard, Michael Moorcock, Brian Aldiss and Christopher Priest were among the best practitioners there were of 'novels of ideas', of 'arguments stated in fictional terms'; because she wanted to stick two fingers up to F.R. Leavis and the whole 'eat your broccoli' school of literary criticism on which she had been force-fed at university; and because Mary Shelley had been sidelined by her husband, through the condescension of posterity.

Abbey Churchyard was in front of Bath Abbey. Angela wrote this at the time:

> I get the most exquisite pleasure from walking through the abbey
> churchyard late at night, when the remorseless pigeons have
> scored their last crumbs and packed it in at last. You can glimpse
> the noble, lichened heads of the statues in the Roman Bath above
> the wall, tranquilly dissociating themselves from the right flank
> of the great church that might have been a cathedral but lost out
> to Wells at the last minute…the church that has the only funny
> façade of any church I know; stone ladders on either side of the

door, with angels climbing up to heaven on them, very sweet – sort of medieval Disney.

When first I looked closely at the Abbey – and the angels – I couldn't help noting that some of the angels were being sent back *down* the ladder – and that the faces of the committee men on high, who were presumably making the decisions about them, had been completely worn away over time from the soft Bath stone – like a faceless bureaucracy. This image later came to haunt me, when I became Chairman of the Arts Council of England. In fact, the staircases of angels on the West Front of the Abbey are a version of Jacob's Ladder from *Genesis* – with the angels linking heaven and earth – as reimagined by a 1500 Bishop of Bath called Oliver. The angels are 'rising and descending' like in Jacob's dream. This was of course the biblical story which inspired the hymn they were playing when the *Titanic* went down: 'Nearer, My God, to Thee'.

Angela Carter moved to Bath in 1972, after she had returned from her two-year residence in Japan, the year she divorced from Paul Carter. At first she stayed with Edward Horesh – a senior lecturer in economics at the University of Bath, whom she'd known since the early 1960s in Bristol days, when Edward had been secretary of the Bristol Film Guild – and then she moved in 1973 to Hay Hill, which she called 'a long thin narrow house in a pedestrian thoroughfare, or alley, of eclectic architectural style'. Eclectic, or rather 'Georgian-infill'. There she lived frugally, even allowing for her slightly puritanical taste for plain living. *The Infernal Desire Machines of Dr. Hoffman* was not selling well, and her royalties from Heinemann (her publisher from 1966 to 1970) amounted in November 1973 to the princely sum of £8.96p. Her essays for *New Society*, the *New Statesman* and the *Radio Times* and on one occasion *Cosmopolitan* – forerunners of the culture and style journalism of today – were a lifeline. In the *Radio Times*, she was billed as 'herself a novelist based in the West Country', a regional novelist from Bristol and Bath. After the broadcast of her radio play *Vampirella* in 1976, she was promoted to 'specialist in horror literature'. I can remember when she came back from London, furious and hurt, after interviewing Iris Murdoch for the *Radio Times*, because her interviewee had asked, at the end of the conversation, 'and what do *you* do?' This was during the period which marked, as she later put it, 'the beginning of my obscurity. I went from being a very promising young writer [the Bristol period, after she graduated from the university there in 1965] to being completely ignored – in two novels'. Which was a slight exaggeration, but only slight. She called *The Passion of New Eve* 'my great bid for the European serious novel' – her own brand of philosophical science fiction – and noted ruefully that her bid was not accepted.

I can also remember how cold Hay Hill could sometimes be. On one occasion, in winter when she had no heat at all, she explained that she had bought a gas fire a while back, but that the men installing it had managed to break the thing and it would take several weeks to repair. Besides, it was no bad thing, she said, to be a bit healthily cold. Provided you wore layers of woollies.

Hay Hill is steep, a kind of hyphen between Lansdown Road and the Circus at the top end, and – past the Baptist church to George Street and over the road to Walcot – gateway to alternative Bath, at the bottom end. It was a hyphen she wrote about in two articles and spoke about often. On the one hand, the Bath of the Crescents, of famous historical characters – or some of them – a city built for pleasure at the high point of an architectural style, a monument to the taste of a certain class which – as she wrote – later became institutionalised as 'good taste'. A bad place to feel sad in, built as it was for the headlong pursuit of pleasure 'which accounts for its ineradicable melancholy'. Like Monte Carlo, or Las Vegas, out of season and with real stone columns. On the other hand, there was subterranean Bath, a place of dishevelled loveliness, some of it half-pulled-down, where dwelt 'occultists, neo-Platonists, yogis, theosophists, little old ladies who have spirit conversations with Red Indian squaws, religious maniacs, senile dements, natural-lifers, macrobiotics, people who make perfumed candles, kite-flyers, do you believe in fairies?' She liked to say that there were a lot of follies in

Bath, and only some of them were architectural ones. Most of them were made of flesh and blood. Nutters had been coming to Bath in their droves since Regency times, to take the waters and gamble away their patrimonies. By the way, the little old ladies and Indian squaws probably came from the film *Night of the Demon* rather than real life. What the hell…those nice Psychical Research people did have an office at the end of Pulteney Street.

Where the Crescents above Hay Hill were concerned, she found Royal Crescent pretentious and self-regarding – 'it makes its pompous and baroque statement across half a hillside, generally giving the impression of knowing just how enormous an architectural occasion it is' – and much preferred Lansdown Crescent, further up the hill, 'a calm eyebrow of stone with before it a sloping meadow', an urbane terrace nestling in a convincing imitation of pastoral seclusion. She compared *this* Bath with a stage set, a place of theatrical splendour, an exquisite back-projection best enjoyed from a horse-drawn carriage rather than a fast-moving car. I can remember talking to her about the front and the back of Royal Crescent. The front – a soft yellow façade, with the strange two-dimensional quality of a dreamscape. The back – with its shantytown of loos and bathrooms and ductwork, stuck on in the nineteenth century, a history of plumbing. The skull beneath the skin. The contrast was a bit like Abbey Churchyard, populated in the daytime not just by visitors to the Abbey and Pump Room but by 'alkies – the people who have moved on from cider to meths, who sit among the pigeons ululating and singing and squabbling and panhandling the tourists'.

Such contrasts gave the city part of its charm, she wrote, in the late twentieth century. 'Charm – the fine-boned, blue-eyed, characteristic English madness; foreigners, who see the charm *and* the madness at the same time, tend to diagnose the combination as hypocrisy'. In Bath, the beautiful people – and rich and famous, the people of taste and fashion – coexisted with the *other* beautiful people. These included at one time or another the earnest arts workshop organisers, the craftspeople, the tattooists, the street marketeers, the flute-players, the émigrés from Notting Hill, the performers and exhibitors in Walcot Village Hall – an old church hall which reopened for arts and community events in April 1975 – the people who placed ads seeking good homes for vegetarian kittens, the people who put notices in the health-food shop offering their organic garbage free to any needy goat, the promotion of Walcot as a kind of nascent Left Bank, the landlord in The Bell (one of her locals) who loved jazz and had a jukebox with Miles Davis and Bix Beiderbecke on it – and who served draught cider which 'you can actually feel making contact with your central nervous system: it's marvellous'. Plus there were the recently arrived students, since Bath had gained university status – Angela went back to College of Advanced Technology days in Bristol, where she taught General Studies to the mathematicians: 'who is this person?' the lecturer in maths had asked Edward Horesh, 'who is teaching them all to smoke pot?' – very unlikely actually, but he may have been speaking metaphorically. Angela was not sure whether the City of Bath had ever really accepted the University, built out of sight just over one of the hills and specialising in science and technology.

These beautiful people – together – were, she wrote, getting the heart of the old place beating again. And they were coming closer and closer. Squatters had moved in next door to her in Hay Hill. 'They used to walk their dog on my roof, gaining access from a convenient window. When they left, they chalked "Cheerio Bath!" in bright-blue letters on the front of the mansion they'd briefly tenanted.' She enjoyed their company.

I arrived in Bath in October 1973, as a lecturer at the University in the history of ideas – and for a time lived way out in the village of Stoney Littleton, then in Raby Place at the bottom of Bathwick Hill. I was 26 and Angela was 33. I had just completed my Cambridge doctorate on Jean-Jacques Rousseau's novel, written in epistolary form, *Julie, ou La Nouvelle Héloïse* – a runaway bestseller in eighteenth-century Europe – and how this, rather than his more overtly political works *Du Contrat Social* and *Discours sur l'inégalité*, was the way in which most readers encountered Rousseau's ideas. Including some of the revolutionary leaders. There were comments in the thesis about the writers who had explicitly 'replied' to Rousseau's novel. There was Laclos with *Les Liaisons Dangereuses* (that's why he wrote it, also as an epistolary novel), which took the same epigraph as *La Nouvelle Héloïse* – 'I have seen the manners of my time and I have published these letters' – only to make it sound much more cynical. And the Marquis de Sade with *Justine, or the Misfortunes of Virtue* – about Justine and her wicked sister Juliette – and *La Nouvelle Justine* – the titles deliberately echoing Rousseau's – which argued that virtue just gets you into trouble in a nasty world, and that being a helpless victim is of no use at all: Justine *and* Juliette draw attention in their different ways to the tyranny of manmade projections onto women, by authors such as Rousseau. De Sade had a copy of *La Nouvelle Héloïse* with him in the asylum at Charenton when he was banged up for something they called 'sexual dementia' in 1803.

I also arrived with a half-finished book on the vampire theme in nineteenth-century literature – and a suitcase full of books and xeroxes on the subject – an interest which arose for me from the reactions of the philosophers of the Enlightenment to an apparent epidemic of vampirism which had broken out in Eastern Europe in the mid-eighteenth century, and which started the whole vampire craze in modern literature. Also, I'd grown up with Hammer Films. One of the first things Angela noticed about me was that I was born on Christmas Day – the day of werewolves, but also (later) of the resourceful Beauty in the story *The Tiger's Bride*. And in a certain light, my eyebrows met in the middle.

So Angela and I had a lot to talk about. Edward had a colour television – which Angela had encouraged him to buy – and the three of us would congregate a couple of evenings a week, to have supper and watch television, go to the pictures or to the opera in Bristol. We went to *The Magic Flute* – Angela wrote in her journal: 'The Queen of the night's sermon': her vampire Countess would be called 'queen of the

night' – and to Verdi's *Falstaff*, after which we fantasised about Falstaff
as a liberal education for Prince Hal – the University of the Boar's Head
Tavern – and what if Prince Charles had a Falstaff to initiate *him* – and
what if Henry V had said to the fat old man at his coronation, 'now
let's *really* have some changes around here' instead of 'I know thee not,
old man'. We went to Weber's 1821 opera *Der Freischütz/The Marksman*,
with its famous scene in the Wolf's Glen – first of the major gothic operas
and an influence on the young Wagner – and talked about transposing
it to the Wild West as a kind of Satanic Western, in which the seventh
bullet in a magic six-shooter would belong to the devil and there would
be a climactic gunfight in a graveyard like in *The Good, The Bad and
The Ugly*, which we also saw, as well as *Pat Garrett and Billy the Kid* –
which she liked a lot, for its strangely anarchic vision of society in the
borderland – and assorted Italian Westerns. This Satanic Western, out
of *Der Freischütz*, eventually turned into Angela's play *Gun for the Devil*.
There was Wagner's *The Flying Dutchman* – Angela's beautiful vampire
Countess would soon believe herself to be living out the myth with roles
reversed 'that she may be made whole by human feeling…with a kiss':
Angela particularly admired the last scene, where the angelic Senta the
Captain's daughter *wants* to join the devilish Dutchman, is excited by
the idea of running with the wolves – but is rejected by him because of a
misunderstanding about her fidelity. Another film she rated highly was
Albert Lewin's very odd fairytale *Pandora and the Flying Dutchman* with
Ava Gardner and James Mason. We watched together J.K. Galbraith's
big BBC TV series about economics round about that time – which had
Karl Marx as the Flying Dutchman (soundtrack by Wagner), sailing
from place to place pursued by his inner demons and the four winds,
until he finally settled in London and a seat in the Reading Room of the
British Museum. And we went to Bristol to see *The Marriage of Figaro*.
On the way back in the car we had an animated argument about the
quality of Mozart's 'class analysis' in the opera, and in particular about
which social class Cherubino was supposed to belong to. He is Count
Almaviva's page, sent off to Seville on army duty to get him out of the

way, seems to be at home with the aristocracy – and yet he is forced to marry the peasant girl Barbarina at the end of Act 3.

Angela couldn't drive – Edward did try to do something about this by teaching her, but his good intentions ended up, sad to say, with Angela driving into a wall. So Edward would drive us to Bristol. When we gathered to watch television in Bath, she would walk from Hay Hill and I would sometimes drive her home.

I can't remember going to the theatre once with Angela in the 1970s; she claimed to have stopped going twenty years before, because classic British acting embarrassed her so much: 'Painted loons in the middle distance, making fools of themselves'. The mopping and mowing, the rolling of the eyes, the false facial hair, the fustian costumes, the irritable vowel syndrome, the middle-class audiences laughing at unfunny jokes – for her, mainstream theatre seemed synonymous with domineering actor-managers and their companies like Melchior Hazard and his dynasty in her *Wise Children*. She must have had some memorably bad experiences at the theatre in the 1950s. Ironically, since her death there have been some lively adaptations of stories from *The Bloody Chamber* for the stage.

She also said, when one of us mentioned the RSC, that she'd much prefer to see the Republican Jonson Theatre, the RJT, which would be considerably more edgy and subversive and *committed*. The so-called University Wits had higher brows, and 'Marlowe had really interesting things to say'. Some of her favourite lines came from the Duchess's seriously disturbed brother Ferdinand in John Webster's *The Duchess of Malfi*: 'the howling of the wolf is music to the screech-owl', and his exit line 'I'll go hunt the badger by owl-light. 'Tis a deed of darkness.' Ferdinand eventually succumbs to lycanthropia, which involves him haunting graveyards, digging up corpses and becoming hairy not on the outside but on 'the inside' – an idea Angela later channelled in *Wolf Alice*, where the necrophiliac Duke has a compulsion to frequent graveyards by night. And all because Ferdinand is in love with his sister. *The Duchess of Malfi* also included a tableau of bloody waxworks or 'feigned statues', an idea that always fascinated Angela. Where the self-taught Ben Jonson was concerned, she much admired his very stylish farewell to writing for the stage, 'safe from the wolf's black jaw, and the dull ass's hoof'. To say that she didn't enjoy going to the theatre is *not* to say that she didn't admire Shakespeare as text and Shakespeare as 'popular entertainer'. It was just that she was very uncomfortable with what had been made of his works on the modern stage. *The Bloody Chamber* collection is full of Shakespearian phrases – 'the beast with two backs', 'he said the owl was a baker's daughter', Juliet's tomb. But on the whole her imagination was certainly more Jacobean than Shakespearian. She would later refer to 'the culture of Shakespeare' – and how he was taught to young people – as turning him into a 'miserable, rotten, reactionary old fuddy-duddy'. And, she added mischievously, 'he was not, I think, terribly clever – but of course he was the great popular entertainer of all time'. Besides, the productions of his plays she had seen never remotely matched what her imagination had already made of Shakespeare's words.

In spring 1974, shortly after Angela had returned on the Trans-Siberian railway from Japan – this time on holiday, and to gather material for an article on a Fertility Festival – Edward, Angela and I went to see F.W. Murnau's 1922 silent film *Nosferatu*. It wasn't a particularly good quality print – it was the French cut of 1926: not tinted, so you couldn't tell which scenes were meant to take place at night and which in the daytime: night-time should have been tinted blue – but the film included one of the most beautiful intertitles of the whole silent era. It comes when the young hero Hutter is first met by the coach and horses from Castle Dracula: 'And when he crossed over the bridge, the phantoms came to meet him.' Angela wrote this phrase twice in her private journal and included it in her radio play *Vampirella*. It was her first written reference to vampires. That intertitle 'And when he crossed over the bridge' had as it happens also particularly appealed to André Breton and his Surrealist pals in late 1920s Paris: Breton called it 'the sentence I have never been able to see without a mixture of joy and terror'; and the phrase 'crossing over the bridge' to the dreamscape became something of a Surrealist mantra at the time. Angela was also much taken with the idea of 'the University of Uppsala', as in the little book by Hutter's bedside at the inn the night before he ventures to the Castle: she later wrote that this book must have been about 'the peculiar habits of the undead, an unpublished Ph.D. thesis lodged in cobwebs in the University of Uppsala since 1731.' For some reason, she thought 'the University of Uppsala' sounded hilariously funny. She was very taken with the scene where the vampire's elongated shadow-hand wrenches Frau Ellen's (or Nina's) heart, and she grimaces with pain. In *Nosferatu*, the pure Ellen (or Nina, depending on the print) must sacrifice herself to keep the vampire occupied until 'the first crowing of the cock'. She is 'inscribed in the corner of sleep…' like Senta in *The Flying Dutchman*.

At that stage, the title 'The Lady of the House of Love' was to have been used for a short story or poem set in Japan, after her 1974 visit – 'the lady of the house of love and the gangster of good fortune'. A bit later, it would become the title of her vampire story, adapted from *Vampirella*, the story which was published in summer/autumn 1975 in *Iowa Review*. I can remember clearly our conversations about *Nosferatu*. Angela borrowed my copy of the script, as well as assorted books about vampires in folklore and literature – all of which she copiously annotated: *The Natural History of the Vampire* by Anthony Masters; *The Romantic Agony* by Mario Praz – especially the sections on 'The Beauty of the Medusa' and 'The Fatal Man'; *La Musée des Vampires*, a strange collection with an emphasis on French necrophiliacs and erotic engravings, with much material on Gilles de Rais, the historical Bluebeard, and Henri Blot; *The Dracula Myth* by Gabriel Ronay (not Egon Ronay, though Angela relished the thought of a Good Food Guide for vampires); *Flesh and Blood* by Reay Tannahill; and *The Vampire: His Kith and Kin* by the eccentric mythographer of the undead the Rev. Montague Summers. We talked about the differences between the vampire of folklore and the vampire of fiction – the upward social mobility of the creature, who in literature was nearly always an aristo; about Sawney Beane the Midlothian cannibal and amateur anarchist who in the 1500s at the time of King James VI together with his ravenous and incestuous clan of children, including roaring girls who wielded clubs, would ambush passing coaches, drag the victims to a cave near Galloway, then enjoy a hearty family meal of, say, roast leg of Justice of the Peace to the sound of bagpipes – Angela's father was Scottish and – as she said – she always felt particularly Scottish when in the company of particularly English people ('my father never *seriously* lived in England'); about the poisoned tree that sprang from the loins of Vlad the Impaler, Vlad Dracula; about the lamiae, the seductive women of legend who could remove their eyes at will; about the changing physical appearance of the vampire in books and on the screen; about the vain vampire lady who can never see herself in a looking-glass – so unlike Snow White's wicked stepmother; about Sheridan Le Fanu's Irish gothic lesbian vampire story *Carmilla* and the bloody Countess Elizabeth Bathory, who had an Iron Maiden torture device constructed to her own design – and who kept the wrinkles at bay by bathing in the blood of virgins. And about how Karl Marx – always called 'Marx himself' in those days – made use of the vampire metaphor in *Das Kapital* to describe the destructive workings of capitalism, the master-slave relationship, and the concept of surplus labour. The phrase 'politically correct' hadn't been invented yet, but we often used 'ideologically sound', which I think came from Joseph Stalin and meant some one or thing toeing the party line. It was always said with a smile. We *didn't* discuss Anne Rice's *Interview with the Vampire*, by the way – whatever most of the literary commentators may say – for the simple reason that the book hadn't been published yet. We did, I remember, discuss whether Vlad Dracula was related to Prince Charles…

Angela wrote this in her *Journal*:

> And when he crossed over the bridge, the phantoms came to meet him.
> 'The Master is Coming!'
> 'The Master is Coming!'
> 'Do not dare to speak his name.'

And this:

> Nosferatu, with his coffin on his shoulder, his fingers like roots, tuberous fingers, the head is like a phallus, with one eye blacked out. Nosferatu at the window of his mansion; Nina at hers; Nosferatu is bent over Nina's body, like a Pietà – parody of a wedding night…a night-sized hallucination, a figure inscribed in the corner of sleep.

Angela made a line drawing of Nosferatu's face, to illustrate this penis with teeth. And she had a film still of the Count standing on the deck of his coffin-ship, the mast and rigging behind him, cut out and interleaved in her *Journal*.

Our viewing of *Nosferatu*, and the many conversations we subsequently had, stimulated Angela's growing interest in vampires – as folklore, as metaphor, as literary construct – and led indirectly to *Vampirella* and *The Lady of the House of Love*, the first story of the collection *The Bloody Chamber* to be written. To begin with, Angela was unsure about what to call the play and the story: *Scarlet Ceremony*; *House of Pleasure, House of Pain*; *Satanic Rhapsody* were all possibles. Then she wrote: 'horror comic superheroine VAMPIRELLA' – 'Vampirella', she later explained in *New Society*, 'the chunky-thighed, horrorzine superheroine with her scarlet garment cut to conceal her nipples while open at the navel'. From then on, that became the title of her radio play. 'I think I shall do a long novella,' she wrote at this time, 'called *Lola Montès* [that was another film we went to see together in late 1973 – Angela had seen it before – set in a circus ring, where the ringmaster invents a life for the celebrated courtesan, which we see contradicted in flashbacks] to go in a book…perhaps with the "Vampirella" story. No. Let's not bother about the book; a Lola Montès story anyway.' *The Loves of Lady Purple*, her short story, has something of *Lola Montès* in it – as would the novel *Nights at the Circus*: the public presentation of femininity: 'is she fact or is she fiction?'; 'how do we know *we* are not imitation human beings?' But *Vampirella* would come first.

Angela then, in her *Journal*, wrote what she called her 'image clusters' – the starting-points for the dense, compacted language of her stories:

the anguish of a sterile, lonely soul,

troubled with diseased imaginings.

claws and teeth are sharpened on centuries of corpses...

disastrous meteors heralded my parturition.

Godfather Dracula...

Note: Schreck is the German for 'terror' [Max Schreck played the character of Count Orlok, the Nosferatu of the title]. Doctor Schreck [he would later become Madame Schreck in *Nights at the Circus*].

women who can remove their eyes.

lapidary fingers: the wind always blows cold over graveyards.

And, eventually, the opening of the play – and its cast of characters – began to take shape:

'Can a bird sing only the song he knows, or can he learn a new song?'

Sad, lonely lady vampire in a castle, the Sleeping Beauty, the Lady of the House of Love.

'Can a bird sing only the song he knows or can he learn a new song,' said the lovely, lonely lady vampire whose hair fell down like tears as she rattled with a gold propelling pencil the bars of the cage in which her pet canary lived...

Later, the propelling pencil would become a long fingernail; the bird would become it rather than he and the canary would become just a bird. But Angela's first radio play, the starting-point of *The Bloody Chamber*, would always begin with the sound of something sharp rattling against the bars of a cage. This began life, she said, with a metallic sound effect: the running of a pencil along the top of a radiator, which to her sounded like 'a long, painted fingernail'. The phrase 'Can a bird sing only the song she knows' – which came to symbolise many things to her – was from 'a film adaptation of Dostoevsky'.

And next:

> Edwardian. Our hero on a bicycle tour of the Carpathians.

> Cast-list
>
> hero
>
> Vampirella
>
> Wardress
>
> peasants
>
> voices of   Elizabeth of Bathory (*sic*) ?
>
>   Gilles de Rais
>
>   Sawney Beane?

At this early stage, hero had a small 'h'. He would soon be given a big 'H'.

At precisely the same time, I was planning a research trip to the Carpathian Mountains in Romania – in the footsteps of Jonathan Harker in the novel *Dracula* – for a chapter in my vampire book. Not on a bicycle but in a hired car, a Dacia 13 or in English a Renault 12, with a notebook and camera on the back seat. As both play and story evolved, the hero became a dashing young chap out of *Boys' Own Paper* circa 1914, who goes on a cycling tour of the land beyond the forest. He is naïve and overly enthusiastic; has studied the good old English tradition of literature at university; looks as though he has 'the head of a lion';

still believes that demons can be redeemed with a kiss and also believes that words are facts – always a mistake in Angela's fiction. Hero has all sorts of erotic adventures in the Carpathians, which was a nice thought. At least, he *almost* does. When confronted by the cloistered vampire Countess in her dark glasses in her glittering castle – the strapping Hero tries to reassure himself by clinging onto the world of facts:

> Soon it will be morning; the crowing of the mundane cock and the first light will dissolve this Gothic dream with the solvent of the natural. Yes, perhaps I shall take her to Vienna; and we shall clip off her fingernails and take her to a good dentist, to deal with her fangs. Perhaps, perhaps…one day, when she is cured… mother, I want you to meet… There are some things that, even if they are true, we must not believe them.

In the end, what protects Hero from the Countess are not the traditional weapons of religion – holy water and the crucifix – or even of folklore and the old religion – garlic and a wooden stake – but the fact that he has been brought up to repress his imagination, and he simply doesn't recognise a bloodsucker when she is staring him in the face. He is not ignorant: he is unknowing. He knows too little while all about him know too much. Desire is best coped with by blessing 'the cold showers of my celibacy – Countess, keep your talons to yourself.' He hopes to cure her by the innocence of his virginal kiss, like in *Sleeping Beauty*. Then off he goes to die – this being August 1914 – in a war that turns out to be more ghastly by far than any superstitious imaginings. 'Next day,' as the story version briskly concludes, 'his regiment embarked for France.'

I can clearly remember talking to Angela about the effects of the First World War on political geography of the land of the Nosferatu – which at the beginning of the War was still on the outer edge of the Austro-Hungarian empire. In the radio play, 'the shadow of the Fatal Count rises over every bloody battlefield'. And also about 'haematodipsomania' – my word for the pathological thirst for blood; like alcoholism only much, much worse – where the drink must always be served at body temperature. I once said to her, just after my return from that motoring tour of Transylvania and Wallachia, 'I couldn't understand a word they were saying,' a line that went straight into the play. And more generally we discussed the vampire as dominance-dependence, and whether human relationships are sometimes 'about asset-stripping'. This became the very gloomy line: 'the shadow of the Fatal Count falls across every marriage bed'.

Hero combats such dark thoughts by concentrating on his bicycle:

Owl hoots, long, lonely sound. The bicycle wheels wobble, click against stone…

HERO. To ride a bicycle is in itself some protection against superstitious fears since the bicycle is the product of pure reason applied to motion. Geometry at the service of man! Give me two spheres and a straight line and I will show you how far I can take them. Voltaire himself might have invented the bicycle, since it contributes so much to man's well-being and nothing at all to his bane. Bicycling is beneficial to the health. The bicycle emits no harmful fumes and permits only the most decorous speeds. It is not a murderous implement.

Yet, like all the products of enlightened reason, the bicycle has a faint air of eccentricity about it. On two wheels in the Land of the Vampires! A suitable furlough for a member of the English middle classes…

Nobody is surprised to see me; they guess at once where I come from. The coarse peasants titter a little behind their hands. Le Monsieur Anglais! But they behave with deference; for only a man with an empire on which the sun never sets to support him would ride a bicycle through this phantom-haunted region.

Hoot of owl...

Now we approach a rustic bridge.

The wheels now rattle as they cross bridge – matching hero's mood.

Something atavistic, something numinous about crossing whirling dark water by no moonlight...

COUNT. (*Very softly.*) And when he crossed the bridge, the phantoms came to meet him...

In Angela's draft version of *Vampirella*, there is also an exchange towards the end of the play which may well have grown out of our strange conversations about Karl Marx and the vampire metaphor. Now that Transylvania has become part of a People's Republic, Eastern European Counts have become stateless persons, and thus legends. In the draft, there is a sudden time-shift forwards from 1914:

BOY. But when I grew up and joined the Party, the secretary told me the only true vampires were the landlords who sucked the blood of the peasantry for a thousand years, and only the clean hail from a machine gun would rid us of their depredations...

COMMISSAR. John Bull is Count Dracula! Uncle Sam is Count Dracula! The vampire of imperialism bestrides the world!

Brisk rendition of THE VAMPIRE TANGO.

But this was cut from the play as broadcast. It was a bridge too far. Marina Warner has suggested that *Vampirella* and *The Lady of the House of Love* may be partly about frustrated desire. If only Hero would let himself go, and allow himself to cross the bridge! Looking back, I am sure there is some truth in this. She has also written of my 'boyish enthusiasm that Angela Carter catches in *The Lady in the House of Love...*'; in the story, 'the beautiful vampire heroine was hoping to suck his blood, but instead meets her doom at his *insouciant* hands'. At the time, when

Angela presented me with the typescript of the play and story, I tended to interpret the story partly through Hero's eyes. And I was a little upset that Hero's greatest protection is his inability to recognise any of the signs. 'Thanks, Angie!' I said to her. But Hero's is of course not at all the author's point of view... The vampire Countess is also protected by her formidable housekeeper Mrs Beane (cue bagpipes) in the play, 'an old mute' in the story; Count Dracula is her father in the play, he almost disappears from the story... 'The narrative line of the short story,' she later explained, 'did not have sufficient space to discuss the nature, real or imagined, of vampirism, nor did it have sufficient imaginative space to accommodate cameo guest appearances by the Scottish cannibal Sawney Beane, with his bagpipes and his ravenous children, nor the unrepentant necrophile Henri Blot... Even Vampirella's father Count Dracula bowed out'.

Angela was kind enough to ask Liz Calder, her editor at Victor Gollancz from 1976 onwards – actually, Liz has recently called it 'an instruction' – to read the manuscript of my book *The Vampyre: Lord Ruthven to Count Dracula*. It was published on the same day as Angela's *The Passion of New Eve* in the short-lived series 'Gollancz Fantasy and Macabre', which was later to include *The Bloody Chamber*. The problem in 1976 was, apparently, that the salespeople and librarians thought of Gollancz books as always yellow-jacketed – rather than in spooky black and red. So the books weren't distributed as widely as they might have been. Angela wrote to me on publication day: 'Congratulations, me old fruit, and here's to the next time... PS *Kaleidoscope* [a BBC radio evening arts programme], too, eh? Lots of love.' She also wrote, following a spiky review: 'don't fret over the *Guardian* review; Pxxxx Rxxxxxxx is a well-known loony, who howls and bleeds when the moon is full. Lots of love.' She always felt she should be attracting more attention from the media, for example from Russell Harty – then a mid-evening television chat show host who knew her brother Hugh. But apart from occasional and usually disconcerting appearances on radio and television, it was not to be. Soundbites were not at all her thing. And she liked long pauses.

In one of the earliest drafts of her vampire play, Angela wrote of the opening:

Cage of blackbirds and clockwork toys.

She was fascinated by puppets, toy theatres, Punch & Judy, china dolls (of which she kept a couple on her shelf in Hay Hill, near the little Craven A poster of a black cat), shams, simulacra, copies and automata – about which she planned at one stage to write a *New Society* article ('try V&A, Horniman Museum', she noted). She had already written the short story 'The Loves of Lady Purple', about an Asiatic professor and his automaton Lady Purple, the Venus of the Orient. Partly I think her fascination had to do with the artificial – beneath the mannequin masks of femininity were there yet more masks, and what then, she wondered: was the *appearance* of femininity in fact part of its essence, or was it yet another form of mimicry? What was image and self-fashioning, and what wasn't? She would sometimes 'remake' herself for social occasions: I remember a party in Stoney Littleton when she wore scarlet lipstick, a brightly-coloured dress, and arranged her hair specially – when everyone else was in jeans, slacks and shirts. She danced the African 'High Life' – not at all characteristic of her. Beneath the warpaint, she was very self-conscious about some aspects of her appearance. The different 'images' on the covers of her books – from young anarchist in wire glasses, anorak and short hair; to romantic Pre-Raphaelite with sidelong glance; to (later) public intellectual with deliberately grey hair when the red dye stopped; all were a succession of masks. Which was the real her? What did the masks say about her? She, too, was in some ways expert in self-fashioning and hyper-aware of it too.

Her fascination with artificial people was partly about puppet-masters and puppets as well, as an image of patriarchal society – although she wouldn't have put it like that. Bluebeard is likened to a puppet-master in *The Bloody Chamber*. Another favourite line at the time, often quoted, was from the social philosopher Theodor Adorno: 'the feminine character, and the idea of femininity on which it is modelled, are products of masculine society.' Her fascination was also about those eighteenth-century thinkers who tried hard to prove that we are just soft machines or meat puppets (Vaucanson's celebrated wooden digesting duck, which ate biscuits and then apparently excreted them onto the floor, convinced some of them – including the royal family at Versailles). And then there was her love of E.T.A. Hoffmann's story *The Sandman*, about the infatuation of the student Nathaniel for the dancing automaton Olimpia, designed and constructed by the evil Coppelius (she always called him Dr Coppelius) with his magic telescope, ably assisted by Professor Spalanzini – a story which was turned into the ballet *Coppélia* by Delibes and the opera *The Tales of Hoffmann* by Jacques Offenbach in 1880. Sigmund Freud put *The Sandman* – and the idea of 'a living doll' – at the centre of his essay on *The Uncanny*, which Angela read in the mid-1970s, together with Freud's *Lectures on Psychoanalysis*. Christopher Isherwood and Don Bachardy's version of *Frankenstein: The True Story*, which was broadcast on BBC television at Christmas 1976, particularly interested her because it added to the cast-list 'a perfect female creation', a dancing creature played by Jane Seymour 'who,' she wrote excitedly, 'is something like the beautiful automaton in *The Tales of Hoffmann*'.

There's something faintly sinister, Angela wrote in her *Journal*, in the utter silence and unresponsiveness of the doll – which confronts the child, for the first time in its life, with the horror of empty space and loneliness. Sinister and attractive. On the other hand, as Honeybuzzard says in the early novel *Shadow Dance*: 'I'd like to have a cupboard bulging with all different bodies and faces.' And, of course, as early as 1967 she had written *The Magic Toyshop*, her second novel and her most popular so far, in which the ogre Uncle Philip much prefers the company of puppets to his more challenging relations. Angela was intrigued by variations on the legend of Leda and the Swan, and in *The Magic Toyshop* Philip recruits the heroine Melanie to play the part of Leda, and be molested on stage by his puppet swan. There was indeed a life-sized solid-silver swan automaton, made in 1773 – that played a tune, then caught a silver fish in its beak before swallowing it – in the Bowes Museum, Barnard Castle, County Durham. I knew about this and introduced Angela to some pictures of it. One cryptic note in her *Journal*, perhaps in response, reads: 'Bluebeard – he is building a swan'. When we all went to a touring production of *Swan Lake* in Bristol, during the interval in the bar, Angela observed in a very loud voice and in a characteristically bawdy way: 'I mean, it's really all about a prince who goes around fucking swans, isn't it?' She liked to say things like that, sometimes. And she added that it made a change from Zeus turning into a swan, in order to do the same to Leda.

Metamorphoses – prince/swan; beauty/beast; beast/prince; grandma/wolf; wolf/grandma; werewolf into husband into werewolf again – were increasingly part of Angela's literary universe in the mid-1970s, as were people who talked to animals. While in Bath, she noted in her *Journal* the phrase 'a man changes into a bird', and she wrote a performance piece about evolution in reverse, as a human being regresses into bird life and sprouts wings – which was produced, with amplified music and especially percussion, in Walcot Village Hall. It was called *Transformations*, and if memory serves it had just one piece of dialogue towards the end spoken in a thick accent by the performance artist: 'Beeg Bird!' Another film we saw together was *The Ruling Class* (1972), based on Peter Barnes's play, in which Peter O'Toole behaves like a bird performing a mating ritual, with flapping wings, to woo his beloved. Angela found this scene 'very beautiful'.

As part of my research into Jean-Jacques Rousseau and eighteenth-century Geneva, I had come across a group of automata, made between 1768 and 1774, by the Jaquet-Droz family of watchmakers to promote their precision watches – which were now housed in the Musée de l'Hôtel de Ville in Neuchâtel: a musician, a draughtsman and a scribe. If you asked the museum technician very nicely, he would occasionally make them go through their paces. Once when I was there, the lady musician was playing her organ – the bellows that powered her were located in her heaving breast – and she played a split note: the technician turned to me and said, 'I think she's tired.' Creepy. The scribe writes, with a goose-quill pen, in neat mid-eighteenth-century handwriting, 'Je pense, donc je suis.' I can well recall talking to Angela about them, and playing her a recording of the organist at her keyboard. She wrote at the time of 'the intricate musculature of wires, the viscera of cogs and wheels' in automata and mechanical toys: 'it is magic but perfectly rational magic – all made by the human hand'. A mimicry of the living. An automaton resembling a soubrette in an operetta – 'the most delicately balanced system of cords and pulleys in the world' – makes a memorable appearance in *The Tiger's Bride*. The vampire Countess is likened to 'a ventriloquist's doll', her voice to 'an ingenious piece of clockwork'.

The finest exponents of handmade model animation in Britain at the time – often using china dolls which looked as though they had been abused by generations of children – were the identical twins the Polish-American Brothers Quay. They were both graduates of the Royal College of Art, and I tried, at Angela's request, to bring the three of them together in the late 1970s. A meeting was arranged, after one of my lectures on film, but sadly it led nowhere. Angela Carter and the Brothers would have been a terrific combination. Another, much later, graduate of the Royal College of Art, the model animator Suzie Templeton, was to make her name with an extraordinary version of *Peter and the Wolf*, made in a Polish studio: it owed a lot to Angela's fairytales and it won an Oscar. The wolf is female, Peter is an adolescent with issues, and the macho huntsman is the bad guy. Hollywood was just beginning to develop post-Carter takes on traditional fairytales in the public domain – and to see the commercial potential of gutsy commonsensical young heroines in mainstream feature films.

Angela's interest in automata was part of her taste for the literature of fantasy and science fiction. Her *New Society* essay on *Bath, Heritage City*, published in 1975, begins with the words:

'...occupying a conspicuous site not fifty yards from the mysterious, chtonic aperture from which the hot springs bubble out of the inner earth...'

In a recent panel discussion about Angela Carter's work at Bath Literature Festival, chaired by her friend and literary executor Susannah Clapp, Carmen Callil – one of the founders of Virago Press and another friend – said she sometimes tried, unsuccessfully, to discourage Angela from using words such as 'chtonic' and that she 'never came to terms with what "chtonic" meant'. Actually, it is a reference to the writings of H.P. Lovecraft, who revelled in such words which – as Angela pointed out in her article about him called *The Hidden Child* in *New Society* that same year – constitute 'a bizarre cosmogony full of ambivalent deities with names that look like typing errors'. Like Cthulhu or chtonic – which means 'subterranean', from the Greek, or 'associated with the spirits of the underworld'. Lovecraft was a sickly, reclusive writer who lived in a clapboard house on a tree-lined street in Providence, Rhode Island, shutting himself away from the modern world and writing very ripe stories with lots of adjectives and orchidaceous prose about journeys into the unconscious – usually involving slime or sludge or lapping, gelatinous *things* emanating from the inner earth. Lovecraft defined the appeal of the tale of terror as 'the rattling at the window – like the scratching of unknown claws at the rind of the known world'. Many of these stories were centred on 'Miskatonic University', which was in fact Brown University, Providence. Angela at that time felt he was in some strange way a kindred spirit. Her *Journal* is full of references to Lovecraft's writings, with an assortment of choice quotes:

'Sometimes, when it is cloudy, I can sleep.'

'My friend had attained a wide notoriety because of his experiments leading towards the revivication of the dead.'

And this one, with which she opened her *New Society* essay:

'We were sitting in a dilapidated seventeenth-century tomb in the late afternoon of an autumn day at the old burying ground in Arkham, and speculating about the unnameable.'

At that time, Lovecraft was absolutely beyond the pale where the literary establishment was concerned. He wasn't even in the box marked 'cult'. Partly for this reason, no doubt, at one stage Angela was tempted to call her collection of short stories – which became *The Bloody Chamber* – 'Weird Tales', after the interwar pulp magazine to which Lovecraft often contributed: 'but,' she added, 'my English publishers found that the idea met with such a general lack of enthusiasm, I abandoned it. Pop Art is more difficult to do in fiction.'

In 1977, Angela persuaded me to contribute to a book of essays and speculations about H.P. Lovecraft, *The Necronomicon*, published a year later and edited by a friend of hers from Bristol days, the science fiction writer and chairman of the H.G. Wells Society George Hay. She contributed another essay, adapted from her *New Society* piece and called *Lovecraft and Landscape*. Mine was about his pseudo-scholarship and his *Dreams of Dead Names*. *The Necronomicon* seldom appears in bibliographies of Angela's writings for some reason. When in 1980-81, Angela went to work as a Visiting Professor on the Creative Writing Programme at Brown University, Providence, I visited her there and we went on a pilgrimage together to find H.P. Lovecraft's grave in the huge manicured and sprinklered cemetery in suburban Providence. It proved to be a long walk – Angela didn't like walking for the sake of walking – and despite wandering around for some time like Eli Wallach in the penultimate reel of *The Good, The Bad and The Ugly*, we never did manage to find it. But we consoled ourselves with some tea with another friend, the American writer Robert Coover – and chatted amiably about that Satanic Western among other postmodern things. ('I *know* you'll get on with him, Christopher.')

In April 1975, I went with Angela to the *Henry Fuseli* exhibition at the Tate Gallery. She stood for ages in front of the *A Midsummer Night's Dream* paintings and drawings – with their libidinous fairies and superheroic Oberon and Titania – while I pondered the visual connections between *The Nightmare*, with its strange squat figure of a mara sitting on the woman's chest and staring out at the viewer, and the design of *Nosferatu*, especially the climactic sequence just before the crowing of the cock. A seed was planted. Many years later I co-curated an exhibition all about *Gothic Nightmares* at Tate Britain, centred on Fuseli's infamous painting. Angela was very struck by a large monochrome poster on the wall of my flat, advertising an exhibition of the lithographs of Odilon Redon in Geneva (June to October 1975). It showed a cosmic battle between a winged devil and a vulnerable, naked girl – with the moon in the background, and a dark river flowing beside them. The winged figure, who has a catlike face, is gnawing at the girl's stomach. The print was called *Beneath The Wings of Shadows* (1891). It is like a Goya drawing updated to the Symbolist era. We discussed it often, what it might mean, and why the decadent aristocrat in Huysmans' *À Rebours* had a particular penchant for collecting Redon drawings. My poster found its way into Bluebeard's Castle in the story *The Bloody Chamber* as the fictional 'Redon engraving I liked best, *The Evening Star Walking on the Rim of Night*'. *À Rebours* did not feature in the story by name, but 'an edition of Huysmans' *Là-bas*, from some over-exquisite private press' did – displayed on a spread-eagle lectern. In the same story, the 'etching by Rops [of] the child with her sticklike limbs…and the old, monocled lecher who examined her' was inspired by three works in a large catalogue I lent Angela – *L'œuvre gravé de Félicien Rops* (Paris, 1975): *Le Plus Bel Amour de Don Juan*, *Le Massage* and *L'Agonie ou Mors et Vita*. The 'postcard with a view of a village graveyard…where some black-coated ghoul enthusiastically dug at a grave', complete with written congratulations on 'this marriage to the descendent of Dracula' – also in Bluebeard's collection – was inspired by the illustrations *Les Amours de Bertrand* and *Le Vampire de Muy* in my collection *La Musée de Vampires*. They all became part of the lush, fin-de-siècle décor of Bluebeard's Brittany castle – intended, she later wrote, to 'half-seduce the reader into this wicked, glamorous, fatal world'. I didn't accompany Angela to the exhibition *The Late Richard Dadd* at the Tate in autumn 1974 –

showing all of Dadd's available works – but we went separately and talked in Bath about Dadd's unnerving painting of 1855-64 *The Fairy Feller's Master-Stroke*, made while he was in a lunatic asylum for killing his father in a fit of madness, and showing in obsessive, tiny detail a fairy splitting a large chestnut for use as Queen Mab's chariot. For me, this was a bizarre parody in miniature of the Pre-Raphaelite painter Ford Madox Brown's huge *Work* (1859-63), showing an idealised road-gang at work in Hampstead, observed by pundits. Angela was working on her radio play about Dadd – *Come Unto These Yellow Sands* – broadcast in March 1979 and partly based on the 1974 Tate catalogue, towards the end of her time in Bath. It includes, in the form of monologues and lectures and witness statements, all sorts of discussions from multiple perspectives on fairies and fairytales and what commentators had made of them. Child psychologist Bruno Bettelheim's Freudian look at *The Uses of Enchantment: The Meaning and Importance of Fairy Tales* – about how such tales help children at early stages, in almost therapeutic ways, to adjust to the realities of adolescent life – was published in 1976, and Angela devoured it, especially the chapters on *Little Red Riding Hood*, *Bluebeard* and *Beauty and the Beast*, *Snow White* and *The Sleeping Beauty*. One of Bettelheim's conclusions was, with the tales' emphasis on the hero and on happily ever after, we are 'left in the dark about the feelings of the heroine'. Angela was shortly to do something about that. Bettelheim also contrasted the *bourgeois*, ornate style of Perrault, 'aware of his courtly audience', with the more down-to-earth, not to say brutal, approach of the Brothers Grimm – fusing the natural world with the uncanny. Angela came to agree with this too, although she had serious doubts about the overall thesis of Bettelheim's book: for her, fairytales were more transgressive, less conformist. About Red Riding Hood, Bettelheim wrote that the tale's basic elements – which went way back – were 'a little girl with a red cap and the company of wolves'. I'm sure that's where Angela found the title of her radio play, story and subsequent film – and the idea of putting a werewolf back into *Little Red Riding Hood*, where he originally belonged. In general, she loved the magic of 'once upon a time', but was not at all comfortable with the conformity of 'happily ever after'. She was also uncomfortable with Bettelheim's tendency to see the meaning of these fairytales as eternal, fixed for all time – rather than as historically located and specific. Of Freud, she once observed – during a seminar at the University of Bath – 'you have to remember that Vienna at that time was a city *full* of syphilitic nutters – so Freud was onto a *really* good thing'. This had the desired effect of embarrassing the more intense research students.

Another book Angela was reading at the time – also published in 1976 – was Max Luthi's collection of lectures and broadcasts *Once Upon a Time: On the Nature of Fairy Tales* which did indeed argue for an *historical* understanding of the stories and began with a thought she must have enjoyed a lot:

> 'For centuries, educated people have looked down on popular fairytales as stories properly belonging to the nursery and the servants' quarters. Yet great writers have repeatedly drawn inspiration from them…'

Aware of the different modes of address used by the writers or compilers of fairytales since the Middle Ages, Angela planned to write the various stories of *The Bloody Chamber*, or *New Mother Goose Tales*, in different literary styles – an idea which to some extent survived to the published version. As she noted:

> *The Snow Queen* – lyrical
> *The Sleeping Beauty* – Walter de la Mare style [presumably *Memoirs of a Midget*, for which she wrote an introduction in 1982]
> *Cinderella* – very primitive, very archaic
> *Puss in Boots* – à la Beaumarchais (and *The Marriage of Figaro*)

And so on. In her notes, Angela was simultaneously thinking about *The Bloody Chamber* and *The Sadeian Woman* – so when she writes 'P in B' it is difficult sometimes to tell whether she has *Puss in Boots* or *Philosophy in the Boudoir* on her mind. Or maybe both. Her finely-crafted writing style, even *within* stories, veered from the lush and sensual to the comic to the satirical to the deliberately bawdy: a rich mix.

In *Wise Children*, Angela would make much of Max Reinhardt and William Dieterle's film, based on his huge stage production at the Hollywood Bowl, of *A Midsummer Night's Dream*. We didn't go and see it in the mid-1970s – as far as I can remember, there was no print available – but we certainly did see Jean Cocteau's *La Belle et La Bête*, designed by Christian Bérard, with the luminous Josette Day as Beauty. The mirrors and billowing curtains and keys and corridor which came to life and bridal bed with flowers and white rose all recurred in the collection *The Bloody Chamber* in various ways. *The Courtship of Mr Lyon* is a parallel text to Cocteau's film. We saw *La Belle et La Bête* at the Arnolfini, which she always took pleasure in calling 'the anal-phoney'. In the late 1960s, Angela had very briefly worked there behind the entrance desk – until she was asked to hoover the floor, at which point she quit on the spot. We also saw *Pandora's Box* (G.W. Pabst, 1929), which Angela had first seen when she was eighteen and had seen again since. On the way home, we discussed whether Louise Brooks as Lulu was playing a subversive kind of free spirit – or whether, as in Frank Wedekind's two plays *Earth Spirit* and *Pandora's Box*, she is meant to be a heartless *femme fatale*, 'who is given Jack the Ripper as a suitable Christmas present' for daring to lift the lid of her box.

The Company of Wolves – the original radio play, broadcast in May 1980 – finishes on a story told by a werewolf about a little girl who is abandoned as a baby on a snow-clad mountainside, and who is suckled by wolves in a cave. All attempts to domesticate her come to nothing. She prefers the company of wild beasts, and understands them. This mirrored the story *Wolf-Alice*. Angela was very interested in feral children when first I got to know her, and she planned to write an article about them for *New Society*. What would happen if someone grew up in the wild, outside social convention and the masks of civilisation, and learned more about life from animals than humans? Her article was to include references to Truffaut's film *L'Enfant Sauvage*, the enigma of Kaspar Hauser,

Mowgli, children and their affinity for animals, the lion lying down with the lamb, and Dr. Dolittle talking to the pushmi-pullyu. It turned instead into a piece about animals in the nursery, in 1976. But a book she would return to, quite often, was Octave Mannoni's *Prospero and Caliban: The Psychology of Colonization*, which presented Prospero as a colonial governor, Ariel as one of his *bourgeois* subject-peoples who feels ready for independence and self-government but is being held back, and Caliban as an indigenous tribesman: 'the island's mine – which thou tak'st from me'; 'you taught me language, and my profit on't is I know how to curse'. With my research interest in Rousseau, I relished chatting with Angela and Edward about the concept of the 'noble savage' – Rousseau versus Hobbes – about Robinson Crusoe and the beautiful and menacing footprint of Man Friday, and about Rousseau's strange ideas about the origin of language, made fashionable again by Jacques Derrida. In Rousseau's view, chimpanzees were in fact quite able to speak – they had the physical equipment for it – but they had collectively decided never to tell anyone else, for fear that the moment human beings discovered this, the apes would inevitably be exploited as recruits to the working class. As it was, they much preferred to live in the wild and in the relative comfort of zoos. There was a famous French engraving in the mid-eighteenth century which had the Archbishop of Paris standing in front of a monkey cage in Paris zoo and saying, 'speak and I'll baptise you'. Another good reason for keeping quiet! We all went to see the film *L'Enfant Sauvage*, originally released in 1971 and based on the physician Dr. Jean Itard's Journal of 1798 about the wild boy of Aveyron he called 'Victor' – who had grown up in the forest and subsequently been rescued by Itard from the National Institute for the Deaf and Dumb. Itard used Victor as a case-study for testing Rousseau's ideas about education: children should never learn things by heart, they should realise it was in their self-interest to learn and understand them – and the tutor should arrange situations where the child could internalise information. The production, which used Vivaldi's Concerto for Mandolin and Flute to accompany moments of elation, cast Truffaut himself as Itard and a young boy called Jean-Pierre Cargol as Victor – and it was simultaneously about how Cargol was turned by the director into an actor, a theme that strongly appealed to Angela.

Susannah Clapp, in her recent book *A Card from Angela Carter*, writes very well about Angela's conversational style.

> …her own tones were unmistakable. Piping, soft, with clipped vowels, at times Angela sounded like a parody of girlish gentility. At other times she skidded into casual south London. You never knew exactly where you were. She was impossible to second-guess. She was a great curser, and took pride in this: 'I am known in my circle as notoriously foul-mouthed.' Yet she was also byzantinely courteous: her most full-blooded protests would often be heralded by an icily disarming 'forgive me'…

Susannah also writes about how Angela laughed or chuckled often and loudly, and how with her 'accuracy paraded itself as irony – and none the less ironic for that'. If she sensed too much 'niceness' or complacency around her, she could be wicked. We went to see the film *Private Vices, Public Pleasures*, directed by Miklós Jancsó of *The Round-Up* fame, at the picture house in Whiteladies Road, Bristol, a film which, much to Angela's amusement, featured a full-frontal Welsh hermaphrodite in the cast – and this, just at the time she was putting the finishing touches to *The Passion of New Eve*, with Evelyn morphing into Eve. *The Passion* features a goddess completely constructed by the rules of cinema; a façade of what men want from their celluloid dreams. Because *Private Vices* was quite a rude film, the accompanying trailer was for one of the *Emmanuelle* series – and I can vividly remember Angela shattering the concentration of the audience by saying in a deliberately loud voice, as she watched it, 'I once met a prostitute in Bangkok who as a party-piece could blow smoke rings through her labia minor.' Or the time when she wrote her article for *New Society* in 1971 on D.H. Lawrence as a stocking fetishist (or in her notes, 'D.H. Lawrence as drag queen') and as she went to post it in Bath, in her oversized coat and a beret at a jaunty angle, she said with glee 'that's nailed the bastard'. She really had it in for Lawrence, and wrote several pieces saying so: his atavistic obsession with 'the phallic wind rushing through the dark' was more than she could stomach. Or her predilection for quoting Chaucer's *The Miller's Tale* (she had studied medieval literature at Bristol), when the wife Alison successfully plays a crude trick on the young man which involves kissing her arse: '"tee hee!" quoth she'. Angela once published a long essay on that 'tee hee'. Only in *her* version, if someone cracked a joke at a dinner table that she didn't find amusing, or paraded some cliché as gospel, she would add an old English word to the mix: 'tee fucking hee'. Her time spent studying Anglo-Saxon at Bristol had evidently lodged some of Chaucer's 'best japes' firmly in her memory. Or her fantasy, which she sometimes shared in public, about a 'Doctor Onan' – she'd seen a brass plaque with that name on a door in Turkey, while on holiday in 1973 or 1974 – and his many adventures in public places. In the story *Puss-in-Boots*, the young Lothario is 'so much in love, he very rarely panders to the pleasures, even of Onan'.

My father was a great fan of the music-hall and pantomime – as was Angela – and he particularly liked a routine he once saw Max Miller perform on the stage which he would often repeat. It was in the 1930s, and Max was the leading stand-up in a declining profession. He would enter with the leg of a shop-window mannequin: 'Mussolini's left leg!' He would then fetch another leg: 'Mussolini's right leg.' Then, having placed them on the stage, he would appear from the wings with two large potatoes in his open palms. Laughter… 'You're all wrong – they're King Edwards.' Angela picked up on this old joke – she may well have heard it from someone else, as a Max Miller devotee – and gave it to 'Gorgeous George: clown number one to the British Empire' in *Wise Children* only with some poetic licence:

> 'He'd started a riot at the Royal Variety Show when he held up a couple of spuds and said, "King Edwards". That was just before the abdication.'

Some commentators have suggested that Gorgeous George was based on Frankie Howerd. He was in fact a reincarnation of Max Miller, with his garish stage costume and cheeky chappie persona, whose recorded performances were sometimes given to Angela by Edward Horesh as presents. Angela enjoyed sending me suggestive Donald McGill-style seaside postcards, when she was on her travels. I have one in front of me. It shows a fireman putting out a blaze with the hose between his legs. 'Blimey – what a man!' says an excited lady onlooker. Angela wrote on the other side: 'nuff said, love Angie'. When first she moved from Bath to Clapham, she sent me a headline from a local paper – 'Rat in baby's pram shock' – pinned to a note: 'This is South London! Lots of love.'

My favourite letter from her was written when Angela had just arrived at Sheffield – on an Arts Council Creative Writing Fellowship at the University, in October 1977 – and was experiencing problems of adjustment. It was at Sheffield that she wrote or completed some of the tales in *The Bloody Chamber*.

> Dear Chris – the winds are wuthering round the arts tower, in which I sit in anomic revery, contemplating a very aged typewriter & a 2-hrs trip back to the commune, where my friends will be hard at work on the next edition of the 'Sheffield Free Press'. I've just retrieved from the (excellent, & I should hope so!) library a book called 'Wolves & Were-Wolves' which reminded me of you – oh, you know what I mean. The first chapter is titled 'The wolf that ate the postman'. I shall take copious notes, & transmit them to you. I may try a cross of were-wolves with 'La Belle et la Bête.'

> Further, there is a course here onto which I've insinuated myself called 'The Gothic Imagination'. The reading list comprises everything from 'Melmoth the Wanderer' to Bram Stoker, & now also includes A. Carter, I'm happy to say. A showing of Nosferatu, too! The man responsible…was very excited to hear I knew an authority on vampires (& even more excited to hear you were an authority on Leone since he is a Clint Eastwood buff & possibly

a consenting adult but don't worry, I will protect you). Anyway, I said you might be willing to do a turn and he bounced & squeaked at the notion. So let me know when you might drop by…

I keep thinking – that's 2 days done; only another three terms of 8 weeks each minus 2 days. I'm sure this is the wrong reaction.

lots of love,

Angela

Terry Pratchett – a great fan of Angela's work: see *The Wyrd Sisters* (1988), for example – once wisely observed: 'She had a way of looking which made you feel whatever you were going to say next, it had better be interesting.' Angela was allergic to clichés and clichéd behaviour. As she wrote of Beauty, in *The Courtship of Mr Lyon*, 'small talk turned to dust in her mouth; small talk had never, at the best of times, been Beauty's forte, and she had little practice at it.' Just so Angela.

So how does my friendship with Angela in Bath in the mid-1970s mesh with the writings of academics and critics, now that her work has become – since her untimely death in February 1992 at the age of 51 – a set text at A Level and since she has become acknowledged as one of the key British writers of the late twentieth century? First of all, I think she has been made into too much of a plaster saint – which she would have detested – and at the same time she has been fitted too snugly into a box marked 'feminism'. As Marina Warner recently observed, 'She was much more independent-minded than the traditional feminists of her time.' Her written dialogues were more often across time with literature, with cinema and with folklore, rather than with contemporary commentators. Because she was usually so clever at embedding her theory and philosophy – and she read a great deal of it: she loved ideas – into her fictional descriptions and characters, she has given commentators a lot to chew on, and sometimes the academic theory has squeezed out the sheer pleasure of the text; the sensual and visual pleasure, the comedy and the rudeness. As Angela wrote, readers could take her books 'on as many levels as you can cope with at the time' and they should be 'read on *your* own terms'. Too often, she has been remade in the image of today's lines in *haute culture* which weren't even around in her day. Her view that culture was one long continuum – high/low, who cares? – has not always fitted the more condescending attitudes of her Eng. Lit. interpreters. One has written that she took over a series of literary sub-genres (science fiction, Gothic, fantasy, pornography, etc.) and 'turned their grubby stereotypes into sophisticated mythology'. That phrase 'grubby stereotypes' would not have appealed to Angela at all. 'I'm up for anything that flickers,' she once said of her enthusiasm for going to the pictures. Even here, some commentators have over-emphasised the importance of art-circuit gods such as Godard and Buñuel – yes, but her *Journal*, matched by my experience, is full of references to *Pat Garrett*, *Dirty Harry* and Hammer Films. She spoke of 'the Hammer films I enjoyed as a child,' and in the mid-1970s she told me she had written to Aida Young – producer of three later Christopher Lee *Dracula* films between 1968 and 1970 – to explore whether they could perhaps work together on a film or television play. Angela once wrote, in an essay on *Fun Fairs*, that academics tended to enthuse about the culture of fairs with all the bloodless assurance of people who had never been near one in real life, or, if they had been near one, they hadn't deep down enjoyed the experience. Others have reduced her iconoclasm – sticking two fingers up at assorted real or perceived establishments and, as it were, swearing in church – and her mockery, to something much more comfortable. Beneath the stylistic flourishes, and the assertions, lay someone much less confident, more brittle, much less sure of herself. And one judgement that particularly irritates me is the critical consensus that before Angela moved to London in the late 1970s she had 'no settled base'. It was only when she settled in Clapham, it is said, that she *really* found her voice. And it was only when she went to Sheffield that she wrote *The Bloody Chamber* (in which the Northern landscapes of the stories apparently reflected the setting of her Fellowship). Both are nonsense. The years in Bath were when *The Bloody Chamber* and *The Sadeian Woman* and most of her best-regarded *New Society* pieces were conceived, researched and partly written – not to mention her edition of Perrault's fairytales, the completion of *The Passion of New Eve* and the writing of *Comic and Curious Cats*. The Bath years were a transforming experience, well before she was comprehensively Virago-ed, if there is such a word. Sheffield gave her the space to complete the process. Marina Warner said to me the other evening, 'You knew Angela Carter before she was Angela Carter': I don't actually think that is right. She was Angela Carter all right, but she needed to launch herself on the London literary scene.

Another piece of critical consensus is that in the first phases of her writing career – the Bristol years, Japan, Bath – Angela was interested in the social and cultural construction of gender – 'femininity' was created, yet palmed off as natural – and focused on deconstructing myths, while after 1979 and the publication of *The Bloody Chamber* she was more interested in celebration and carnival and symbolic acts of resistance; locating self-creation in performance and public presentation. Again, this is nonsense. She started taking notes on *Nights at the Circus* – including the name Fevvers – in 1976, in Bath. As we've seen, she was already well into wings and swans and metamorphoses. Even that conversation on the way back from the opera about *The Marriage of Figaro* and the social class of Cherubino found its way into *Nights at the Circus*.

Above all, I think, commentators on the writings of Angela Carter have tended to downplay her strong streak of socialism, a word that post-modernists dare not utter if it isn't in quotation marks. She could be solemn about it too – another forbidden word. She once reminisced that her political formation grew partly from her childhood experiences in South Yorkshire and its coalfields during the War, and partly from conversations with her anarchist friends in Bristol who would meet at the Berkeley Café opposite the university. She was to write of 'fairy tales, folk tales, stories from the oral tradition...are all of them the most vital connection we have with the imaginations of ordinary men and women whose labour created our world'. This also connected with her background (with then-husband Paul Carter) in the Bristol folk-music scene of the 1960s, where she helped make recordings, knew Shirley Collins, visited folk clubs, wrote liner notes for records, and is said to have had a good folk-singing voice herself. She read studies of popular ballads – especially Celtic ones – and their connections with archetypal stories. For some reason, the phrase 'and the larks they sang melodious' would always reduce her to a fit of giggles. This chimed at some level with her aesthetic of funfairs, canal boats, seaside postcards, tattoo artists, toy-makers, carnival colours and old sardine tins. It was sardine tins which first introduced her to her regular illustrator and good friend Corinna Sargood (then Grey), who shared her taste and then lived in Bristol. It was Festival of Britain and Ealing comedies rather than slick Pop Art. She liked her socialism to be full-blooded – preferred Danton to Robespierre; Trotsky to Lenin; Joe Gormley to Arthur Scargill in the miners' strike – and she later reminded several interviewers if they went on about her status as a New Age role model and what did she feel about being a latter-day Mother Goose, 'Look, I'm a socialist, damn it – how can you expect me to be interested in fairies?' or 'This world is all there is, and in order to question the nature of reality one must move from a strongly grounded base in what constitutes material reality...I'm in the de-mythologising business.' When she spoke of Fine Art, she prophesied that unless it had some point to make it would soon become a decorative irrelevance. Of Trotsky, she liked to say that after he was murdered with an ice-pick in August 1940, it was discovered that he had an extra-large heart as well as a brain 'of extraordinary dimensions'. This, from Isaac Deutscher's biography.

Chuckle. The characters in her fiction, she later admitted, 'have a tendency to be telling you something'.

I can vividly remember an informal evening talk she gave to postgraduate students in the Education Department at the University of Bath in 1976. She reminisced about her own primary school in South London – run by 'a perfectly awful woman [called Miss Cox] who looked and dressed like Queen Mary' – all pastel-coloured satins and beaded fronts – but 'who did a wonderful job' – and then launched into a tirade about the embourgeoisification of the working-class child and the reinforcement of traditional values by the current education system; and its tendency to treat people as children long after they had grown up. Children, she said, are often more experienced about life, have more sophisticated problems, than their teachers, who still go on about the niceties of Jane Austen: Jane Austen, a provincial maiden lady who probably knew little or nothing about the actual mechanics of sexual intercourse, and who was more interested in table-manners. None of her characters had a clue about sexual desire, or how to express it. Schools, she added, stood too far outside the community – alienated from the 'urban barbarism' that surrounded them. During question time, one intrepid graduate student asked her: 'So, having said those things, how would you go about teaching English to today's schoolchildren?' Pause. 'With a King James Bible in one hand and a lash in the other.' Consistency in such matters wasn't always her strongest suit. Her 'fire and brimstone' approach to teaching Creative Writing would later become legendary.

When I was reading Angela's diaries and journals, in preparation for this essay, the most emotional moment I had was when I came across – in her *Big Red Diary* for 1974 – a listing of the bus times from the City Centre to the University of Bath and back again. Because in 1974, Angela would sometimes come and sit at the back of my lectures at the university on political theory, or Soviet cinema, or the history of European socialist thought – our of sheer personal interest – and smoke her way through the lecture then leave. Ex-students of mine, who sat near her, have recently let me know that this happened more often than I had remembered. It must have been one of the reasons she noted the bus times.

In May 1976 – the fiftieth anniversary of the General Strike, which happened from 4-13 May 1926 – I put together an audio-visual presentation on the Strike and its legacy for the Bath Labour Party at Century House in Pierrepont Street. Angela was at the time Secretary of the Bathwick ward of the Party (even though it wasn't her ward – it did make the meetings more lively!) and Edward was the Bath Party's political education officer. I was an ordinary member. There was a taped soundtrack, which involved Angela, Edward and I reading from *The Penguin Book of Socialist Verse* – Thomas Hood, William Morris, Bertolt Brecht – intercut with newspaper accounts of what was happening day by day on the streets. The juxtaposition of pictures was based on Eisenstein's writings about Soviet cinema and the collision of images, about which I was lecturing at the time: bosses in top hats, frock coats and spats; uniformed soldiers manning busses; special constables looking conflicted; a man herding sheep down Whitehall while a voice-over spoke of the bourgeoisie. Those sorts of collision. The musical soundtrack, meanwhile, included *England Arise* – for the coalminers – and *The Black Bottom*, the dance-craze of the mid-1920s, for the strike-breakers. It was all a bit sentimental, and certainly solemn, but as Angela once wrote of her childhood South Yorkshire, 'I'm a sucker for the worker hero, you bet…of course I romanticise it, why the hell not?' We had all watched Ken Loach's dramatised history of the labour movement *Days of Hope*, in autumn 1975. Ken was another Bath resident, and gave a talk – on the media's coverage of strikes and how they were 'threatened' rather than 'promised' – to the Bath Labour Party at around the same time, which we all attended. Bernardo Bertolucci's two-part epic *Novecento* or *1900* – about the history of the rural Left in Italy from 1900 to 1945 – made a strong impression on Angela. The credit titles were played over a large painting of 1901, by Giuseppe da Volpedo – his best-known painting in Italy, called *The Fourth Estate* – with a rousing Ennio Morricone anthem on the soundtrack. At the end of this credits sequence, Angela turned to me and said, 'This is really hopeful' – which is not the kind of thing she said very often. Several tales in *The Bloody Chamber* reflect her political views: Signor Pantaleone riding off once a week to 'extort most-grasping rents from starving peasant farmers' and, later, to devote his afternoon to 'usury, bankruptcy, here, a small tradesman, there, a weeping widow, for fun and profit' (in *Puss-in-Boots*); Bluebeard rushing away to clinch 'a deal, an enterprise of hazard and chance involving several millions' and deserting his vulnerable new bride in the process (in *The Bloody Chamber*); the 'grave-eyed children [who] tend the little flocks of goats that provide the homesteads with acrid milk and maggoty cheese' (in *The Company of Wolves*). 'I think my work is deeply political,' she later observed. 'A lot of people don't. That's fine. I like creeping up on people from behind and sandbagging them.'

Angela moved to London in 1977, to The Chase in Clapham – she regularly returned to Bath for the next two years or so – and I became a Professor at the Royal College of Art a couple of years later. For many reasons, we went our separate ways. Angela sometimes came to the RCA to view student exhibitions and give readings – one of them *The Lady of the House of Love* – and when I was finding my feet she introduced me to some artist friends of hers such as Gillian Ayres. And a year later in 1980, she had a gentle go at me in *New Society*, in an article on *The Recession Style*. Her conclusion to this was that fashion designers – and those consumers who had a steady job and could afford new clothes – were now hyper-aware of the *meaning* of what they were wearing. Everything was now in inverted commas. We were living in an age of lost innocence.

> Semiotic theory has clearly permeated the whole business. I blame the art schools, especially their general studies

departments… Not only has the idea of the 'language of fashion' become a boring shibboleth, but much of the apparel you see about is clearly intended to be 'read', in no uncertain terms, as complex statements of affection and disaffection.

I wrote a card to her, saying 'that's how I earn my living these days, Angie.'

Shortly before she moved from Bath, she presented me with a collage – cut-out paper on thick hardboard – based on the colours of a well-known brand of sweets. It was called, she explained, 'It Takes All Sorts To Make A World'. In my view, Bath City Council should commission and install a plaque to Angela Carter, at Hay Hill – as the most significant writer actually to *live* in the city, rather than just look in, since Mary Shelley wrote *Frankenstein*…

Thanks to:

Edward Horesh, Corinna Sargood, Susannah Clapp (and her *A Card From Angela Carter*, Bloomsbury, 2012), Marina Warner, the modern manuscripts department at the British Library, and the Bristol Festival of Ideas.

3

Freud's Nightmare

Introduction

IN APRIL 1975, *I visited the pioneering* Henry Fuseli *exhibition at the Tate Gallery (now Tate Britain) with Angela Carter. The show was largely organised around literary themes and authors: Shakespeare, the Classics, Milton and the Bible, Dante, Northern Poets and Legends. Angela was particularly fascinated by Fuseli's various versions of Titania's bewitching from* A Midsummer Night's Dream *- including his huge painting of the subject (1785-9),* Cobweb *(1785-6),* Titania and Bottom *(1789-90) and* Oberon squeezes the flower on Titania's eyelids *(1793-4) - and incidentally by Fuseli's obsessive hat and hair fetishism. Some of his fairies, surrounding Titania, are full-blooded libidinous little creatures, who pose and preen and look knowingly at the viewer. Others are cat-like. Fuseli's paintings of the* Dream *were part of the then-new Shakespeare industry, which flourished from the 1780s onwards - inspired by David Garrick. 'The judicious adoption of figures in art' - with this 'poetical painter' using earlier paintings by others as sources, rather than the life room - struck a distinct chord with Angela's literary aesthetic at the time. She would revisit Shakespeare's* A Midsummer Night's Dream *several times in her work - 'I've written various adventures with it' - and considered the play 'a mixture of fertility festival, formal masque, silliness, invention and music…this is what all art should be like'. Her* Overture and Incidental Music for A Midsummer Night's Dream, *first published in* Interzone *in 1982, and anthologised in the collection* Black Venus, *opens with a bawdy fairy known as 'The Golden Herm' (for hermaphrodite) complaining about the wetness of an English midsummer, in the woods, and trying to find out what* *'desire' means. The Golden Herm predates the 'nostalgic, disinfected' fairy wood invented by the Victorians, and owes much to Fuseli's treatments of the* Dream. *When visiting the exhibition, I was more drawn to Fuseli's* The Nightmare *(1781), his various versions of* An Incubus leaving two sleeping girls, *and his treatments of* Macbeth. *When we returned to Bath, Angela gave me Frederick Antal's* Fuseli Studies *(1956) and – later – a book of colour reproductions she had found in a museum bookshop in Italy,* L'Opera Completa di Fuseli *(by Gert Schiff, Rizzoli, 1977). I wrote this essay in the wake of the exhibition* Gothic Nightmares – Fuseli, Blake and the Romantic Imagination *(Tate Britain, February to May 2006) which I co-curated with Martin Myrone and which encouraged me to dig deeper.*

Freud's Nightmare[1]

In 1926, the forty-three-year-old American writer and socialist Max Eastman visited Sigmund Freud in his office at Berggasse 19 – 19 Hill Street – a street in the residential sector of Northern Vienna. Number 19, an apartment block, was a large turn-of-the-century building. Eastman had published, ten years before, the first popular non-specialist introduction to Freud's teaching for American readers, in *Everybody's Magazine*. He had also published a chapter on 'Marx and Freud' which Freud had judged to be 'really important; probably also correct'. So when he found himself in Vienna in 1926, Eastman made an appointment with the great man. His fact-finding tour of the Soviet Union, a couple of years earlier, had helped to shake his faith in Marxism – and he was also beginning to have serious doubts about Freud.[2]

He went up the stairs to the landing of Berggasse 19, then turned right to the door of Freud's compact suite of offices. Through the foyer outside Freud's waiting room – with its metal bars on the doors, for security reasons – to the waiting room itself.[3] Eastman recalled his first impressions of the waiting room some sixteen years later in 1942, as part of a chapter on Freud – 'the crotchety greatness of Sigmund Freud' – in the book *Heroes I Have Known*:

Berggasse 19 was a big roomy house full of books and pictures, the whole mezzanine floor padded with those thick rich rugs in which your feet sink like a camel's in the sand. I was not surprised to see hanging beside Rembrandt's *Anatomy Lesson*, without which no doctor's office would be recognisable, a picture of *The Nightmare* – a horrid monster with a semi-evil laugh or leer squatting upon a sleeping maiden's naked breast. Freud's early speciality had been anatomy, and he had in him the hard scientific curiosity suggested by Rembrandt's picture. But then he had too, in my belief, a streak of something closely akin to medieval superstition… Freud's discovery that impulses suppressed out of our thoughts can continue to control those thoughts, both waking and sleeping, and also our actions and bodily conditions, was certainly a major event in the history of science. But what a lot of purely literary mythology he built around it! Mental healing always did and always will run off into magic.[4]

For Max Eastman, this big roomy house – actually an apartment – with its professional offices looking away from the street towards an inner courtyard, with its offices crammed to bursting point with books, journals, paintings, prints, photographs, antique sculptures and oriental rugs – an 'embarrassment of objects', as Peter Gay was to call it[5] – this environment was a kind of protection by a middle-class family against the world outside; it was also in some ways a metaphor for the psychoanalytical process itself. Freud had indeed likened his psychoanalytical work in the early text *Studies on Hysteria* (1895), to 'clearing away, layer by layer, the pathogenic psychical material which we liked to compare with the technique of excavating a buried city.'[6] Eastman also thought there was something obsessional about Freud's collecting mania; so many objects and pictures crammed into such a small space. The two men discussed among other things whether the unconscious was a thing or a concept; the role of metaphor in Freud's science; the question of whether psychoanalysis was a science at all; the relationship between physical and psychological explanations; and why Freud seemed to dislike America so much – 'I don't hate America', Freud replied, 'I regret it'. After the meeting, which ended cordially, Max Eastman left the apartment convinced of two things. First, that Freud's dislike of America had something to do with 'our rather hard-headed scepticism about some of the more mythological of his reported discoveries in 'the Unconscious'.[7] Eastman much preferred the phrase 'unconscious brain states' to 'the Unconscious' because he felt the use of the word as a noun rather than an adjective made it seem too much like a thing rather than a concept, 'a scheming demon for which anatomy certainly finds no place'. Second, that Freud was at the same time a scientist and a latter-day demonologist:

> 'Freud would not let his discoveries be a contribution to psychology. They had to *be* psychology – "Freud's psychology". And there had to be quite a little of the infallibility of the Pope in his pronunciamentos.'

Freud, concluded Eastman, was a man who veered from scepticism to credulity, a thin-skinned man who tended to see criticism as betrayal of the cause.[8]

The whole of Eastman's chapter is in fact centred on these two levels of analysis: the science, the anatomy, the external symptoms, the measurable; and the metaphorical, the archaeological, the literary, the mythological – even the demonological. Which brings us to that framed print of *The Nightmare* which he saw hanging against the dark floral wallpaper of Freud's waiting room, and which he misremembered as of 'a sleeping maiden's naked breast'. It may also have been seen there by 'HD' – Hilda Dolittle, the American poet and friend of Ezra Pound – who was in analysis at Bergasse 19 between March 1933 and December 1934, and who published her *Tribute to Freud* in the mid-1950s:

> I waited as usual in the room, with the round table, the odds and ends of old papers and magazines. There were the usual framed photographs… There was the honorary diploma that had been presented to the Professor in his early days by the small New

England university. There was also a bizarre print or engraving of some nightmare horror, a 'Buried Alive' or some such thing, done in Düreresque symbolic detail. There were long lace curtains at the window, like a 'room in Vienna' in a play or film. The Professor opened the inner door after a short interval. Then I sat on the couch.[9]

This '"Buried Alive" or some such thing' was almost certainly Fuseli's *The Nightmare*.

The first question is: which version of *The Nightmare* by the Zürich-born artist Henry Fuseli – or Johann Heinrich Füssli, as he was originally called – did Eastman and maybe HD actually see? Of the original paintings by Fuseli, two separate versions had entered Western culture. The first was exhibited at the Royal Academy summer show in 1782 (painted the year before), where it caused a sensation – as it was probably intended by the ambitious artist to do. This one is now in the Detroit Institute of Arts. The second, an upright replica painted to order by Henry Fuseli, was made in 1790-1791, ten years after the original, and is now in the Goethe Museum Frankfurt. Freud's Welsh disciple Ernest Jones, when he used a plate of Fuseli's *Nightmare* on the title spread of his book *On the Nightmare* (1931, second impression 1949),[10] actually confused the two. He printed the Frankfurt version of 1790-1791, and wrote below it 'by J H Fuseli 1782'; a surprising error because Jones also acknowledged the help of Professor Paul Ganz of Basle – a distinguished inter-war Fuseli scholar – in getting permission to reproduce the painting and 'providing assistance'. In fairness, there were still muddles about the dating of the two pictures at the time. But, which *was* the printed version hanging in Freud's waiting room? We know from Max Eastman that it was already there in 1926. It was probably there in 1933-1934, when HD was in analysis. But it does not appear in Edmund Engelman's celebrated photographs of the interior of Berggasse 19 which he took in May 1938, the month before Freud left Vienna 'to die in freedom', as the apartment was about to be dismantled. In fact, while Engelman was busy photographing Freud's offices and apartment, some Gestapo officials were equally busy watching him do so from the upper floors. But the print *was* there, in December 1937, when Freud's close friend and colleague Madame Marie Bonaparte (whom he always called 'the Princess': she was Princess George of Greece) filmed some home movies – including footage of the waiting room – which were subsequently to be edited together for the American Psychoanalytical Association after the raw footage had been unearthed by Anna Freud in the early 1970s. These home movies, slightly out of focus, contain two separate shots of *The Nightmare*, the first static, the second moving. The first – of five seconds – shows the framed print on the wall against the floral wallpaper; the second, of three and a half seconds, pans up a large jar from antiquity – probably Egyptian, designed to rest in the sand – which stands in front of the print, and which was presumably moved for the earlier shot. Anna Freud's voiceover, added later, explains that the shots with their French intertitles were taken by Marie Bonaparte – who appears in one of them 'waiting for her analytic hour' and that 'all the pictures in the waiting room…all these pictures are still there – that's all the waiting room. And the waiting room is now, in Berggasse, very much restored as it was then'.[11] Actually, *The Nightmare* is an exception to this. The version of the print hanging today in the Sigmund Freud house in Vienna was placed there in the 1970s. Maybe Marie Bonaparte was drawn to this particular image, because of her own interest in the psychopathology of horror, and in the works of Edgar Allan Poe about which she was to write a celebrated study. She had known Freud since 1925 when she first entered analysis in Vienna.

The print was possibly given to Freud by Ernest Jones, who made his name by publishing some key works on the nightmare – essays written in 1909-1910, while he was reorganising the medical section of the University of Toronto Library, expanded to book length in 1926 and first published as a book in 1931. Most of the 1931 book was written some twenty-two years earlier, by Jones's admission. Jones first met Freud towards the end of April 1908, at the Hotel Bristol in Salzburg, and then visited Freud in Vienna the following month.[12]

He later recalled that Freud said to him at the time, 'what we most need is a book on dreams in English; won't you write one?' So a second possibility, an attractive one, is that Jones saw the print of *The Nightmare* on the walls of the Berggasse apartment in May 1908, and that this – plus Freud's question – first aroused his interest in the subject. If so, the print was already there as early as 1908 – and it may no longer have been there in May 1938, unless Edmund Engelman omitted to photograph that particular angle of the waiting room. Engelman later recalled, of his single photograph of the waiting room, 'in my eagerness to get on into the "important rooms", I rushed through this one, stopping only for a quick shot of the pictures and diplomas on one wall.' He also recalled that the angles he chose were partly to do with 'the positions where Freud usually stood or sat', and partly with where he could place his bulky tripod without damaging anything.[13] So the print *may* after all have been there in May and June 1938. It is thought that Freud must have presented his framed print of Fuseli's *Nightmare* to Marie Bonaparte when he emigrated, which would explain two things: that it didn't travel to 20 Maresfield Gardens, his last refuge in Hampstead; and that a Fuseli print with a Freud dedication 'to M.B.' was auctioned in Geneva a few years ago – where it was bought by a French psychoanalyst.[14] I like to think it now hangs in *her* waiting room. Marie Bonaparte died in 1962.

Back to the print itself. Freud makes no mention of it in his published works but he does refer to a collection which includes a related print. This print was one of an undated folio of eighteen pieces in a small folder called *Le Poitevin: Les Diableries érotiques*, which he had in his library. The collection – by the French printmaker Eugene Le Poitevin (1806-79) – had been published in the 1830s, in France – a series of images of devils, sometimes alone and sometimes in groups, enacting the erotic fantasies of young girls. The example which related to *The Nightmare* shows a small leering devil lifting the nightdress of a woman who lies half-naked across her bed while clutching his penis – a direct, and more obviously erotic, transcription of Fuseli's originals. Following the popular success of Fuseli's *The Nightmare* in the 1780s, the image

– specially the 1782 version – soon entered the bloodstream of popular culture, and the result was a small industry of parody 'nightmares', in the form of political satires or erotic prints or illustrations to horror novels. Fifteen direct transcriptions have been unearthed, dating from between 1783 and 1823, not to mention less direct ones. Le Poitevin's take on the theme dates from a time when *The Nightmare* had become a popular inspiration for French book illustrations.[15] Le Poitevin's 'erotic sorcery' was a late example, before the craze petered out. It seems likely that Freud already possessed this folio in 1909, because he mentions the Le Poitevin collection in his case history of the 'Rat Man', published in that year. In the final section of his published case notes – called 'The Father Complex and the Rat Idea' – Freud describes how this highly intelligent twenty-nine-year-old lawyer called Ernst, who introduced himself in October 1907 and stayed in analysis for eleven months, was obsessed to the point of neurosis with a torture involving rats in a pot and open buttocks which he'd been informed while serving in the army was 'a horrible punishment in the East'. Freud then free-associates around some of the symbolic meanings and verbal connotations of rats: dread of disease, guilt about money ('*raten* = instalments'), fears of anal penetration and even the rat as penis. There is then this footnote: 'If the reader feels tempted to shake his head at the possibility of such leaps of imagination in the neurotic mind, I may remind him that artists have sometimes indulged in similar freaks of fantasy. Such, for instance, are Le Poitevin's *Diableries érotiques*.'[16] Including the transcription of *The Nightmare*. It is worth noting that in Freud's equally celebrated 1908-09 case history of the cheerful five-year-old 'Little Hans', the boy has a phobia about being bitten by a white horse…

Marie Bonaparte's footage of the Fuseli *Nightmare* shows it to have been printed back to front – the opposite way round to all known official printed editions, for example the edition of January 1783, a stipple engraving by Thomas Burke – the one which indelibly associated Fuseli in the public mind with *The Nightmare*, a bestseller at five shillings a time in a first edition of 2,000 which quickly sold out.[17] At first I thought that this particular shot in the home movie must have been flipped – as sometimes happens – but it is the same way round behind the antique jar, and in neighbouring shots the writing is the correct way round, for example on the spines of books. The out-of-focus inscription is on the left side of the border, the more common position, with the writing aligned to the edge of the image. So this was probably a pirate version or even a photograph of the Fuseli print which had been reversed in the printing. The reversal made it look more like the 1790 version, which is also reversed, the victim's head on the left, nightmare on the right. There was something of a Fuseli revival in the Tens and Twenties of the twentieth century – with the attention paid to *The Nightmare* by the Surrealists, for obvious reasons, with the reinvention of Switzerland as a cultural destination, and with the William Blake renaissance – plus the purchase of many Fuselis, good value in those days, by the Kunsthaus in Zürich, which became the biggest collection of this 'local artist made good'. So maybe this print was a part of that fashion. Maybe Freud purchased it in Switzerland. Or maybe it was purchased at a print-seller's in London.

If it was, then it is likely that Ernest Jones purchased it, a gift to his master and teacher from Freud's closest British adherent – and one of his most uncritical disciples. Jones was part of the 'inner circle' around Freud, the only colleagues from whom he was willing to take criticism. And – like Max Eastman – Jones was later (in his biography, published 1953-57) to recall that Freud could be credulous as well as a good late-nineteenth-century scientific positivist. In 1931, Ernest Jones's *On the Nightmare* was published by Leonard and Virginia Woolf at the Hogarth Press. Jones was by then well in with the Bloomsbury set,[18] via the writer James Strachey, brother of Lytton, who had contacted him in 1920 offering to translate Freud's writings into English. Jones had explained to Freud that the dynasty was 'a well-known literary family'.

In *On the Nightmare*, Jones outlined the various 'explanations' of nightmares which had been in common currency from medieval times to the early twentieth century, and then contrasted them with 'the epoch-making work of one man – Professor Freud – on the psychogenesis of dreams and the relationship of them to the neuroses'.[19] For Jones, writers on the nightmare had for centuries mistaken for the true *cause* of the malady various superficial factors or symptoms 'that play a part, of varying importance, in the evocation of a given attack'.[20] In the Middle Ages, the causes tended to be projected outwards, onto 'external personal agents' such as lewd demons or grimacing dwarfs, incubi visiting women by night and succubi visiting men by night. St Augustine, for example, in *The City of God*, wrote of fiends of hell tempting frail humanity. The more cynical Geoffrey Chaucer, in *The Wife of Bath's Tale*, preferred to observe that visits by incubi had become a lot rarer since mendicant friars started preaching within the walls of convents. Then, from the early seventeenth century onwards, the causes tended to be projected onto bodily processes or physical factors – 'non-mental and non-sexual' – which physicians began seriously to study for the first time. So, various writers in the Age of Enlightenment rejected the timeworn folkloric explanations as 'superstitious' and instead debated which bodily process held the key to nightmares: sleeping on one's back or left side, eating difficult-to-digest or undigested food (favourites included cucumbers, West Indian pears and under-done pork), an over-full stomach, circulatory disturbances, breathing difficulties, menstruation and reading anxious-making books too late at night. All these were eighteenth-century 'explanations' of the nightmare experience. The thing was to reduce superstitions to 'natural causes' and then explain them away. Ernest Jones began *On the Nightmare* with an epigraph from Erasmus Darwin, the physician and poet, and grandfather of Charles – and it was the same literary epigraph the first four lines of which had appeared beneath the original print of Fuseli's *The Nightmare* in 1783. In Jones's epigraph:

> So on his Nightmare, through the evening fog,
>
> Flits the squat fiend o'er fen, and lake, and bog;
>
> Seeks some love-wilder'd maid with sleep oppressed,

Alights, and grinning, sits upon her breast –

Such as of late, amid the murky sky,

Was marked by Fuseli's poetic eye

This was the folkloric version of the nightmare with a vengeance, originally part of Erasmus Darwin's scientific poem *The Botanical Garden*, subtitled 'The Loves of the Plants' (1789-91) – where it illustrated Darwin's thoughts on the suspension of willpower, in sleep, while the senses remain alert – so you experience 'the painful desire to exert the voluntary motions' which leads to all sorts of imaginings. 'In vain she wills to run, fly, swim, walk, creep.'[21] Such thoughts were part of what was known as 'the new psychology', and they show that the unconscious was already topical in the late-eighteenth century; it is just that it wasn't called that yet. Darwin's lines were also a misunderstanding or a misreading of Fuseli's painting. He evidently thought the nightmare was the horse – 'so on his Nightmare...flits the squat fiend' – rather than the mara (a completely different word, from the old Teutonic for 'devil' and the Anglo-Saxon for 'crusher') squatting on the woman's breast. It was a confusion which has survived to this day, between a female horse and a 'nightmare'. In the painting, the sightless horse is the vehicle of the mara – it even wears a collar – and could just as well be a stallion: a blind creature leading the mara to random places. In what may well be Fuseli's original drawing of March 1781, the horse isn't even there at all.[22] Perhaps Freud, unlike Jones, would not have fully comprehended this linguistic and gender confusion: he would have thought of *The Nightmare* as *Der Alptraum*. But Ernest Jones was fascinated by the connections between the two traditions – even if they were purely linguistic – and his one reference to Fuseli in the entire text is in a chapter on the mythology of horses, riders, human-animal metamorphoses and night-flights – which he sees as examples of 'interchangeability'. So he cites a Swiss folk legend, in which:

> ...the mara penetrates through the keyhole into the bedchamber
> in the guise of a steed, lays her fore-hoofs on the sleeper's breast,

and with glaring eyes stares at him in the most alarming fashion – a description which might well have been written in reference to one of the versions of the frontispiece by Fuseli in the present volume.[23]

Actually, it might not. The steed in the painting is a background figure, the mara is either a monkey-like creature (in the first version) or a cat-like creature (in the second), the victim is female and the eyes are glaring out at the viewer rather than at the sleeper. So he was wrong on all counts. No version of the Fuseli remotely resembles Jones's account of the folk legend. And the 'horse-mara' connection in the painting may even have been intended as a joke – as a visual pun on the word 'mare'. Fuseli did like macabre jokes.[24]

The conclusion of Ernest Jones's *On the Nightmare* is *not* that such folk wisdom is mere mumbo-jumbo – on the contrary, modern medicine he says has in some ways 'unlearned' folk explanations which are still very useful to the psychoanalyst. The conclusion is instead that, surprising as it may seem, if you go to your physician today complaining of nightmares, he or she is still liable to give you irrelevant advice about hygiene or indigestion or sleeping posture which goes right back to the 'explanations' of the eighteenth century: 'the explanations of this condition still current in medical circles, and which ascribe it to digestive or circulatory disturbances, are probably further from the truth than any other medical views'.[25] Again, it is not that the Enlightenment hypotheses are completely off-beam: it is just that they confuse symptom with deep causes. These superficial symptoms often happen to people without causing nightmares; and nightmares often happen without these superficial symptoms. Clearly a deeper explanation was needed. Strangely, while Ernest Jones was rigorous in his interrogation of scientific and medical sources, he tended to be slapdash in his use of literature and visual art. He misdates and misreads the Fuseli painting, and he misquotes Erasmus Darwin: it should be 'squab' not 'squat' – a much better word – and the maid should be oppressed 'by sleep' not 'with sleep'. Be that as it may, in order to reach the deeper explanation for which Jones was searching, we need to go back to the reception of Fuseli's *The Nightmare*, amongst critics and commentators, at the time it was first exhibited.

The first-ever review of the painting was in the London *Morning Herald* on Wednesday 8 May 1782, the exhibition having opened at the Royal Academy then in Somerset House on Monday 29 April, the review went straight to the confusion between 'mare' and 'mara'.

> There is a wildness of conception in Mr Fuseli's picture of the Night Shade at the Royal Academy, which teems with that usual concomitant of genius, inaccuracy. He has introduced a mare's head into the piece, to characterise his subject. Now the personification of that disorder, which attacks the human frame in sleep, is borrowed from a word of northern origin; Mair or Mère, a witch or sorceress. Shakespeare's Mad Tom [in *King Lear* Act III sc iv] mentions her in that character from some legendary ballad…
>
> St Withold footed thrice the wold,
>
> He met the Night Mare and her nine-fold;
>
> Bid her alight and her troth plight
>
> And aroynt thee, witch, aroynt thee![26]

So, according to this critic of *The Nightmare* – the first – Fuseli had confused the man with the horse: the *Lear* reference suggests that the critic had been reading Dr Johnson's *Dictionary* on the subject. Johnson was still the authority in the 1780s, and could be depended on to cite interesting literary references as usage. He wrote:

> NIGHTMARE [*night*, and *mara*, a spirit that, in the northern mythology, was related to torment or suffocate sleepers]. A morbid oppression in the night, resembling the pressure of weight upon the breast.
>
> Saint Withold footed thrice the wold

He met the *nightmare*, and her name be told;

Bid her alight, and her troth plight...

MARE, on the other hand, was a completely different word. It was 'the female of a horse'.[27]

The confusing thing for critics was that *The Nightmare*, unusually for Fuseli, did not make explicit reference to a specific literary or classical/mythological source: there was no subtitle and no clue in the title. Exhibition-goers were accustomed to paintings by various artists since the Renaissance of specific dreams experienced by Old Testament sages, Trojan warriors, Renaissance artists or Shakespearean kings – but a generic nightmare – *The Nightmare* – perhaps set in the present day was something new. Surely, given Fuseli's reputation up to now,[28] this must have a Shakespearean meaning – maybe to do with *King Lear*? *The Morning Chronicle*, of the following day, acknowledged that *The Nightmare* was a virtuoso performance but was more turned off by the subject-matter:

> *The Nightmare*, by Mr Fuseli like all his productions has strong marks of genius about it; but hag-riding is too unpleasant a thought to be agreeable to anyone, and is unfit for furniture [i.e. as decoration] or reflection – *Qui bono?*... Yet surely a disagreeable subject, well executed, is preferable to the most engaging one ill described...[we have] another proof how artists sometimes lose themselves, and mistake their talents...[29]

'Hag-riding' – the review went on – could indeed be a reference to Mad Tom's song in *Lear*, or even to *Paradise Lost* (6ii) – a reference to the witch supposed to wander in the night 'lur'd with the smell of infant-blood'. So John Milton maybe – on the other hand, it could perhaps be a reference to the Queen Mab myth, as Dr Johnson had also written under the word 'mare', a reference to Mercutio's speech from Act I, Scene 4 of Shakespeare's *Romeo and Juliet*:

And in this state she gallops night by night

Through lovers' brains, and then they dream of love;

…This is the hag, when maids lie on their backs,

That presses them and learns them first to bear,

Making them women of good carriage.

This debate in the journals of 8 and 9 May – which created an aura of mystery around the picture – may well have stimulated public interest in *The Nightmare*. The picture wasn't from any agreed literary source, or from nature – so exactly where did its nobility reside? What was its point? There was an immediacy about *The Nightmare* which Horace Walpole, for one, found 'shocking', and he wrote that single word in his copy of the Academy catalogue next to the Fuseli entry. [30] But the publicity was working: over six and a half thousand people could have seen *The Nightmare* on Saturday 1 June and Monday 3 June alone – and they probably did. On Thursday 9 May 2,713 people were recorded as visiting the Royal Academy exhibition, the highest figure for a single day of the entire run and even higher than the existing all-time record for daily attendances.

So far the debate about the painting had concerned its 'wildness', whether the subject-matter was 'disagreeable' or acceptable, and possible sources of inspiration in Shakespeare or Milton. The critical consensus seemed to be that Fuseli had personified an idea. The question was, what exactly *was* the idea? Where paintings of visions were concerned, the critics seemed much more comfortable describing the visual conventions than they were at explaining what all this might *mean*. It took a Church of England vicar, Rev Robert Anthony Bromley, Rector of St Mildred's in the Poultry, to be the first to suggest that *The Nightmare* might after all be about sex. In the first volume of his *Philosophical and Critical History of the Fine Arts - Painting, Sculpture and Architecture* (1793), Bromley included in his chapter on 'the qualifications essential in the constitution of moral painting' an elaborate sideswipe at Fuseli's picture. He didn't mention the artist by name but he didn't need to:

...the dignity of moral instruction is degraded, whenever the pencil is employed on frivolous, whimsical, and unmeaning subjects... The *Night-mare, Little Red Riding Hood, The Shepherd's Dream* [exhibited by Fuseli at the Academy in 1786] or any dream that is not marked in authentic history as combined with the inspiring dispensations of Providence, and many other pieces of a visionary and fanciful nature, are mere speculations... What good has the world, or what honour has the art, at any time derived from such light and fantastic speculations? If it be right to follow Nature, there is nothing of her here. All that is presented to us is a *reverie* of the brain...mere waking dreams, as wild as the conceits of a madman. [A recent commentator] very properly calls such artists 'libertines of painting': as there are libertines of religion, who have no other law but the vehemence of their own inclinations...[31]

Bromley had evidently been reading the critics. But, in strongly implying that Fuseli was among the 'libertines of painting', Bromley was breaking new ground. Maybe *The Nightmare* was an example of the kind of libertine art which had been exhibited in recent Paris *Salons*, or was known to be collected for private consumption by well-heeled connoisseurs and even the seedier members of the royal family. *A Philosophical and Critical History* continued – at great and ponderous length – to enunciate the principles that 'whatever is outré and extravagant can never be beautiful', and 'whatever is empty or poor of sentiment cannot instruct any persons'.[32] Fuseli was furious. He took bitter offence at Bromley's attack on *The Nightmare*. It was one thing to encourage a public reputation for eccentricity and even for being 'Painter in ordinary to the Devil' – Fuseli did that whenever the opportunity arose, and on one occasion said of his diabolic reputation 'Aye, he has sat for me many times' – it was quite another to be publicly accused of being a libertine. Especially to accuse someone who was as desperate to be accepted by the artistic establishment as Fuseli was. So Fuseli wrote an ill-tempered and anonymous review of Bromley's book in the journal the *Analytical Review* of July 1793 and then encouraged a debate at Somerset House which resulted in the Royal Academy cancelling its subscription to the second volume of Bromley's *History*. How could a commentator use 'so little delicacy' as to liken a living artist to a libertine? Whatever next?[33]

Apart from possible literary or mythological sources – or 'figures in art' as he called them[34], which might have served as models for Fuseli, and there was much debate about these as well – there is another intellectual context which helps to clarify the contemporary meaning of *The Nightmare*, namely the ways in which the painting could have been 'read' at the time of its first reception. Fuseli was fascinated by visions and dreams, play-acting and orating, larger-than-life superheroes and curvaceous heroines, and painterly gloom, but in a quieter more private way he was almost equally fascinated by aspects of applied science and medicine. He was well-informed about entomology and liked to study it over breakfast, he wrote a number of articles about insects for the *Analytical Review* (usually over the signature 'R.R.'), he made a surprising number of drawings of entomological subjects which he called his 'favourite study and amusement' and he tended to lose himself in the close analysis of butterflies and moths when he was feeling particularly depressed. He also knew a great deal about the Linnaean system of classifying plants, insects and animals, and how 'his divisions and subdivisions are crumbling every hour to dust', especially when viewed through the latest microscopes.[35] Ever since he first arrived in London in the mid-1760s, from Zürich, Fuseli had particularly enjoyed mixing in medical circles. On one occasion he surprised his friend the painter Joseph Farington when the conversation turned to the subject of madness. Instead of waxing lyrical about Lady Macbeth and King Lear, he talked statistics:

> Fuseli mentioned that a Medical man who attended Bedlam had said that the greatest number of these who were confined were *Women in love*, and the next class in respect of number was *Hackney* and *Stage Coachmen*, caused it was supposed by the

constant shaking exercise to which they are subject which affects *the pineal gland.*[36]

One of Fuseli's closest friendships in London was with Dr John Armstrong – notoriously waspish medical practitioner, poet and friend of John Wilkes – of whom the painter 'always entertained a high opinion', and who returned the compliment by 'praising him in the Journals'.[37] In 1744, Armstrong had published his best-known poem *The Art of Preserving Health* (it was often reprinted), a polemic in favour of regular exercise, moderation in all things, fresh air, honest toil, thinking pure thoughts and eating sensibly.[38] In the long section devoted to *Exercise* (Book III), Armstrong wrote of nightmares:

> Oppress not nature sinking down to rest
>
> With feasts too late, too solid, or too full…
>
> Not all a monarch's luxury the woes
>
> Can counterpoise, of that most wretched man,
>
> Whose nights are shaken with the frantic fits
>
> Of wild Orestes; whose delirious brain,
>
> Stung by the furies, works with poisoned thought…

Ways of avoiding nightmares, Armstrong went on, included going to bed early, avoiding rich food, engaging in 'pleasing talk' just before going to bed and as a very last resort reading Homer aloud. Indulging in 'sickly musing', 'hideous fictions' and nasty paintings, especially when alone, were not recommended. In the part of *The Art of Preserving Health* which was about over-eating Armstrong went on to cite the researches of a Dr John Bond who was soon to publish a full-length *Essay on the Incubus, or Night-mare* (1753).[39]

Bond claimed that this was the first-ever full-length work on the subject of nightmares, which it was not. Ernest Jones was to find on the library shelves sixteen earlier works dating from the period 1627 to 1740, mainly published in Germany and nearly all in Latin. But Jones was to cite Bond more often than anyone. In his essay, Bond contrasted the old folkloric and moral explanations of the nightmare with the new medical ones. He made this the centrepiece of his argument. He began by dismissing superstitions 'that did not appear serious or probable', and explaining why he would confine himself instead 'the laws of animal economy'.[40] This was the enlightened position:

> I have therefore omitted an inquiry into the origins of many odd epithets and quaint names commonly given to this Disorder; such as Hag-riding, Wizard-pressing, Mare-riding, Witch-dancing & c… In our language it is generally known by the name of the Night-mare; which strange term probably arose from superstitious notions which the British had, and perhaps still have, of it…[41]

The popular confusion between 'mare' (female horse) and 'night-mare' (bad dream) was, apparently, part of this superstition. Bond also excluded the thesis that 'the Night-mare is an imaginary Disease, and proceeds from the idea of some demon, which existed in the mind the day before'. Instead, he carefully listed the symptoms – people lying on their backs, having bad dreams, breathing with difficulty, experiencing a violent oppression on the breast and losing voluntary motion – and explained them all as relating to blockages in the circulation of the blood. In particular, he noted, nightmares occurred when the head was lower than the legs, when the victim had turned onto the left side, and when too much blood was flowing into the brain. So each of the folkloric explanations was 'really internal'. For Dr Bond, the kinds of people who were likely to have nightmares were relatively easy to classify:

> 'Young persons of gross full habits, the luxurious, the drunken and they who sup late, are most subject to the night-mare. Also Women who are obstructed; girls of full, lax habits before the eruption of the Menses.'[42]

Bond was writing in the 'sensory' tradition of John Locke, who in his *Essay Concerning Human Understanding* (1689) had treated dreams as 'Waking Man's Ideas, though for the most part oddly put together' rather that 'the Soul [having] ideas of its own'.[43] So the transition from theological or moral to medical explanations was well under way by this time. But still within this frame of reference, Bond's thesis about blood circulation was to be explicitly challenged by another Lockean Dr Robert Whytt in his *Observations on the nature, causes and cure of those disorders which have been commonly called Nervous* (1765, reprinted 1777). Whytt reckoned that Bond's conclusions were 'far from being satisfactory' – they begged many more questions than they answered – and proposed instead that the causes of nightmares lay not in the blood but in the stomach: indigestion, wind, excessive phlegm, eating too late, 'certain medicines or poisons' including nervous medicines, in short 'strange ideas excited in the mind in consequence of the disordered state of the stomach, not then corrected by the external senses as they are when we are awake'. Whytt agreed with Bond's list of symptoms – and his thoughts about 'a suppression of the menses in women' – but:

> '…neither a horizontal posture, sleep, nor heavy suppers, do ever produce the night-mare, at least in any considerable degree, unless the person be predisposed to it from the particular condition of the nerves of the stomach.'[44]

Fuseli's painting *The Nightmare* clearly refers in many detailed ways to the contemporary debate about the causes of nightmares and – in parallel – includes most of the folkloric explanations as well. The victim is sleeping on her back, turned to her left side, with her head below her legs and with a pressure on her stomach. On the bedside table is a jar of liquid, maybe a 'nervous medicine'. But the sightless horse and the *mara* are there as well – the superstitious notions, as Bond had written, 'which the British had, and perhaps still have, of it…'[45] Fuseli really enjoyed British superstitions, particularly the ones he'd seen enacted in Shakespeare's plays and most particularly imps, elves and fairies. His *A Midsummer Night's Dream* paintings and drawings celebrated them.

Like so many other aspects of *The Nightmare*, this medical debate even found its way into Fuseli's reputation. In the year he became a full Royal Academician, in 1790, the *Public Advertiser* started a rumour that the artist's imagination did not spring from refinement of taste at all but from 'an animal process, and is brought about after regular intervals by Mr. Fuseli's eating raw pork for supper'.[46] This rumour was evidently still in the ether when one of his biographies appeared in 1830, three years after Fuseli's death; the biographer felt the need to dismiss it: 'The story of his having supped on raw pork chops that he might dream his picture of the nightmare has no foundation.' On the contrary, wrote the biographer, Fuseli ate two frugal meals a day (the Armstrong diet, perhaps) and always avoided supper if he could.[47] But – he added, casting a shadow of doubt over the frugal Fuseli – the artist did once drop in on William Blake, probably around the time of the *Advertiser* allegation, and discovered him eating a plate of cold mutton: 'Is *that* what you do it on?' Fuseli asked.[48]

By the time of this biography – Allan Cunningham's *Lives of the Most Eminent British Painters* (1830) there was a growing craze for books about geniuses, and the more eccentric the better. It had long become a mantra among Romantic writers to see dreams as gateways into the darkness (so that, as Novalis put it, 'world becomes dream; dream becomes world'). In popular biographies a number of visual and literary artists was said deliberately to have induced their nightmares: the poet Southey was reputed to have used laughing gas, the novelist Anne Radcliffe indigestible food late at night, while others opted for portions of undercooked meat after prolonged periods of vegetarianism. Not all of which had the desired result. The 'romantic agony' could simply take the form of serious indigestion. Thomas De Quincey could not understand why Fuseli bothered to eat 'raw meat for the sake of obtaining splendid dreams'. 'Better,' he suggested, 'to have eaten opium.'[49] The rumour about raw pork gained some of its currency from the shocking *immediacy* of *The Nightmare*, and its concrete details: the image must have come from somewhere, and Fuseli was known to be very choosy about his sources. Where did it come from?

Today, post-Freud and Ernest Jones, we can see that the painting is also and perhaps primarily about sex – although whether it is about submission, empowerment or voyeurism is still being hotly debated by art historians. At the time, the thought that nightmares might have deep sexual connotations

– and causes – whether openly expressed or disguised, was not yet thinkable. We have seen how the art establishment in the form of the Royal Academy ganged up on a hapless vicar who dared to suggest that the painting might have something to do with sex. Sigmund Freud's interpretation of Fuseli's *Nightmare* has not been recorded. We know that, by his own admission, he derived far more pleasure from the subject-matter of paintings and the stories they told than from their 'formal and technical' qualities: 'I may say at once,' he famously wrote in *The Moses of Michelangelo* (1914), 'that I am no connoisseur in art, but simply a layman. I have often observed that the subject-matter of works of art has a stronger attraction for me than their formal and technical qualities, though to the artist their value lies first and foremost in these latter.'[50] So he would no doubt have related Fuseli's painting, at the level of subject-matter and story, to his own theory of dreams. Since Ernest Jones's conclusions, in *On the Nightmare*, were based partly on *The Interpretation of Dreams* (1900), partly on Freud's writings about *Angst* and *Superstition*, we can confidently speculate that he would have agreed with them at that stage in his career. And Freud would have been reminded of them, every time he looked on the wall of his waiting room. For Freud, as we know, dreams were the 'guardians of sleep', the carriers of waking wishes or repressed desires which could not for various reasons emerge in any other way, usually wishes and desires from childhood. As a rule, these were in his view 'erotic wishes…and sexual desires', and they emerged through the freedom of the dream state in *displaced* or *symbolic* or *condensed* or *represented* forms.[51] Taking these ideas as his starting-point, Ernest Jones outlined the history of the explanations of nightmares pre-Freud which we looked at earlier, then added – following Freud – that in nightmares these erotic wishes and sexual desires were 'transformed into anxiety', and the more forbidden the sexual desire the greater the anxiety: nightmares embraced the terror which the sleeper feared the most, and had buried the deepest. In one way, this contradicted Freud's theory of dreams, which were supposed to be about wish-fulfilment, whereas for Jones they were about anxiety. How could they be about repressed wishes *and* anxieties, both at the same time? Well, said Jones, the *latent* content of the nightmare was wish-fulfilment – buried very deep – but the *manifest* content, the bit the dreamer remembered, was anxiety. That terror came, he said, or rather asserted, 'from the deepest stirring of mental life, which has the primordial conflict over incest'.[52] This was an unacceptable desire 'of such vehemence, that it threatens to overpower the repressing force', and in general the more intense the repression, the more distorted, perverted or disguised the dream. So 'an attack of the nightmare is an expression of a mental conflict over an incestuous desire', which had indeed been repressed since childhood.[53] The folkloric explanations had 'a kernel of truth' in them, said Jones, because they described in their own ways the symbolic language of nightmares – and 'the structure of myths and dreams are related in respect of the unconscious mechanism at work'. Hence Jones's chapters on the incubus, the vampire, the werewolf, the devil, the witch, beauty and the beast – and indeed the horse. The physical or organic explanations also contained 'a modicum of truth', provided one accepted that they were about '1 per cent not 99 per cent' of the nightmare experience.[54] Incest was for him the key. He didn't attempt to prove this. He simply took it as the final turn in his argument, as fact. At the core of nightmares lay Oedipus and incest, the very deepest of unmentionables.

Art historians, writing about Fuseli's *Nightmare* since the publication of Ernest Jones's study, have tried to relate some of his ideas back to the painting itself. So we have one influential historian, H.W. Janson, agreeing that *The Nightmare* was really a displacement of the artist's sexual fantasies – about his friend's young niece, a girl called Anna Landolt who had recently married someone else: so the victim was a projection of the artist's dream-girl, while the incubus-demon took the place of the artist himself.[55] It may even have been a self-portrait – a pretty far-fetched idea! Since then most commentators have more or less taken it for granted that the fantasy in the picture is a sexual fantasy – with the mara as a form of grinning penis with ears. A specialist in the study of sleep patterns, from the Department of Psychiatry at the State University of New York, has adopted a different tack by arguing that the painting depicts several of the distinctive features of 'sleep paralysis', as distinct from nightmares and often confused with them: 'sleep paralysis' is an anxiety attack which happens just when one is falling asleep or waking up, and which is apparently accompanied by hallucinations of 'someone sitting on my chest'. '[*The Nightmare*] actually represents a specific phenomenon…which long after the painting appeared was described in clinical terms and given its specific name.'[56] So it shouldn't be called *The Nightmare* at all. It should be called *The Sleep Paralysis*.

Another specialist, from the Department of Neurology at McGill University, Montreal, has argued that nightmares in fact occur during confused states of arousal rather than dreaming sleep: for this scientist, the painting depicts a literal belief in nocturnal demons pressing upon the sleeper's chest, and at the same time illustrates the etymology of the word: 'the monster sitting on the patient's chest and the female horse (sic) leering in the background refer to the ancient Teutonic word *mar*, meaning devil, and the English word mare, which it suggests.'[57] And so on. Such analyses of the painting tend to be circular, self-reinforcing, and they tell us much more about the writer than the visual image. They look for reinforcement of their science in the painting.

Whether, every time he walked past it, Freud thought *The Nightmare* was about the repression of incestuous desires – or about the ancient and medieval mythologies which interested him; about the metaphorical rather than the psychological – we don't know. His print may well have been one of his 'tools of thought, the kitchen utensils of his imagination', as Marina Warner has put it.[58] And *was* it entirely coincidental that in summer 1938 he settled in 20 *Mare*sfield Gardens, Hampstead, leaving the picture behind? Well, one thing's for sure. When Freud's patients arrived for their daily appointments at Berggasse 19, in Vienna, and sat in the waiting room looking at that framed print on the wall, they must certainly have known they had come to the right address.

(ENDNOTES)

1   This essay was first given, as a paper in draft form at the *Fear* conference (Trinity College Dublin, 19 May 2006,) and then as a lecture to the Friends of the Freud Museum, (London, 17 November 2006.)

2   Eastman, Max, *Heroes I have known* (New York, 1942), pp. 262-73.

3   For photographs of these locations, taken some twelve years later, see Edmund Engelman, *Berggasse 19 – Sigmund Freud's home and offices, Vienna 1938* (Chicago, 1981), plates 2, 7, 8, 9 & 10.

4   Eastman, Max, *Heroes I have known* (New York, 1942), p. 264.

5   Gay, Peter, *Freud – for the marble tablet.* In Engelman, *Berggasse 19*, pp. 13-54.

6   Gay, Peter, *Freud*, pp. 19-20. *Studies on Hysteria* was written by Freud with Josef Breuer.

7   Eastman, Max, *Heroes I have known* (New York, 1942), esp. pp. 215-66.

8   Ibid., pp. 267, 272-3.

9   Doolittle, Hilda, *Tribute to Freud*, 'Writing on the Wall' (New York, 1974), pp. 60-1.

10   Jones, Ernest, *On the Nightmare*, illustration opposite the title page, (London, 1931; reprinted London, 1949).

11   Freud, Anna, voiceover in the home movies, screened as part of the permanent exhibition at 20 Maresfield Gardens.

12   See Brenda Maddox, *Freud's wizard – the enigma of Ernest Jones* (London, 2006), pp. 61, 68-89. Also Ernest Jones, *On the Nightmare*, pp. 7-8.

13   Engelman, Edmund *Berggasse 19 – Sigmund Freud's home and offices, Vienna 1938* (Chicago, 1981), pp. 136-7.

14   Communication from Michael Molnar, acting director of the Freud Museum (London, May 2005).

15   See Christopher Frayling, 'Fuseli's *The Nightmare* – somewhere between the sublime and the ridiculous' in Martin Myrone (ed.), *Gothic nightmares* (London, 2006), pp. 13-15, 45-51. Also, David H. Weinglass, *Prints and engraved illustrations by and after Henry Fuseli* (Aldershot, 1994), section on *The Nightmare*, pp. 55-72. A print resembling the Le Poitevin print, in the form of a small lithograph vignette attributed to Charles Ramelet (1805-51), from the journal *Macedoines* in 1830, is reproduced in Peter Tomory, *The life and art of Henry Fuseli* (London, 1972), plate 227. In this version, the devil is not lifting the victim's night-dress, which covers most of her right thigh. It is also left-to-right rather than right-to-left, another example of reversal. The Le Poitevin seems to have been an erotic parody of the Ramelet, which was presumably quite well-known at the time.

16   Freud, Sigmund, *The case histories – 'Little Hans' and the 'Rat Man'. Standard edition of the complete psychological works, vol. X, 1909* (London, 2001), p. 214. The 'Rat Man' case is described pp. 154-249, including that 'horrible punishment in the East'; 'Little Hans', pp. 22-100.

17   See Martin Myrone (ed.), *Gothic Nightmares*, p. 49.

18   See Brenda Maddox, *Freud's wizard*, p. 160.

19   Jones, Ernest, *On the Nightmare*, 'Pathology of the nightmare', (London, 1931; reprinted London, 1949) pp. 13-54.

20 Jones, Ernest, *On the Nightmare*, (London, 1931; reprinted London, 1949) pp. 30, 37, 50; section on 'medieval superstitions', pp. 57-97.

21 Continuation of Erasmus Darwin quote above, seventeen lines later. See Myrone, *Gothic nightmares*, p. 43.

22 Frayling, Christopher, 'Fuseli's *The Nightmare*', p. 11. See Nicolas Powell, *The Nightmare* (London, 1973), pp. 58, 97-8 for a reproduction and possible explanation. There is no bottle on the table either.

23 Jones, Ernest, *On the Nightmare*, p. 256, part of the chapter 'The horse and the night-fiend', pp. 248-73.

24 On other critical confusions surrounding *The Nightmare* at the time, see Christopher Frayling, 'Fuseli's *The Nightmare*', pp. 11-15.

25 See, among many other references, Ernest Jones, *On the Nightmare*, (New York,1971) pp. 13-14.

26 *Morning Herald*, 8 May 1782.

27 Johnson, Dr Samuel, *A dictionary of the English language*, vol. 2 (London, 1755).

28 Fuseli's earlier exhibits at the Royal Academy, for example, had included visualisations of scenes from *Henry VI Part II*, *Macbeth* and *Henry VIII*.

29 *Morning Chronicle*, 9 May 1782.

30 See Frayling, Christopher, 'Fuseli's *The Nightmare*', pp. 10-12.

31 Bromley, Revd Robert Anthony, *A philosophical and critical history of the fine arts*, vol. 1 (London, 1793), pp. 36-7, 56-61.

32 Frayling, Christopher, 'Fuseli's *The Nightmare*', p. 12.

33 For the anonymous review, see Eudo Mason, *The mind of Henry Fuseli* (London, 1951), pp. 278-9. For the controversy, see Joseph Farington, *The diary*, vol. 1 (eds) Cave, Garlick & Macintyre (New Haven, 1978-84), p. 165.

34 Fuseli's third Royal Academy lecture 'on Invention' about 'the judicious adoption of figures in art', printed in John Knowles, *The life and writings of Henry Fuseli*, vol. 3 (London, 1831).

35 On Fuseli and entomology see for example Mason, *The mind of Henry Fuseli*, pp. 332-6, the source of the quotations on the subject in this paragraph.

36 Farington, Joseph, *The diary*, vol. 6, (New York, 1926) p. 228, entry for 2 April 1804.

37 On Fuseli and Armstrong, see Mason, *The Mind of Henry Fuseli*, p. 127.

38 Armstrong, John, *The art of preserving health – a poem* (London, 1744), Book III, pp. 84-6, Book IV, pp. 108-9, the source of the quotation and subsequent references.

39 Armstrong, John, *The art of preserving health*, Book II, pp. 38-9. See also John Bond, *An Essay on the Incubus, or Night-mare* (London, 1753), pp. 1-83.

40 Bond, John, *An Essay on the Incubus, or Night-mare*, pp. 2-5.

41 Ibid., pp., 2-5, 24, 46-51, 79-82, the source of the rest of this paragraph.

42 Ibid., pp. 46-51.

43 Locke, John, *Essay concerning human understanding* (London, 1689), in *Works* (1714), vol. 1, pp. 36-7.

44 Whytt, Robert, *Observations on the nature, causes and cure of those disorders which have been commonly called nervous* (London, 1765), pp. 315-18, the source of all the Whytt quotations above.

45 See footnote 44.

46 *Public Advertiser*, 31 May 1790.

47 Cunningham, Allan, *The lives of the most eminent English painters*, vol. 2 (2nd ed. London 1830-3), pp. 358-9, the source of the 'no foundation' quote as well; also Peter Tomory, *The life and art of Henry Fuseli*, pp. 181-4.

48 Peter, Tomory, *The life and art of Henry Fuseli*, p. 184, citing Allan Cunningham.

49 de Quincey, Thomas, *Confessions of an English opium eater* (London, 1823), p. 118.

50 Cited in Anthony Storr, *Freud* (Oxford, 1989), p. 93, from the *Standard edition of Sigmund Freud's works*, vol. 13, trans. James Strachey & Alix Strachey (London, 1953-74), p. 211.

51 On Freud's *The interpretation of dreams*, with quotations, see Storr, *Freud*, pp. 41-51.

52 Jones, Ernest, *On the Nightmare*, (New York, 1971) pp. 42-4, the source of the next sentence as well.

53 Ibid., pp. 42-4, 75-7.

54 Ibid., p. 52.

55 See, among many others since, H.W. Janson, 'Freud's nightmare', *Art and Science* (New York 1963), pp. 23-8.

56 See Jerome M. Schneck, 'Henry Fuseli, nightmare, and sleep paralysis', *Journal of the American Medical Association*, 207:4 (27 January 1969, pp. 725-6), the source of the above quotations.

57 J. Broughton, Roger, 'Sleep disorders: disorders of arousal?' *Science*, 159 (1968), pp. 1070-8, on the 'nocturnal demons' and the etymology of the word 'mara'.

58 Warner, Marina, 'Preface' to *20 Maresfield Gardens* (London, 1998), pp. vii-ix..

4

The Funeral March of a Marionette

Introduction

Angela Carter was intrigued by Gounod's opera Faust *(1859), with its transposition of a sixteenth-century set of legends, via Goethe's* Faust *part one, into a mid-nineteenth-century Parisian idiom. She once said that she would like to see a production of* Faust *in a double-bill with Béla Bartók's one-act* Bluebeard's Castle *(1911) based on Perrault's story – though it has to be said this would make for a very long evening indeed, especially if* Faust *were to be performed in its optional five-act version complete with wild orgiastic ballet on Walpurgis night. These days, most audiences probably associate* Faust *mainly with Gaston Leroux's* The Phantom of the Opera, *during which it is performed in Garnier's wedding cake of an opera house.*

Amongst the countless fin de siècle *and libertine literary and visual references running through the short story* The Bloody Chamber, *music – folk and classical: a relatively neglected aspect of Angela Carter's work – provides a rewarding way into the experience of reading it. The seventeen-year-old heroine-narrator is a student at the Paris Conservatoire; she is taken to Wagner's* Tristan *at the opera, the night before her wedding; the Brittany landscape, on the way to the moated castle on Mont St Michel, is described as having 'all the deliquescent harmonies of Debussy, of the études I played for him'; there is the welcome wedding present of a Bechstein grand in the living room; a page from the score of* Tristan, *the* Liebestod *in the secret file; the naked corpse of the opera singer – the heroine's predecessor as bride – lying in the elaborate catafalque within the bloody torture chamber itself; the therapeutic task of playing 'all Bach's equations' from* The Well-Tempered Clavier, *to recover from the shock; the blind piano-tuner who becomes the bride's close companion – a healing figure; and the little music school they set up together on the outskirts of Paris, with occasional visits to the Opéra.*

No wonder David McVicar's now-classic production of Gounod's Faust *at Covent Garden in 2004 – which set the story in decadent 1870s Paris, rather than sixteenth-century Germany, and included in act 5 a ballet of delightful tutued vampirettes – seemed to belong within the post-Carter universe of* The Bloody Chamber.

The Funeral March of a Marionette

BETWEEN October 1955 and May 1965, Alfred Hitchcock's television shows – *Alfred Hitchcock Presents* (1955-62) and *The Alfred Hitchcock Hour* (1962-5) – made him the best-known film director in the history of the movies, created an image of the director which would colour the rest of his film career and turned him into a multimillionaire as well. Each episode would be introduced with Hitchcock in rotund silhouette stepping into a life-sized outline of a profile caricature, which he had drawn, as the show's logo. He would then move off-camera to the left. The accompanying music – following a drumroll – an excerpt from Charles Gounod's *Funeral March of a Marionette* – would create an atmosphere of macabre charm sustained when Alfred Hitchcock then proceeded to address the viewers, face to face, with some acerbic and witty comments about the upcoming show, beginning with the words 'Good eeeevening.' At the beginning of the debut episode *Revenge*, aired on 2 October 1955 and directed by the man himself, he raised the curtain in characteristic style.

> 'Good evening. My name is Alfred Hitchcock and tonight I'm presenting the first in a series of stories of suspense and mystery called, oddly enough, *Alfred Hitchcock Presents*. I shall not act in these stories, but will only make appearances – something in the nature of an accessory before and after the fact – to give the title

to those of you who can't read, and to tidy up afterwards for those who don't understand the endings. Tonight's playlet is really a sweet little story. It is called *Revenge*. It will follow… *{Looks to the right}* Oh dear, I see the actors won't be ready for another 60 seconds – however, thanks to our sponsor's remarkable foresight, *{bitterly}* we have a message that will fit in here nicely…'

The New York Herald Tribune critic echoed American public sentiment when he wrote a month later, 'the best thing about *Alfred Hitchcock Presents* is Alfred Hitchcock presenting'. The format of the introduction had been suggested by Hitchcock himself, just after the series idea was first mooted, but they were usually written for him by comedy scriptwriter James B. Allardice and filmed ten at a time at Universal. Over the years, Gounod's short piece would become known as 'the Alfred Hitchcock theme' – just as the excerpt from Rossini's *William Tell Overture* had become known as 'the Lone Ranger theme'. Hitchcock became identified in the public mind with this sinister and jolly funeral march. Predictably, Hitchcock chose the Gounod as his eighth record on the BBC radio programme *Desert Island Discs* in October 1959. His favourite, though, was not the *Funeral March* but his fourth selection, *Siegfried's Horn Call* by Richard Wagner. The second episode of *Alfred Hitchcock Presents*, called *Premonition*, was about a man who fantasises that he has been to Paris to study music at the Conservatoire…

The Funeral March of a Marionette had a suitably bizarre gestation. It was originally written by Charles Gounod in late 1871/early 1872 as part of a 'Suite Burlesque' for piano, which was never completed: the *March* was to have contributed to one of the movements. The piece, in the key of D minor, was intended as a satirical musical portrait – for solo piano – of the *Athenaeum* critic Henry F. Chorley, against whom the composer had developed a strong grudge. Chorley had translated much of the French libretto of Gounod's *Faust* for its English première in 1863, and had then publicly slated the passages which he *hadn't* translated – his words having been adapted in rehearsal to fit the music. Maybe that was one of the reasons. Or the fact that Chorley had started by praising Gounod to the skies, then changed his mind. He was by all accounts a short-fused, abrasive, spiteful sort of critic – of whom Gounod's benefactor at the time, the redoubtable Georgina Weldon, wrote that his voice was 'thin, sour, high-pitched, sopranish' and his bodily movements were like 'a stuffed red-haired monkey'. She was greatly amused by the composer's satire on his personality and thin physique with its jerky movements. '[Gounod] made me nearly die of laughter by playing over the piece to me.' At that stage, the piece lacked the first four bars and 'the fugued bit in the middle'. The composer himself declared, 'I have seen in a piece the *very image* of Charles.' Mrs Weldon was an amateur soprano, music teacher, enthusiastic litigant and vociferous champion of good and sometimes lost causes. Charles Gounod was living with the Weldons at Tavistock House in Bloomsbury, London, at the time (they had met in March 1871, shortly after the composer arrived in England from Paris). He, too, was embattled and busy – in the midst of well-publicised rows, encouraged by Georgina or 'Chère Mimi' with the Albert Hall, the publishers Novello's, and assorted concert promoters. Mrs Weldon wrote that 'we were bothered by a great many people' at Tavistock House – not to mention the orphans she was helping to use their singing voices in the room beneath Gounod's – and that the composer somehow managed to ignore all the turbulence and intrigue around him, with remarkable powers of concentration. He often liked to compare his many adversaries in the music world (real and imagined) with vampires – sucking his very life-blood by sharing his royalties:

> At the present day, vampires are said to inhabit only certain villages of Illyria. Nevertheless, it is by no means necessary to undertake so long a journey in order to engage in conflict with monsters of this kind. They come across us in all parts of civilised Europe under the form of Music Publishers and Theatrical Managers.

When Chorley died, on 16 February 1872, it was agreed *not* to dedicate the piece to him – part of the original joke – and to uncouple it, where the public was concerned, from the original satire. 'His death put a stop to that.' Instead, Georgina Weldon wrote a narrative 'programme' for the piece; she also inspired a new title:

> I told him it was a little like 'Marionette' music and a few mornings later, Gounod, radiant with delight, told me that he had found [a title to give it], and *The Burial of a Marionette/L'Enterrement d'une Marionette* (changed by me to a *Funeral March*) was thus christened.

As she was also to recall, ten years later, in her inimitably stilted style 'translated from the French':

> I helped M. Gounod in every imaginable way... I am the author of the following trifle. Am I, for this reason, to divide M. Gounod's profits on *The Funeral March of a Marionette*? The *March* is a fragment of an unfinished movement of a 'Suite Burlesque'.
>
> At the beginning of this movement...it is supposed that two actors of the [Marionette] troupe have had a quarrel, during which one of them is killed. The troupe is lamenting the unhappy fate of their companion. They organise a ceremony to carry the remains of their friend to the cemetery.
>
> *Music.*
>
> The procession starts, and on the way the mourners begin to lament the vicissitudes of human life. How sad to think that a single blow on the nose of so clever an *artiste* should kill so noble a soul! Such talents!
>
> *Music.*

As it happens to be in the heat of summer, a few stragglers begin to think the journey long and wearisome, and to express the desire of quenching their thirst in a neighbouring tavern of alluring aspect. They naturally observe to each other that it is not the place of the living to die for the dead, and this encourages them to revive their drooping spirits by a few drops of agreeable and stimulating beverage.

Music.

The tipplers then set to work to discuss the various qualities of the deceased. A few good fellows praise him; others (as usual among *artistes*), full of bitterness, begin to run down the qualities of their late companion…'a more vulgar-looking devil I never knew.'

Music {disdainfully}.

In the middle of this argument, they forget that the procession is approaching the cemetery. They immediately hasten to join the procession, avoiding, however, with dignity, any appearance of undue haste.

Music.

They rejoin their comrades and enter the cemetery, the band repeating the theme at the beginning of the March.

Music.

The last two bars seem to remind one of the shortness of life! So easily extinguished.

Sic transit gloria mundi.

This 'programme' became – in much less prolix form – a series of inscriptions on the musical score: 'the Marionette is broken', 'the funeral procession' and so on. The music was published by Goddard and Co., London, in 1872. The unintentional murder; the walk to the cemetery; the noble sentiments followed by the visit to a pub; the drunken argument; the tragi-comic race to rejoin the procession; the swaggering *March* which seems to put things right; the sad moral to the tale after all the jollity… The anecdote, with its double mood, reads just like the ones which Alfred Hitchcock would later deliver, in deadpan style dressed like an undertaker, at the opening of his television programmes.

Gounod, meanwhile, decided to include this 'trifle', 'this little skit' – minus the narrative – within the incidental music he composed to accompany the poet and librettist Paul Jules Barbier's drama *Jeanne d'Arc*, which opened at the Théâtre de la Gaîté in Paris on 8 November 1873. The *March* was to be the ballet interlude. Barbier had co-written the original libretto of *Faust*. Gounod penned a strong letter of complaint to the conductor of the orchestra, shortly before the première, because he had been informed by a friend that 'at the general rehearsal, the *Funeral March* in *Jeanne d'Arc* had not been played at the place designated by the author': he had strong views about exactly where the ballet was to be performed, and had dedicated the score of *Jeanne d'Arc* 'to my dear and courageous friends Henry and Georgina Weldon'. Over in England, the piece was already becoming a favourite with drawing-room pianists, and in concerts of programme music, after a slowish start. At first, publishers had thought it was 'not suited to the English taste' and in any case were minded to give the volatile composer a wide berth. But this soon changed. Georgina Weldon continues the story:

> I am the co-laborator of this composition which, in England, has brought Gounod (by 1st November 1875) nearly £350.00 (Gounod's share till this date) (perhaps double that sum); and in France, only 250 francs…because I had not thought of sending to the Théâtre de la Gaîté, or to the Paris papers, this little joke. It had been played, however, every night for three months at the representations of *Jeanne d'Arc* in Paris, and in London we had no such chance… Gounod later on [in 1879] scored it [for orchestra],

and I used to ruminate over and over again how we could make the public swallow this silly *stuffed* music, which was like Chorley… [When] I invented my little tale, I advised Gounod to add the four first bars to imitate a fight, and, as I considered it necessary to have some music to describe the conversation on the way to the cemetery, he added the fugue [in D major]. This dodge was successful, the *March* was encored and applauded…the critics, who understood the story not the music, were absolutely *forced* to confess that the spirit and interest of the composition were inspired by the subject. "French wit, cleverness etc. etc."

So, she concluded, the piece had been introduced to the British public – and the critics – by a sort of musical confidence trick. Where the question of 'spirit' was concerned, there was a postscript. Shortly after Charles Gounod died in October 1893, Mrs Weldon – by then deeply involved in Spiritualism – claimed to have made contact with him on the other side during a séance. Whether or not they discussed the share of royalties for the *Funeral March* she did not, however, record for posterity. When Alfred Hitchcock was growing up in East London, the *Funeral March* was still a staple in the repertoire of Edwardian parlours. How he first encountered the piece has been the subject of much speculation. Was it at a recital somewhere – as it was with Baroness Orczy, the author of *The Scarlet Pimpernel*? Hitchcock once recalled: 'I am a very good listener…from an early age I was a devotee of symphonic music. The Albert Hall on Sunday, The Queen's Hall…' Was it through the recording by John Philip Sousa, made in 1903? Or through a Laurel and Hardy two-reeler of 1928, *Habeas Corpus*, in which a nervous Stan Laurel – working as a part-time body-snatcher for a mad scientist – digs up a grave in a spooky cemetery, to the brief orchestral accompaniment of Gounod's *Funeral March*: this was the first Hal Roach film to be released with synchronised music and effects, on discs – which may have stayed in the technically-minded Hitchcock's memory. Or was it suggested by composer Bernard Herrmann, shortly after he had finished writing the score for *The Trouble with Harry* (1955): the macabre humour in *Harry* is very close to that in Hitchcock's spoken introductions. By then, Hitchcock had a large collection of classical records. I heard the definitive answer from the man himself – though I did not know it at the time – when he was visiting Cambridge University shortly after his epic twenty-five hours of interviews with François Truffaut had first been published in France, and the year before they were published in the English language, in summer 1966. Hitchcock was over in England 'promoting the title of *Torn Curtain* – making it known'. I was a second-year undergraduate at the time. After his question-and-answer session in the Lady Mitchell Lecture Hall on the Sidgwick site, he left the building surrounded by an excited flurry of young cinéastes – no bodyguards in those days – and made for his waiting Rolls limousine in Sidgwick Avenue. He was dressed in trademark plain dark-blue suit, crisp white shirt, dark silk tie, with a copy of *The Times* poking out of his jacket pocket – all five foot eight inches of him – and close-up, he looked apprehensive, ill at ease, with a complexion rather like the colour of *The Financial Times*. I found myself standing face to face with him for a brief moment, and – tongue-tied – I hummed a few bars from the main melody of Gounod's *Funeral March*, the bits used at the beginning of his shows. Pom-pom pom-pom-pom pom-pom-pom. He smiled, turned to go, then turned back and with a deadpan expression said one word to me in reply: 'Sunrise.' I hadn't a clue what he meant by this. Like 'Rosebud', I supposed. It was only forty years later, when I played the DVD of F.W. Murnau's film *Sunrise* (1927) with the original score restored, that the mystery was solved. The sequence where the peasant couple visit a city photographer's studio – and accidentally knock over a headless 'Winged Victory' sculpture, one of the photographer's props, then guiltily search for the head – was accompanied by the jolly funeral march slightly speeded up. The juxtaposition evidently stuck in Alfred Hitchcock's mind, and he remembered it. The couple is scared (ominous music), but the search for a head is a joke at the expense of their lack of sophistication (jolly music). The film was made just as the talkies were about to emerge: thirteen days after *Sunrise* was released in September 1927, *The Jazz Singer* opened. The score for *Sunrise*, and accompanying sound effects, were recorded-on-film via a 'Movietone soundtrack' printed on the left-hand side of the image – as distinct from the rival 'Vitaphone' system used by Warner Brothers involving playback of records more or less synchronised with the image. Again, Hitchcock may have been attracted to this, as a technical innovation. The original score, and effects, were by Hugo Riesenfeld. With that one word 'Sunrise', Hitchcock was, I believe, trying to let me know – with a characteristically mysterious flourish – that it was a distant memory of viewing *Sunrise* that first suggested to him the idea of using Gounod's music. In this, as in so much else, the heyday of the 'silent' era in the mid to late-1920s was to be his crucible. Hitchcock had visited UFA studios near Berlin in Autumn 1924, and observed Murnau at work first hand; later, he acknowledged the key influence of Murnau on 'how to tell a story without words', and how best to move a camera. His first two films were in fact Anglo-German co-productions. *The Pleasure Garden* and *The Mountain Eagle* were 'made in Munich': 'my German was enough to order a good meal, you know…' *Sunrise* was designed in Germany, and shot in Hollywood on the Fox backlot.

Clearly, Hitchcock saw the central section of *The Funeral March* as the musical equivalent of the distinctive persona he wanted to project, and of his brand of humour: for the trailer of *Psycho* (1960), he took the audience on a genial conducted tour of Bates Motel and the Victorian clapboard Gothic mansion on the hill where Norman's mother lived, while the music on the soundtrack played something like the song 'We're busy doing nothing' in a merry rearrangement which strongly resembled the Gounod; when he reached the shower-room and opened the see-through curtains, Bernard Herrmann's shrieking strings took over. The mansion had already appeared in several episodes of the television series, but the motel was specially built for the film. Hitchcock referred to this style as 'a typically English type of humour; even a typically London type of humour. It's of a piece with such jokes as the one about the man who was being led to the gallows to be hanged. He looked at the trap door, in the gallows, which was flimsily constructed, and asked in some alarm, "I say, is that thing safe?"… That's an example of the kind of humour I'm talking about.' Dry, macabre; a tad formal as well. Alfred Hitchcock, the son of a Leytonstone greengrocer, born above his father's shop, who in his late teens became a trained graphic designer, had an instinctive flair for branding long before the word entered common parlance. His first television series was launched in the same year as he was granted American citizenship.

It was Bernard Herrmann's jaunty arrangement of the *Funeral March*, transposed up a third and played by eight bassoons – 24 seconds at the beginning, 56 seconds under the end credits – which became the most celebrated version to accompany the television series. This was recorded in September 1963, and all subsequent episodes of *The Alfred Hitchcock Hour* made use of it. Herrmann also composed the scores for seven Hitchcock features between *The Trouble with Harry* (1955) and *Marnie* (1964), most notably for *North by Northwest* and *Psycho*. Earlier episodes of *Alfred Hitchcock Presents* and the *Hour* had featured four different orchestral versions, by four different arrangers – including the British composer/arranger Lyn Murray, who had recently written the score of *To Catch a Thief* (1955): Murray's orchestration opened the hour-long version of the show in 1962-3, to be superseded by Herrmann's. The first arrangement, for *Presents*, seems to have been not scored but 'tracked' from the CBS music library by 'music supervisor' Stanley Wilson – pruned to fit into the allotted time. Gounod's *Funeral March* lasts for four minutes in all, including the half-minute introduction which – following Georgina Weldon's 'programme' – suggests an animated argument ending with a marionette falling to the ground: this is followed by the march proper, a *danse macabre* in quick-march tempo. Then, for the conversation in the pub, the 'fugue' section in D major, followed by a reprise of the march. The Alfred Hitchcock television shows only featured the main melody. Gounod was never credited.

His topping and tailing not only set the tone and made 'Hitch' more recognisable than the stars in his films, it also created the impression that he had directed and written every single episode himself: in fact, he only directed twenty out of three hundred and sixty-five. The opening moments introduced to the viewer Hitchcock the film-maker, Hitchcock the character and Hitchcock the master of illusion – and Hitchcock the roly-poly raconteur who could get away with outrageous stories. Thereafter, he would usually appear in person on posters for his new films, or for re-releases of older ones, with a message for potential customers. On one of the *Psycho* posters, he was pointing at his watch and saying, 'No one…will be admitted to the theatre after the start of each performance.' For *The Birds* (1963), he stood with his hands clasped and warned, 'Remember, the next scream you hear may be your own'; for *Marnie* (1964), cut-out effigies of his portly figure were sent out to cinemas as lobby displays, as if he was welcoming visitors into a funeral parlour; for *Frenzy* (1972), the same effigy had a necktie draped over the left hand (with Hitchcock's famous caricature on the tie) and a cartoon bubble with the words, 'My new thriller *Frenzy* will tie you in knots.' Before the mid-1950s and the television series, his posters would usually include the words, 'Directed by Alfred Hitchcock' below the title (in the 1920s and 1930s) or the words 'Alfred Hitchcock's…' above the title (from *Saboteur* onwards). But after the series had proved such a huge public success, even re-releases of his films began to feature a promotional image of Hitchcock himself: for *Strangers on a Train* (originally 1951, re-released 1960s), he held the letter 'l' above the word 'Strangers' – suggesting 'Stranglers', while for *North by Northwest* (originally 1959, re-released 1966), Hitchcock was carrying a huge designer-hand with a finger pointing roughly in a ten o'clock direction – the graphic equivalent, presumably, of 'north by northwest', although there is no such point on the compass – and saying, '…so we brought it back.' The standard photo portrait which was used in much of his promotional material – showing Hitchcock talking and pointing with his left hand – was created in the early 1960s while the television series was on the air and used until the end of his life. Throughout his career, from *The Lodger* (1926) onwards, he made a brief personal appearance in all his films: this signature started out according to Hitchcock as a means of 'filling in the screen'; then it became 'a superstition'; finally – at the time of the television series – it 'eventually became a gag'. In *The Birds*, for example, he is seen leaving a pet-shop with two small curly white terriers on leads (his own dogs); in *Torn Curtain* (1966), he is sitting in a hotel lounge with an infant on his knee – as John Addison's music makes reference to Gounod's *Funeral March* – and in *Frenzy* (1972), he is standing in a crowd listening to a speech about the 'necktie murders', while wearing a bowler hat and looking like a 1920s city gent. The original idea for these momentary cameos came – by Hitchcock's admission – from Charlie Chaplin's brief appearance on a poster carrying a trunk in *A Woman of Paris*. After *Presents* had made his appearance well-known in every American living room, he said, his appearances in films became increasingly difficult: 'one's visage is so familiar that I have to get into the picture and out as quickly as possible so as not to spoil the story.' At the 'earliest possible moment'.

But Gounod's music was more than just a piece of branding. It expressed in aural form Hitchcock's basic philosophy of film-making which he had formed many years before. The idea that actors were to be treated like puppets, with the director as the puppet-master – an idea he had first articulated in the mid-1920s. The idea that 'all that matters, all that exists for the audience, is what is on the screen' – hence the key importance of pre-planning, storyboarding, framing and above all montage, and the fact that the actual shooting was, he claimed, the most tedious part of the process. Hitchcock had learned a lot during his apprenticeship years not only from the German Expressionists but also from Eisenstein's films and Pudovkin's writings; a favourite story he liked to tell was about the famous experiment where a close-up of a Russian actor's face was intercut with a shot of a dead baby, then back to the face, then to a shot of a plate of soup: 'you read compassion on his face…then he looks hungry…and yet in both cases, they used the same shot of the actor; his face was exactly the same. Just like a close-up of James Stewart looking out of the window [in *Rear Window*, 1954]'.

He dreamed of making a 'purely cinematic film', or of not bothering to watch the rushes; many of his most memorable sequences make sense as pieces of celluloid projected onto a screen rather than by reference to the real world: the glass ceiling in *The Lodger*; the chase across the roof of the British Museum in *Blackmail*; Cary Grant carrying a glass of milk up the stairs in *Suspicion*; the opening three minutes of *Vertigo* – another chase across the roof, this time in San Francisco; the shower sequence in *Psycho*; the crop-duster and the cornfield in *North by Northwest*; the first fourteen seconds of *Strangers*, which tell us all about the two leading characters by showing us their shoes; the crows on the playground climbing-frame in *The Birds*, with Tippi Hedren sitting and smoking in front of them while the children sing a repetitive nursery rhyme. Sometimes – especially towards the end of Hitchcock's career – such virtuoso cinematic flourishes seemed to stand out from the increasingly static and overlit stories which surrounded them, as if they had involved an extra dose of imagination. In his heyday, though, they were integrated into films which seamlessly blended visual experiences with handcrafted dialogue – dialogue which was much more than just talk. By his own admission, he did not read novels. They were, he said, too complete. He preferred original screenplays, short stories or even 'vague ideas' as a starting-point, and categorised his approach as anti-literary: for him, the screen was empty and he had to fill it; the cinema was empty and he had to fill it; films were celluloid containers to be filled with visual ideas. The screenplays and storyboards he worked with resulted from weeks of conversation, guidance and invention. The conferences would usually begin by evoking images and the sensations they were intended to create, and 'then the themes would emerge'. Hitchcock's favourite painter – ever since he first saw the work at an exhibition in the 1930s, just after the artist left his teaching post at the Bauhaus – was Paul Klee, who at that time was struggling to find a visual equivalent of musical notation and words on the page. Even before that, at the time of his first film as a solo director (*The Pleasure Garden*, 1925), Hitchcock had spoken of the film director as an impresario introducing the press, the distributors and the public to his own distinctive visual world. 'Actors come and actors go,' he said to the London Film Society and in a letter to the press predicted that moving pictures would one day be created by one man – like a composer creating a piece of music, or like a visual artist. By 1926, *Picturegoer* magazine was already calling him 'Alfred the Great'.

So both the marionettes and the funeral march in Gounod's music in significant ways reflected Alfred Hitchcock's aesthetic as well as his persona. His television series made *Funeral March of a Marionette* as famous worldwide as Paul Dukas' *The Sorcerer's Apprentice* acted by Mickey Mouse in *Fantasia*. Mickey Mouse was the only other movie-related character – with the exception of Charlie Chaplin – who could be identified by nothing more than his silhouette; those two circular ears surmounting a circular face which have since become one of the most powerful global brands of the twenty-first century. Hitchcock often celebrated Mickey Mouse as the ideal film performer for a director to work with: 'Mr Disney has the right idea. If he doesn't like them, he just tears them up.' Mr Disney also had the right idea when he hosted – on camera – his own television series, and – through his success – encouraged the other studios to come to terms with television rather than badmouthing it. When Alfred Hitchcock uttered such lines as the one about tearing them up – sadistic in implication, sardonic in tone, relished in the delivery – he somehow managed to make them sound benevolent. Having seen and heard him at that 'lecture' in Cambridge University (1966), I can vouch for the fact that both the sadism and the relish, the darkness and the jocularity, were brilliantly communicated face-to-face. It was difficult to know by then whether you were meeting Alfred Hitchcock or a clever construct who shared the same name: Hitchcock or 'Hitchcock'.

The film which was screened on that occasion was *Shadow of a Doubt*, made in 1943, which he had often said was his favourite because it most fully combined suspense, psychological depth and film technique. It also had a strong sense of place, small-town America in the form of

Santa Rosa California which reacts to the presence of *The Merry Widow* serial killer Uncle Charlie played by Joseph Cotton, as seen through the eyes of his young niece Charlie played by Teresa Wright. 'And I enjoyed working with Thornton Wilder.' This was one of the few films where Mrs Hitchcock – Alma Reville, his long-term wife and collaborator – received a full screenplay credit: Hitchcock had been directing films for 42 years, and had been married to Alma for 40 of them. And it contained one of the great Hitchcock moments, when Joseph Cotton goes up the stairs and realises that he has just unwittingly confessed his crime to Teresa Wright. But Alfred Hitchcock was in playful mood that afternoon. He started the proceedings by saying that *Shadow of a Doubt* might not really be his favourite film at all: he had just said that to please 'the plausibles' among film critics, because the story was among his most plausible and logical.

The question-and-answer session which followed the screening continued to reveal the usual Hitchcock contradictions. The accent, a mixture of Leytonstone and twenty-six years' worth of California: he never lost the accent of his roots, the carefully corrected vowels and the cockney tradesman's slow, droll and deliberate delivery of them. It didn't take Professor Higgins, who by the way spent a lot of research time with cockney greengrocers, to notice where this man originated from. Then there was the schoolboyish relish with which he described nasty murders, especially English ones gleaned from published anthologies of Famous Trials: he still had the London *Times* delivered every day, a newspaper which – he said – was rather dry but contained many humorous snippets, such as the headline 'Fish Sent to Prison' above a story about a small tropical aquarium which had been donated to Holloway Prison in London. On this occasion, he told the stories of two cases he had read about, which together gave him the idea for the details of the murder in *Rear Window*: the cases of Patrick Mahon (who killed a girl, chopped up her body and threw it out of a train window, and then burned her head in his living-room fireplace) and Dr Crippen (who murdered his wife and cut her up, but who made the mistake of allowing his girlfriend to wear his late wife's jewellery). His excitement when describing film technique – especially the importance of editing when creating tension, one of the reasons his films contain such great stills – was combined with the usual, not entirely plausible, dismissal of the whole business of actually making films. Then there were the by-then characteristic jokes about actors and cattle and the clarification that what he *really* said was 'actors should be *treated* like cattle'. There was the often-told story about his being locked up for a minute or two in a police station near his father's shop, when he was a small child of four or five, because he had been sent to the local Chief Constable with a note which said 'that's what we do to naughty boys'. He told anecdotes about his Jesuit education at St Ignatius College in Stepney London from 1909-13 (his mother had Irish Catholic roots) which taught him 'a strong sense of fear', a prudishness in sexual matters and also 'taught me about analysis'. He hinted at the rich and strange mixture of English music hall, silent films, cockney humour, skill at planning and German Expressionism which were component parts of his apprenticeship: his earliest films, he said, following his visit to UFA, were filmed on exotic locations in Europe (Genoa, San Remo and Lake Como for *The Pleasure Garden*; the Tyrol for *The Mountain Eagle*), and he still liked to visit the Palace Hotel in St Moritz where in December 1926 he and Alma had spent their honeymoon. After arriving in Hollywood, he continued to set many of his films all or partly in England, to use 1930s-style English actors (from *Rebecca* to the tweedy lady ornithologist in a beret in *The Birds*, who seems to have walked to Bodega from off the set of an Agatha Christie movie), and to use English writers as well. His television production company was called 'Shamley Productions', after the beloved tudor house in the country he bought in 1928 at Shamley Green – called Winter's Grace – and had since sold. He spoke of the time he spent at evening classes in technical college, during the First World War, learning to make engineering drawings, combined with his graphic work 'in the ad department' as a designer of advertisements and 'art titles' for films – which, he said, helped him to understand that film was fundamentally about the organisation of the image. He recounted the origins of the famous outline caricature drawing he had made which was featured every week in his television series, and which started life way back in 1927 when he sent it to friends as a Christmas present, in the form of a wooden jigsaw puzzle inside a small linen bag: 'I drew it myself,' he said, 'and with one exception there's been very little change since then – just that at one time I had more hair; all three of my hairs were wavy in those days!' He described the difference between suspense and shock – between Hitchcock thrillers and the 'creaking-door type' of horror movie – illustrated, as ever, by the story of how to present a potential bomb explosion to audiences: 'the point is to let the audience know where the bomb is, but not let the characters in my story know'; the point was also *not* to let the bomb go off (unlike with the child on the bus in *Sabotage*, 1936). He wasn't interested in quick thrills that lasted ten seconds, he said; six or seven reels of audience worry was what he was after. He said that he felt he was beginning to become a victim of type-casting: 'if I made *Cinderella*, the audience would start looking for a body in a pumpkin coach'; if his films attempted more than just 'spine-tingling', they were treated by critics as disappointments. And yet, at the beginning of his career he had scripted five romances and directed two more before his first thriller *The Lodger*; then there were six more dramas before his second thriller *Blackmail* (1929). At that time, he had a reputation as a 'quality' film director, rather than as a director of thrillers. Much more recently, *Vertigo* and *Marnie* had also been 'dramas rather than thrillers'.

Looking back, there was very little discussion of the films which are among his most highly rated today – *Vertigo*, *Rear Window* and his then-recent *The Birds* and *Marnie*, which did indeed disappoint and confuse his fans when first they were released. *Vertigo* and *Rear Window*, in fact, had been withdrawn from circulation, so we couldn't get to see them – except on bootleg black-and-white 16mm copies – following some argument or other Alfred Hitchcock had had with Paramount. They were lying in a vault. No one mentioned this. The idea of Hitchcock as a moralist – 'crime and punishment', 'the transference of guilt' – surfaced at various moments in the conversation (the book *Hitchcock* by Rohmer and Chabrol, first published in 1957, was still the standard text). But the themes which have intrigued critics and writers since the re-evaluation of Hitchcock's work in the 1960s were all to come in the future: so there was no mention of his humanism (Robin Wood's book), his voyeurism and fetishism (feminist critics from the 1960s onwards), his supposed misogyny and cruelty, especially towards chilly blondes (Donald Spoto's biography), his murderous gaze which forces viewers to feel guilty, which focuses on the male point of view and casts women as objects of spectacle; the compulsive quality of his films which makes people see some of them over and over again (especially the ones which are themselves about repetition and remaking); the idea of a frightened film-maker (morally, socially, sexually) who overcomes his fear by manipulating both actors and audience. With the publication of Truffaut's interview book about Hitchcock, the process of re-evaluation had only just begun. From memory, someone had read the French edition and asked whether he felt comfortable being asked such detailed and complicated questions – sometimes a whole page's worth, followed by a one-line answer, for example when Truffaut describes 'the prayer sequence' in *The Thirty-Nine Steps* (1935) for twenty-five lines, and Hitchcock simply replies 'Yes, that was a nice scene' – when he seemed so much happier describing his craft and reminiscing about his early life. He replied that he was very flattered that the *Cahiers du Cinéma* people had 'lionised' him as he put it: the celebrated special issue of October 1954 with articles by Bazin, Chabrol and Truffaut; the often reproduced photograph of him standing next to the Sphinx, taken on his world tour promoting *Psycho* in 1960. As an inveterate riddler himself, this seemed just right. Even the stone face – which occasionally creased into a smile. But he was characteristically dismissive of attempts to make him seem an intellectual of any sort – and spoke of the young French film-makers with a mixture of respect, distance and humour. Then, after a question about a murderer who may or may not have taken *Psycho* a bit too seriously – I can't recall the details – to which Hitchcock replied 'and he drank a glass of milk after seeing the film; that's probably much more significant' – he finished on his ideal role as the ultimate puppet-master engaging in what he called 'mass hypnotism': the audience could become like 'a giant organ to be played' by the all-powerful director. It would be like planting electrodes in the brain. At the start of the film, he would plant the appropriate emotion – affection, fear, anxiety: then he might begin to mix things up, so that – for example – the audience would feel pleasure during a murder scene. That, he said, would become interesting. And it would 'save me a lot of trouble!' His main concern as a director, he said, was with the audience 'identifying themselves with a character': 'I suppose the ultimate in that will be the theatre of the future, where we'll all go into a darkened room, we buy a ticket and say "I want to be this character" and then we go through the *actual experiences* under hypnotism… It's only an extension beyond the identification.' As a postscript, he told a terrific joke about a woman who wrote to him about her daughter's washing habits: after seeing Clouzot's *Les Diaboliques* – the sequence where the goggle-eyed corpse of the husband sits up in a bathtub – the girl had apparently given up baths, and after seeing *Psycho* she had given up showers as well. Afterwards, and closer up, the most striking contradiction was between the impish, swaggering showman who fronted *Alfred Hitchcock Presents* on television – which had turned him into a brand and a franchise – and the plainly ill-at-ease man in a plain blue suit who was a lot cleverer than he pretended to be. After making his way through the crowd of students, he got into the back seat of his waiting Rolls-Royce limo – with uniformed chauffeur.

In retrospect, the mid to late-1960s when his visit to Cambridge took place seem very like a watershed in Alfred Hitchcock's career: not just his career as a film director, but his critical career as well, which impacted on his films. For it was around this time that he was promoted by critics from the ranks of popular entertainers into the exclusive club of serious artists; from master craftsman to distinguished 'auteur'. It was also around this time that the 'auteur theory', an Americanised and softened version of Cahiers' 'politique des auteurs', came to be accepted by newspaper critics and academics; and that the suspense thriller came to be taken as seriously as the earnest social-problem film. The result of all this was a widespread reappraisal of Hitchcock's aesthetic status. The films he had made during the television decade – *Vertigo, North by Northwest, Psycho, The Birds* and *Marnie* – which on first release had either been praised as mere entertainments or dismissed as pretentious failures (the conjuror over-reaching himself, for example with the inconclusive ending of *The Birds*), were to be redefined as stages in a complex artistic journey. There was less debate about 'shock versus suspense' or 'quick excitements versus seven reels of worry' and more about 'the act of looking', 'meditations on the processes of film-making' and even 'the English period versus the American period'; less emphasis on paperback collections of crime stories, and more on hardback university monographs. The Truffaut book, a major retrospective with book by Peter Bogdanovich at the Museum of Modern Art, maybe the visit to the Film Society at Cambridge University, were all part of the canonisation process. There were even discussions about whether or not the unconvincing special effects in *Marnie* were deliberate – like the unconvincing special effects in Truffaut's *Fahrenheit 451*, which were seen as a homage to them. Some commentators have argued that Hitchcock himself connived in this re-evaluation, that he was as in control of his new image as he had been of his television persona. If so, his business strategy was startlingly successful. Everyone began taking Hitchcock very seriously indeed. His penultimate film *Frenzy*, written by Anthony Shaffer, was a deliberate compendium of many of the themes which critics had for twenty years been claiming were his obsessions. A Hitchcock sampler.

At times, when thinking about this inflation of Hitchcock's reputation – into areas where he would certainly not have felt at home – I am reminded of the sequence in *The Trouble with Harry* (1955), in which an absent-minded doctor walks through the countryside reading a book: so engrossed is he in the words on the page that he twice trips over Harry's outstretched corpse without realising it. The first time he doesn't notice the corpse at all; the second time, he apologises to it. Many of the recent academic commentaries on Hitchcock's films have strongly resembled that absent-minded doctor: the feeling I get from these studies which attempt to psychoanalyse the absent director is that the authors cannot forgive Hitchcock for scaring them so much; the only way for them to exorcise the demon is to theorise him out of existence.

The Trouble with Harry, with its macabre sense of humour and plot twists, was the nearest in tone among Hitchcock's feature films to his weekly television series, which first appeared a year after *Harry* opened in cinemas. When James Allardice was hired to write Hitchcock's episode introductions, he was shown a rough cut of *Harry* as the best guide as to what was wanted. Which takes me back to the jolly, deadpan showman dressed like an undertaker – with the cockney vowels and expressive hands – who visited my university so many years ago, and whose artistic credentials were not yet the subject of learned dissertations; they were still convincingly embodied in the funeral march of a marionette.

He concluded that first episode with the cheery thought:

> Well, they were a pathetic couple! We had intended to call that one "Death of a Salesman" but there were protests in certain quarters. Naturally Elsa's husband was caught, indicted, tried, convicted, sentenced and paid his debt to society for taking the law into his own hands. You see, crime does not pay…not even on television. You must have a sponsor. Here is ours…

Then, cue the Gounod.

He introduced the second episode he directed – *Breakdown*, with Joseph Cotton, aired on 13 November 1955 – with the cheery thought that the story would

> '…point a little moral – advice like mother used to give: you know, like walk softly but carry a big stick or strike first and ask questions later. That sort of thing…'

Cue the Gounod again…

THANKS TO:

Dan Auiler: *Hitchcock's Secret Notebooks* (Bloomsbury, London, 1999)

James Harding: *Gounod* (George Allen and Unwin, London, 1973)

Evan Hunter: *Me and Hitch* (Faber, London, 1997)

Robert E. Kapsis: *Hitchcock: The making of a reputation*
(University of Chicago Press, Chicago, 1992)

Donald Spoto: *The Dark Side of Genius* (Little Brown, Boston, 1983)

John Russell Taylor: *Hitch: the life and times of Alfred Hitchcock*
(Da Capo, New York, 1996)

François Truffaut: *Hitchcock* (Simon and Schuster, New York, 1967;
first published in France, 1966)

Georgina Weldon: *My Orphanage and Gounod in England*
(translated from the French, The Music and Art Association, London, 1882)

The account of Hitchcock's Cambridge lecture of summer 1966 is based on my
notes taken at the time, supplemented by indelible memories.

5

The House That Jack Built

Introduction

SHORTLY AFTER *the publication of* Nights at the Circus *(1984), Angela Carter said 'You know, sometimes when I read my back pages, I'm quite appalled at the violence of my imagination. Before I had a family and stuff.' In some ways I feel the same way about this article* The House That Jack Built, *which was first published – in an earlier form – in 1986, and which inspired a BBC2 TV* Timewatch *documentary in September 1988, to mark the centenary of the Whitechapel murders, a programme I wrote and presented. It was called* Shadow of the Ripper. *The article was written in an attempt to understand the contemporary fascination with the story of the murders, and to explore why certain 'solutions' seemed to work, and others did not, in the absence of any sustainable or credible evidence. Angela Carter was fond of G. W. Pabst's film* Pandora's Box *(1929) – which updated the story to the 1920s – and after writing an article (1978) in* New Society *about the film, wrote a review article about the life and times of Louise Brooks: Angela always reckoned that Brooks' astonishingly impetuous performance in* Pandora's Box *played against Frank Wedekind's vision of a destructive, deceitful* femme fatale *in interesting ways. Much of Brooks' behaviour showed 'evidence of human feeling'. Angela also adapted the two 'Lulu' plays by Wedekind (1895 and 1904) into a new version for the National Theatre in 1987, based on a literal translation. In Act 7 of this* Lulu, *at the end of the play, Jack the Ripper 'a dishevelled man with red-rimmed eyes and – yes – the mark of Cain upon him' arrives in the attic studio which Lulu now shares with her bedraggled friends. She is about to turn, in desperation, to prostitution, and agrees to go into her bedroom with Jack for next to no payment. There is a terrible scream offstage. 'Lots of spirit, that one,' muses the murderer. 'Jack certainly knows how to pick 'em.' Sadly, although commissioned, Angela Carter's* Lulu *was never performed.*

The House That Jack Built[1]

31 August 1888

The body of Mary Ann Nichols is found by two cart-drivers in Buck's Row, Whitechapel at 3.30 a.m. – her throat cut and with serious wounds to her abdomen.

8 September 1888

The body of Annie Chapman is found in the yard of 29 Hanbury Street, Whitechapel, at 6.00 a.m. by one of the house's tenants – her throat cut and with partial disembowelling; some of her internal organs, including her uterus, are missing.

30 September 1888

The 'double event'. Elizabeth Stride's body is found at 1 a.m. by a pedlar in costume jewellery and steward of the Club, in Dutfield's Yard off Berner Street near the Commercial Road, outside the International Working Men's Club – her throat cut, but no other injuries. She was killed between 12.30 a.m. and 12.50 a.m. At 1.45 a.m., in Mitre Square, some three-quarters of a mile away and just inside the City Police jurisdiction, the body of Catherine Eddowes is found by a police constable – her throat cut, deep incisions in her face, extensive abdominal injuries, and her uterus and left kidney are missing.

9 November 1888

Mary Kelly's body is found indoors – in a room in Miller's Court, Dorset Street, Whitechapel, at 11.45 a.m. – with very extensive mutilations; she had evidently died at about 4 a.m. the previous night. There was not enough flesh left on her face or neck for the consulting surgeon to be certain whether she had been strangled or stabbed – though the 'arterial blood which was found on the wall in splashes' did suggest that Mary Kelly's throat had been cut.

THE MYTH-MAKING PROCESS started while the murders were actually being committed. The crimes attracted a great deal of publicity at the time – it was, for example, unique for both *The Times* and the *Illustrated Police News* to lead with the same story – and, after the Catherine Eddowes murder, this publicity was matched by angry demonstrations on the streets of Whitechapel. Thanks to the nameless journalist who wrote to the Central News Office on Friday 28 September, the murderer had a name: 'Yours truly, Jack the Ripper. Don't mind me giving the trade name.' And thanks to the law and order reporters, the murders of Stride and Eddowes, both on the same night, were linked for the first time with a whole series of previous prostitute murders in Whitechapel: Emma Smith (Monday 2 April 1888), Martha Tabram (Tuesday 7 August 1888), Mary Ann Nichols (Friday 31 August 1888) and Annie Chapman (Saturday 8 September 1888).

At the time of Emma Smith's death in Osborn Street, Whitechapel (she had been assaulted by a gang of four men, and subsequently died of a haemorrhage from stab wounds to her vagina), the London Hospital had not considered the case significant enough even to inform the police until four days later, while the newspapers had not bothered to report an event which was clearly thought by some editors to be common enough in the brutal East End of London. Nothing special to interest readers here – particularly since the East End had come to be associated with an utterly different image during the previous five years: stories about upper-class 'slummers', university settlements, charity organisations, and exposés of appalling housing conditions or the sexual immorality of 'outcast London' made good copy in 1883-88; stories about the brutality of the East End were thought to be either out of date (harking back to Tales of Newgate and the Ratcliffe Highway) or dangerous (just over two years after the unemployed dock and building workers had marched to Trafalgar Square). Ten years before 1888, the East End would almost invariably have been described in terms of 'Curses', 'Wilds', 'Deeps', 'Pits' and 'Hell': by the mid-1880s, a less dramatic image of that economically and socially run-down sector of London was beginning to emerge.[2] Even the popular press had cottoned on to the idea of viewing Whitechapel as less of a slaughterhouse, and more of a deadly dull, sickeningly monotonous place to inhabit. Whether through fear (after the events of February 1886, when, in the words of *The Times*, 'the West End was for a couple of hours in the hands of the mob'), 'a new consciousness of sin' (as Beatrice Webb, among others, supposed) or a simple change in fashion (the 'Corinthians' of the 1820s, who went East to watch the gore, turning into the better-intentioned 'slummers' of the 1880s), the 'men of intellect and property' (newspaper editors among them) no longer thought it wise to view the East End through blood-tinted spectacles by 1883-88. But this 'new consciousness of sin', or whatever it was, quickly evaporated when 'the Ripper' came on the scene. A good story was a good story, whatever damage it did to the image of the East End in the eyes of those up West, or indeed of those who lived there.

Emma Smith and Martha Tabram had been killed within 300 yards of where Mary Ann Nichols' body was discovered in Buck's Row. Here *was* something special: in retrospect, Stride and Eddowes were reported by the popular press as being the Ripper's *fifth* and *sixth* victims – and detailed information about Smith and Tabram was printed for the first time in September 1888 (with suitably graphic illustrations of Tabram having her throat slit and being punctured with a bayonet, 39 times). After the night of 30 September, a pattern – the Ripper's 'form' – had been created by the press, and extreme reaction was, understandably, not long in following. (Even today, estimates of the number of murders committed by Jack the Ripper range from 20, the highest, to 4, the lowest: the general consensus is that 'Jack' struck five times). A Mrs Mary Burridge, of Blackfriars Road, was so overcome by the *Star*'s lurid account of one of the murders that she dropped dead on the spot.

Scotland Yard's policy in autumn 1888 seems to have been to release as little information as possible in the press; Frederick Abberline, the recently promoted Detective Inspector (First Class) in charge of the Ripper investigations, was expressly forbidden from granting publishable interviews about the crimes. The reporters covering the case for the popular press (who were not the specialised crime correspondents they would be today) constructed a sensational story as best they could from the scant materials at their disposal – a story which had to conform to the (already) well-tried conventions of dramatisation, personalisation and simplification. In the absence of the staple ingredients for such crime stories in the 1880s – the dramatic court case, the sentimental letters from the condemned cell, the 'last words' which could be distributed as souvenir brochures at the time of the execution – these reporters tried at first to get as much mileage as they could out of what seemed to be a very saleable feature of this case, the horrible mutilations. Full details of the post-mortem examination of Mary Ann Nichols' corpse were published by many popular newspapers. After that, some pressure seems to have been brought to bear on Dr George Bagster Phillips, the Divisional police surgeon, perhaps by representatives of the Home Office, to prevent him from making such information so readily accessible in the future. At the inquest on Annie Chapman, Dr Phillips referred to 'various mutilations of the body' about which 'I think I had better not go into further detail': a fortnight later, at another hearing, he was pressed by the Coroner, Wynne Baxter, to be more explicit 'in the interests of justice'. Phillips still thought 'it a very great pity to make this evidence public. These details are fit only for yourself, sir, and the jury,' but after the court had been cleared of women and children, and after Phillips had again expressed the view that such publicity would in fact *thwart* 'the ends of justice', he reluctantly agreed to present the results of his post-mortem examination. The Coroner then appealed to the 'responsibility of the press' and the popular newspapers responded by printing only a few choice details (a fuller account was later to appear in *The Lancet*, a journal that was actually permitted to mention the word 'uterus').

At the inquest on Mary Jane Kelly, the issue of publication was raised yet again. On this occasion, the remains of the victim were moved from the Whitechapel district to Shoreditch mortuary, perhaps in order to prevent Wynne Baxter from having anything to do with the inquest. The Coroner was now to be Dr Roderick Macdonald, who, as an ex-police surgeon, K division, was likely to prove much more cooperative. Two of the jurors complained about this at the opening of the inquest, but to no avail: Macdonald silenced them ('I am not going to discuss the subject'), rushed through the preliminary part of Dr Phillips' evidence, admitted he was suppressing the rest ('there is other evidence which I do not propose to call, for if we at once make public every fact in connection with this terrible murder, the ends of justice might be retarded'), and abruptly terminated the proceedings with the words 'it is for the police authorities to deal with the case'. *The Illustrated Police News*, whose reporter seems to have been present when the police broke into Miller's Court, published a full account of the mutilations (with characteristically gory artists' impressions), but most other newspapers, notably the *Daily Telegraph*, were content to criticise both the Home Office and Dr Phillips for what they considered to be a blatant 'insufficiency of inquiry'. It was a pity, wrote the *Telegraph* correspondent, that Phillips was not a 'free agent' in this matter. More details would surely have been in the public interest...

More recent commentators have interpreted Phillips' actions as part of a 'cover up' of one sort of another. There is no need for so elaborate an explanation. Quite simply, the police were not prepared to cooperate with the press.[3] This may have been because they felt their inquiries would be 'thwarted' by publication, because they were concerned that others might copy the Ripper's style, because they were keen to avoid public disorder in the Whitechapel area (several senior police officers expressed alarm about the spread of 'silly hysterics', which could easily turn into a backlash against the Jews, or in their view worse, another Bloody Sunday), or because they did not like the way the popular press was exploiting the story. Whatever the reason, Phillips' behaviour was quite consistent with the Yard's view of how reporters should be treated, in autumn 1888.

So it was not surprising that the press, at all levels, should focus its attention on the tensions that already existed between the Metropolitan Police Commissioner, the Home Secretary, the head of the CID, the Metropolitan Police (the Met), the City Police and members of the medical profession concerned with the case. Basically the reporters had very little else to write about if they wanted to keep the story going, and even the administrative aspects of the 'Ripper' inquiry made good copy. Accounts in *The Times* and the *Telegraph* of the various demarcation disputes which the Commissioner at the Met (Sir Charles Warren) had brought out into the open seem at times to have become a substitute for in-depth reporting of the actual crimes – and editors of the more popular newspapers were quick to sniff out further scandals, perhaps as a way of getting revenge on Scotland Yard officials for their lack of cooperation. The 'leg men' employed by these editors had not always encountered such hostility in the past, it seems, when the stories they were covering concerned developments *after* the arrest of the criminal. A good example of this 'sniffing out' process concerns the story about two champion bloodhounds which Sir Charles Warren thought might be usefully employed in the hunt for the Ripper, in October 1888. The story went around that these bloodhounds had been lost in the fog during a training session on Tooting Common. They had not in fact been lost (one of them was in Scarborough at the time), Sir Charles Warren was not even present, and the whole story was based on a misunderstanding, but this did not stop several newspapers from printing a full account of the bizarre incident, complete with engravings (of Warren as a mindless bloodhound).

Another way in which the popular press could exploit the crimes, at the same time as indirectly criticising the conduct of the police, was to publish 'suggestions' as to how the Ripper might be captured, suggestions which the Met could then be attacked for not implementing. W.T. Stead's *Pall Mall Gazette*, an evening newspaper and review, represents the most extreme example of this process: the paper took advantage of London readers' interest by collecting ideas suggested in the morning dailies, and revamping them *all* with trimmings. In between a serialisation of Conan Doyle's latest mysteries ('the central figure is a haunted General. Who haunts him and why he is haunted will be wrapped in judicious mystery for seven or eight weeks'), reviews and articles about Mr Richard Mansfield's performance as Dr Jekyll and Mr Hyde, currently packing them in at the Lyceum ('The transformation in Jekyll and Hyde – how it is done by one who knows'), and short stories by Grant Allen (who was soon to create the first super-villain of modern crime literature, with master of disguise Colonel Clay, the con-man hero of *An African Millionaire*), the *Pall Mall Gazette* gave an exhaustive list of 'suggestions of the public'. These included 'everyone in Whitechapel to report to the police, before going to bed' (which would have had the unfortunate side effect of giving the murderer all sorts of chances as they went home), issuing rubber shoes to policemen, disguising them as prostitutes, dressing up prize pugilists in drag, and issuing East End prostitutes with lockable steel collars (perhaps attached to a 'powerful storage battery' which could shock).

On 1 October 1888, the *Gazette* used the opportunity of the Ripper's double murder to criticise Lord Salisbury's Irish policy, and for the next month offered a whole range of suggestions about the murderer's identity: he was an army doctor suffering from sunstroke, who had seen the play *Dr Jekyll and Mr Hyde* once too often; he was a crazy occultist who was seeking to achieve supreme power by these fiendish means; he was an anarchist, perhaps of French, Russian, or Jewish origin; he was an unhinged English clergyman; he may even have been a member of the detective force. 1887 was the year in which Booth first launched his survey of the London poor in the East End, and on 24 September 1888 the *Gazette* jumped on this bandwagon by suggesting that the 'political moral of the murders' was that they were performed by a 'scientific humanitarian', 'capable of taking a scientific survey of the condition of society, and indifferent to the sufferings of the individual, so long as he benefits the community at large' (by drawing attention to shocking conditions in the Whitechapel area).

On 10 September they had cited at length De Quincey's *Essay on Murder Considered as one of the Fine Arts* to the effect that the Ripper might well have 'a benevolent aspect, a gentlemanly bearing, and a peculiarly soft and pleasant voice': 'De Quincey relates how a maniac once asked a girl what she'd think if he appeared by her bedside at midnight with a knife in his hand. "If it was anyone else," she replied, "I should be terribly frightened, but as soon as I heard *you* speak, I should be reassured."' The *Gazette* continued:

> It is to be hoped that the police and their amateur assistants are not confining their attentions to those who look like 'hard ruffians'. Many of the occupants of the Chamber of Horrors look like local preachers, Members of Parliament, or…nurses. We incline on the whole to the belief…that the murderer is a victim of mania which often takes the awful shape of an uncontrollable taste for blood. *Sadism*, as it is termed from the maniac marquis, is happily so strange to the majority of our people that they find it difficult to credit the existence of such powers of mere debauchery. The Marquis de Sade, who died in a lunatic asylum at the age of 74, was an amiable-looking gentleman, and so, possibly enough, may be the Whitechapel murderer.

Since the *Pall Mall Gazette* synthesised all the 'suggestions' made by the morning newspapers, its articles on the Ripper present a broad cross-section of opinion about his possible identity. Other, less broad, cross-sections may be found in the correspondence columns of *The Times* and in the Home Office files (which contain among other things suggestions penned by self-appointed guardians of law and order at the time).[4] *The Times* letters, in particular, were mainly sent in by retired members of the professions, elderly clerics and trigger-happy representatives of the armed forces, who were quick to express their moral outrage on behalf of 'all honest folk', and who sought a cure for all the ills besetting beleaguered Britain by the passage of laws against 'anti-socials' of all descriptions: clearly, they had not had such a good time since the riots of February

1886. Putting all these sources together, we find that the 'suggestions' fall into three main categories.

The Ripper as decadent English Milord.[5] Perhaps, like de Quincey's connoisseurs, Wilde's Dorian Gray or the Goncourts' bizarre version of Lord George Selwyn, this gentleman of leisure was seeking after luxurious cruelties which could stimulate his jaded sensibilities. Perhaps, as was suggested by an amateur sleuth who wrote to Scotland Yard, he was one of those 'upper or wealthy sort' who think that the working-class world exists purely 'for their pleasures – that of revenge being included – as a life business; without regard to any law but their own will'. E.W. Hornung's *Raffles* (1899) was also convinced that the Whitechapel murderer fitted this description:

> To follow crime with reasonable impunity you simply must have a parallel ostensible career – the more public the better. The principle is obvious. Mr Charles Peace, of pious memory, disarmed suspicion by acquiring a local reputation for playing the fiddle and taming animals, and it's my profound conviction that Jack the Ripper was a really eminent public man, whose speeches were very likely reported alongside his atrocities. Fill the bill in some prominent part, and you'll never be suspected of doubling it with another of equal prominence.

Raffles' assumption is, of course, that the 'eminent public man' who murdered whores was practising his art for art's sake: there is no suggestion that any 'lower' motives came into it. In other words, the gentleman cracksman is relating the Ripper's motives to his own:

> *Necessity*, my dear Bunny? Does the writer only write when the wolf is at the door? Does the painter paint for bread alone? Must you and I be driven to crime like Tom of Bow or Dick of Whitechapel? You pain me, my dear chap; you needn't laugh, because you do. Art for art's sake is a vile catchword, but I confess it appeals to me. In this case my motives are absolutely pure…[6]

The nonconformist and reformer W.T. Stead, whose *Pall Mall Gazette* had cited de Quincey's *Essay on Murder*, was also 'under the impression for more than a year' that 'the veritable Jack the Ripper' was a decadent occultist who called himself Roslyn D'Onston Stephenson, and that the crimes represented the application by a gentleman of leisure of some esoteric art. Stead's deduction is particularly interesting, in that his halfpenny evening newspaper had recently made its name by specialising in lurid exposés of East End child prostitution (complete with two innovations on the newspaper scene, the interview and the cheaply printed illustration). When Stead opted for the 'decadent Milord' explanation, he was, on the face of it, destroying the very image of the East End which his paper had struggled so hard to present, since July 1885: an image of a place where people were exploited for cash rather than butchered for kicks.

But Stead had also been one of the many who campaigned 'with moral indignation' against the publication of Emile Zola's naturalistic novels in England. He had argued that Zola's frank presentation of sex, violence, cruelty and slang were liable to injure public morals, if translations were made easily available. In October 1888, much to the *Gazette*'s delight, Henry Vizately was summonsed for publishing three 'indecent' novels (including *Nana*) in translation, was fined £100 and placed on probation for 12 months. Stead, and his National Vigilance Association, had temporarily won the day, ensuring that 'slum novels', dealing among other 'putrid filth' with drunkenness and prostitution, would not be available to those who could not read French.[7] So, in a sense, Stead's explanation of the Ripper murders fitted neatly into the moral position on the role of the artist which the *Pall Mall Gazette* had promoted in the previous year, and which, to judge by sales, may well have been a popular one. It was simply a case of transposing the arguments against Vizately to the editorials on Whitechapel, and full mileage could still be got out of the 'modern Babylon' at the same time. *The Lancet* of 27 October finally made explicit the connection between the two campaigns: in an article on 'the exploits of Jack the Ripper, as detailed for our delectation at the breakfast table day after day', the writer noted with suitable disgust 'the same drift towards sensationalism in the popularity of the realistic novel'. *The Lancet* continued:

> The realism which E. Zola has popularised in France, and which threatens to invade us in England, does not consist in the truthful portraiture of all aspects of human life, but in the deliberate and systematic choice of what is vile and corrupt for the purposes of fiction. It is as if a painter, determined to paint nature and nature only, were to neglect the wood, the stream, the ocean and human beauty, and fill his canvas with nothing but sores and ulcers and deformities. Such art would be realistic at the expense of sacrificing its true ends – namely, the promotion of pleasure by means *that elevate and ennoble.*

'A healthy all-round genius, like SHAKSPEARE', *The Lancet* went on, was 'sure to paint man as a rational, self-controlling being, and not as a wanton savage': this, in contrast to 'our French neighbours' who tended to worship people like the author of *The Beast in Man*.

Over the coming years, the novelist George Gissing and the poet Algernon Swinburne were actually to be named as possible Ripper 'types' – ironically, in Swinburne's case, since he too had campaigned against the Zola translations. It was almost as if the Gothick tradition of the penny-dreadfuls had joined forces with the fin-de-siècle realism of the novel: so the murderer had to be presented in the stock role of the 1820s Corinthian, the man of leisure who visited the Ratcliffe Highway to watch the rat-fighting and the drunken brawls, or to find a torture garden which catered for his particular taste in flesh. La bête humaine in a democratic setting…

In Paris, where Stead's exposé 'The Maiden Tribute of Modern Babylon' had been something of a *succès de scandale*, the murders were immediately related to another literary phenomenon which was almost equally chauvinistic – the fictional celebration of 'le sadisme anglais': 'Jack' became easily absorbed into a perverted pantheon of English Milords which had included George Selwyn, Lord Byron, Algernon Swinburne and the 'Marquis of Mount Edgecumbe'. 'Le vice anglais', if enjoyed to excess outside the confines of public schools, could so easily get out of control. Most of the monographs published by Professor Lacassagne's Institute at Lyons had been about French 'vampires', necrophiliacs and sadistic murderers; now at last an Englishman could be added to the list.

The moral context for the *Pall Mall Gazette*'s coverage of the Whitechapel murders to some extent explains both the appeal of the 'decadent artist' or the 'decadent aristocrat' thesis, and the reasons why the paper had an interest in promoting it in autumn 1888.

Less explicable is the recent fascination with 'solutions' that belong to the same category: in the past few years, the names Frank Miles and Walter Sickert have been linked with the Ripper crimes, as have those of the Duke of Clarence, his tutor at Cambridge (James Stephen) and Montague Druitt, an Oxford-educated barrister who was an active member of the MCC and Blackheath Cricket Club – a true heir to the *Raffles* tradition. Apart from the obvious advantage which these candidates share over the man-on-the-Whitechapel-omnibus – there is plenty of archive information about them, so it is not difficult to construct a full-scale biography with photo as part of the 'solution' – the attraction of this category today may well have something to do with revelations about 'the other Victorians'[8] which were first published in the 1960s. Plays about real-life eminents in a fictional setting (such as Graham Greene's *Return of A.J. Raffles*), films about fictional detectives in a real-life setting (such as *A Study in Terror*, and *Murder by Decree*, both featuring Sherlock Holmes and both opting for the Clarence 'solution'), books about the Whitechapel murders (naming Druitt, Clarence, James Stephen, and, most recently, the unlikely trio of the medic Sir William Gull, the painter Walter Sickert and the coachman John Netley as perpetrators of the crimes) have all proved popular in recent years, as have television series about assorted royal scandals of the nineteenth century – perhaps an indication of the power which the idea of 'the other Victorians' has over popular entertainers, and of the fact that the idea is not nearly as subversive as it looks.[9] The only certain thing that can be said about 'the Ripper as other Victorian' is that there is not a shred of hard evidence to link the crimes with *any* of the blue-blooded suspects named. No matter: Stephen Knight's *Jack the Ripper: the Final Solution*, which named three eminent names, sold a lot of copies; Joseph Sickert's admission that the book was based on an elaborate hoax ('it was a whopping fib') was given a few lines in *The Sunday Times*. Readers of *The Final Solution* had all been gulled – perhaps because they wanted to be.[10] There are still people who seriously believe that Walter Sickert had something to do with it.

The Ripper as a mad doctor. In this school of thought – the first to be suggested, at the time – he was a crazed medical student who had caught syphilis from a prostitute (possibly even 'had his privy member destroyed'), and sought revenge on the whole pack of them. Or he was an American physician who was collecting as many specimens of the female uterus as he could find, to include as a free hand-out with a monograph he was writing on diseases of the womb. He was a ship's doctor, or perhaps an amateur whose only practical experience came from filleting fish. If he was not exactly a doctor, then he *might* have acquired his knowledge of anatomy from the slaughterhouse – thus he was a slaughterman, a Jewish ritual slaughterman, or even a woman disguised as a slaughterman. This category seems to have gained legitimation from at least some of the evidence given at the inquests on the Ripper's victims: speaking of the Nichols murder, Dr Rees Ralph Llewellyn suggested that the mutilations were 'fairly skilfully performed'; of the Chapman murder, Dr Phillips opined that 'the mode in which the uterus was extracted showed some anatomical knowledge'; Dr Frederick Brown thought that the murderer of Eddowes showed 'a good deal of knowledge as to the positions of organs in the body cavity and the way of removing them'. But other professional observers were by no means so convinced. Doctors Sequeira and Saunders disagreed with Brown about the Eddowes murder, others reckoned that Kelly had been so severely mutilated that it was impossible to judge the 'skill' of the murderer, while Dr Thomas Bond of the City Police was certain that in each case the mutilations were done 'by a person who has no scientific or anatomical knowledge. In my opinion he does not even possess the technical knowledge of a butcher or horse slaughterman or any person accustomed to cut up dead animals'.

Whether or not the evidence pointed in the direction of 'some anatomical knowledge', the mad doctor category proved the most popular both in the press, and among commentators from the reading public at large. After all, the dramatisation of *Jekyll and Hyde* was very much in the news at the time (one suggestion in the files actually names Richard Mansfield the actor as the murderer, since his 'transformation' was *so* convincing), and the idea that the Ripper might be a doctor who was leading a double life seemed to 'work' in much the same way: the London Hospital in the Whitechapel Road could provide a secure base for his operations. There was a concurrent scandal in the press, about the bad behaviour of over-excited young surgeons in operating theatres, and especially those in London hospitals.

Robert Louis Stevenson's *Jekyll and Hyde* metaphor for 'the beast in man' was first published two years before the murders, and had gone through several editions by autumn 1888. The Lyceum adaptation opened in August. In the book, a successful society doctor who mixes in all the right social circles (and some of the wrong ones – there is a suggestion that he knows all about Cleveland Street) unleashes his alter-ego, a brutal counterpart who represents what Jekyll calls the other side of his 'dual nature'. The doctor is tall, pale and thin – of what the Victorians called 'refined features' (features with which the Ripper was associated by several eye-witnesses interviewed by the police). The beast is sallow, small and squat, rather like the 'hard ruffian' archetype mentioned in the *Pall Mall Gazette*. Hyde is, in other words, the physical embodiment of Jekyll's great discovery, 'that man is not truly one but truly two'. The doctor's lecture on the subject has been featured in suitably abridged form at the beginning of all the major film versions of the story:

I say two, because the state of my own knowledge does not pass beyond that point. Others will follow, others will outstrip me on the same lines; and I hazard the guess that man will be ultimately known for a mere polity of multifarious, incongruous and independent denizens. I for my part advanced infallibly in one direction and in one direction only. It was on the moral side, and in my own person, that I learned to recognise the thorough and primitive duality of man… It was the curse of mankind that these incongruous faggots were thus bound together – that in the agonised womb of consciousness these polar twins should be continuously struggling.[11]

At a time when neither Freud nor Krafft-Ebing had filtered into popular consciousness, when forensic medicine was still in its infancy (after one of the murders a rumour went round that an official photograph had been taken of the victim's eyes, since it had apparently been suggested by some European forensic experts that the retina at the moment of death would reflect the face of the murderer),[12] the Jekyll and Hyde model represented the most accessible 'explanation' for newspapers to exploit: an 'explanation' which had as its subtext something about 'the female principle' battling it out with 'the male principle'. Jekyll himself does not interpret the 'dual nature' of man in sexual terms at all: rather, he stresses that it is on the 'moral side' and has something to do with being just and unjust. Whatever the deeper meaning of the metaphor, in 1888 it seemed to newspapermen and their reading public to fit the idea that the Ripper could be an 'amiable-looking gentleman' *and* 'a hard ruffian' both at the same time. He was a bright young doctor who had gone off the rails; he was a soft-spoken gentleman who heard voices in his head in the night; he was Mrs Belloc Lowndes' *Lodger*, Mr Sleuth (1911), Stevenson's Dr Jekyll, the *Pall Mall Gazette*'s version of the Marquis de Sade. This 'either…or' explanation might account for the fact that the Ripper was likely to be as normal as thee or me – except when the dreaded beast in man came to the surface: for, apart from anything else, dialectical psychology was, of course, a thing of the future. It appears that Stevenson may have had William Gull, MD, DCL, LLD, FRS, Queen Victoria's Physician Extraordinary, in mind when he created the character of Henry Jekyll, MD, DCL, LLD, FRS: if so, it could explain why Gull, who by 1888 was aged and hemiplegic, has come to be associated by some recent writers with the Ripper murders; plus the fact that he seems to 'fit'.

The Ripper as anarchist, socialist or philanthropist.[13] If one literary correlative of our first category is Wilde's *Picture of Dorian Gray* (decadent young thing indulging in murder as one of the fine arts), and of our second is Stevenson's *Dr Jekyll*, this third category has more to do with the image of the East End that had been constructed by the press in the few years before 1888. The 'mad doctor' thesis represented the most accessible 'explanation' at the time, but the Ripper as foreign agitator ran it a close second.

The fact that several of the eye-witness accounts stressed (for whatever reasons) the murderer's 'foreign' appearance, while some of the senior police officers associated with the case were on record as suggesting that the murderer was a 'Jewish Socialist', were used to legitimate this thesis. He was a Jewish agitator, an Irish revolutionary, a 'low-class Asiatic', a Thug, a Russian Jew seeking to discredit the English police, an insane Russian doctor, 'a low-class Polish Jew', a Polish Jewish shoemaker, King Leopold of the Belgians, and a Portuguese sailor. Anyone who could write 'Mishter Lusk' – as in a letter 'from Hell' to George Lusk of the Whitechapel Vigilance Committee, of Tuesday 16 October – must be Irish. Anyone who could mutilate in the Ripper's fashion must either be Portuguese (according to Napier's *History of the Peninsular War*, it was 'characteristic' of them), or a Malay running amok ('probably primed with opium'). He was certainly not one of us.

This category of explanation relates to the image of the East End in 1888, in two important ways: it fed off the 'anti-alienism' which had paralleled the economic decline of the dockland areas of East London and it mirrored more general fears about the spread of Socialism among members of the 'true working class'. That the economic depression of the East End – and the concomitant rise of overcrowding, sweat-shops, and exploitation – had occurred at much the same time as the peak years of immigration from Eastern Europe, was a fact duly noted by those commentators who were concerned about the 'dilution' or 'degeneration' of good old English stock in the 'outcast' areas of London. There may have been structural reasons for this depression – the shift in patterns of employment around the docks, the competition from regional factories, the changing face of industrial London – but the immigrants provided a ready-made, and simple, explanation of it all which could displace more searching questions about the root causes of economic decline in East London. The 'economy of makeshifts' which was so characteristic of the people of the abyss was thus presented as a *racial* characteristic, in the popular middle-class press. Moreover, the Ripper struck at much the same time as these connections were first being formulated. The *East London Observer* of 15 September 1888 duly noted:

> On Saturday in several quarters of East London the crowds who assembled in the streets began to assume a very threatening attitude towards the Hebrew population of the District. It was repeatedly asserted that no Englishman could have perpetrated such a horrible crime as that of Hanbury Street, and that it must have been done by a JEW – and forthwith the crowds began to threaten and abuse such of the unfortunate Hebrews as they found in the streets…

Then, on 30 September, Elizabeth Stride was discovered outside the International Working Men's Educational Club, by a Jew. The result was, in one commentator's words, 'the nearest thing to an East End anti-Jewish pogrom, prior to the advent of Mosley'.

When the *Church Times*, no less, suggested that the Ripper might well be a Jewish Anarchist, the *Arbeter Fraint* retaliated with the words '…such homage to the Holy Spirit!' When *The Times* reported that a Jew named Ritter had been arrested near Cracow for the ritual murder of Christian women, and that 'the evidence touching the superstitions prevailing among some of the ignorant and degraded of his co-religionists remains on record and was never wholly disproved', the Chief Rabbi, Dr Herman Adler, wrote in to 'assert without hesitation that in no Jewish book is such a barbarity even hinted at'. Adler wisely added, 'the tragedies enacted in the East End are sufficiently distressing without the revival of moribund fables and the importation of prejudices abhorrent to the English nation'. But some members of the police force took more convincing than that. Sir Charles Warren thought the murderer might well be a 'Jewish Socialist'; Abberline thought he was George Chapman, a Pole whose real name was Severin Klosowski: Robert Anderson, Assistant Commissioner of the Met., stated as 'a definitely ascertained fact' that the Ripper was 'a low-class Polish Jew'; and Melville Macnaghten, who was soon to become Assistant Chief Constable at the Yard, named a certain Kosminski ('a Polish Jew resident in Whitechapel') as one of three key suspects (Kosminski had apparently 'become insane owing to many years' indulgence in solitary vices').

Official visits were made to kosher abattoirs, two ritual slaughtermen were arrested, and the special knife used by the shochet was examined by Dr Brown to see whether it could have inflicted wounds of the type found on the victims' bodies. The most highly publicised arrest in the whole case was that of John Pizer, or 'Leather Apron', a Polish Jewish shoemaker, and of the 130 arrests, made in the London area alone, a significant proportion were of Jews; following Pizer's arrest, the Ripper became more and more 'foreign in appearance' by the hour. So, when Sir Charles Warren ordered a chalk-written message about the 'Juwes' to be rubbed off a wall near Goulston Street – near where the bloodstained fragment of an apron was found shortly after the Eddowes murder – he was being far more responsible than many commentators have since suggested. It was strange, however, that he did not agree to let the words be photographed (by City Police photographers, significantly enough), and it may have been an error of judgment that prevented him from simply erasing the word 'Juwes', but the fact remains that, had he allowed the message to stay, he might well have had a riot on his hands (the message was written above a common stairway leading to a tenement block occupied mainly by Jewish immigrants). This was certainly the explanation he gave to the Home Secretary – who was furious – and it seems a reasonable one. (The police file implies that if the writing *was* done by the murderer, it may have had the intention of casting suspicion on three Jews who claimed to have seen him.) Dr Adler immediately wrote to congratulate Warren on his prompt action, reassuring him that the word 'Juwes' did not appear in any Yiddish dialect, and informing him of his conviction that 'the writing emanated from some illiterate Englishman who did not know how to spell the word correctly'. Warren's response was to publish this information in *The Times* of 15 October.

The recent thesis that Warren was 'covering up' for someone when he rubbed out the message, that the message referred to a different form of ritual slaughter based on Masonic mythology, seems not only to ignore the realities of East End history at the time, but also to fall prey to exactly the same mode of argument as led many to accuse the Jews in 1888. In the absence of any 'explanation' of the Ripper's actions, at the time of the murders, harassed police officers and sharp newspaper editors, as well as correspondents from the reading public, were irresistibly drawn to the 'secret ritual' argument: but there seems little excuse for doing so today.

If the murderer was not Jewish, then he must be Irish (the next worst thing), or Oriental. Failing that, he must be an English Socialist. Warren could not make up his mind whether the Ripper was Jewish, Socialist, or both; he was sure the Socialists had *something* to do with it – even if it meant suggesting that the murders were intended by one wing of the International to 'bring discredit' on another wing – but he could not work out exactly what. We have seen how Stead's *Pall Mall Gazette* put forward 'a scientific humanitarian' as the possible culprit. Others were more specific, implying that the Reverend Samuel Barnett founder of Toynbee Hall, the signwriter to General Booth of the Salvation Army, and even Dr Barnardo were possible 'types'. John Burns, who was to lead the dock strike of 1889, was detained by the police as he walked home from a late-night workers' meeting.

In a sense, this line of thought represents the other side of the 'alien' thesis. For, if one feature of the East End which was constantly in the news was the peril of unrestricted immigration (and suggestions as to how immigrants might most humanely be deported), another was the danger that pernicious socialist ideas might spread from 'outcast London', the 'residuum of labour', to more respectable or 'true' members of the working class. Once the good old English aristocrat of labour, or the artisan, found socialist ideas attractive, then the Trafalgar Square incident, and its aftermath, would seem like a side-show. Warren, who had given the orders which resulted in 'Bloody Sunday', was more aware of this than anyone. It was bad enough to watch the emergence of the Independent Labour Party, and the dramatic increase in trade union membership: something had to be done, preferably by non-political action, to seize the initiative from the socialists before their ideas spread *too* far.

In the popular press, the 'non-political actions' of 1884-88 were all treated with a greater or lesser measure of enthusiasm, for they seemed to provide ways of resolving the problem dramatised by Trafalgar Square without actually confronting it. The foundation of Oxford House (in 1884) and Toynbee Hall (a year later); the beginning of Charles Booth's survey of the East End, and the inauguration of the People's Palace in the Mile End Road (both 1887); the announcement of the Salvation Army's new policy of social reform in 1887; the much-publicised increase in the number of 'settlers' (or 'slummers') from the upper rungs of society, all these were easy enough to ridicule (Henrietta Barnett's 'all class' East-West tea parties at the Vicarage being an obvious target, almost as obvious, in fact, as the social worker who smugly declared: 'charity presents no difficulty to me; I took a First in Moral Philosophy at Cambridge'), but there were urgent reasons why they should be encouraged nevertheless. When the Ripper struck, the 'slummers',

Salvationists, university settlers, social analysts and 'do-gooders' of all descriptions were accused of murderous intentions with equal enthusiasm. Perhaps their work *was* actively dangerous, after all. More importantly, the Whitechapel murders gave editors the opportunity to associate socialism, or just plain philanthropy, with 'outcast' activities – the old-fashioned, sensational image of the East End as a den of vice – and thus to drive a wedge between the 'outcasts' and the 'respectables'. This distinction had been on the hidden agenda ever since Trafalgar Square, and the implied association between ripping and socialism brought it into focus.

If Jack was not a social analyst (like Booth), a settlement man (like Barnett, or, as has been suggested more recently, Druitt), a charity organiser (like Barnardo), a Salvationist (like General Booth's signwriter), or a revolutionary (probably Jewish – enough said), then there was always the danger that the socialists themselves would seize the initiative by using the crimes for their own propagandistic purposes. Jack, with a fiendish sense of timing, had succeeded in undoing the efforts of many well-intentioned people to publicise a less sensational image of the East End, just at a time when Beatrice Webb (among others) was beginning to realise that these efforts were merely the *first* stage: the East End, as a city within a city, was still little understood and much neglected.

Those who enthused over the 'non-political actions' of 1884-88, suggesting that they represented some kind of *solution* to the problem, were, predictably, shocked when various wings of the Socialist movement *did* use the Ripper crimes as a symbol of the evils of capitalism. *Justice*, the organ of Hyndman's Social Democrats, thundered 'the real criminal is the vicious bourgeois system which, based upon class injustice, condemns thousands to poverty, vice and crime'. Bernard Shaw presented a more whimsical Fabian view, in a letter headed 'Blood Money for Whitechapel', which he sent to the *Star* (a more radical evening paper than the *Gazette*) on 24 September 1886. To him, the identity of the murderer was quite simple – he was a social reformer 'of independent genius'. 'Less than a year ago, the West End press was literally clamouring for the blood of the people, and behaving as the propertied class always does behave when the workers throw it into a frenzy of terror by venturing to show their teeth': but since the beginning to the Whitechapel murders, he said, the West End press had undergone a change of heart:

> Whilst we conventional social democrats were wasting our time on education, agitation and organisation, some independent genius has taken the matter in hand, and by simply murdering and disembowelling four women, converted the proprietary class to an inept sort of communism. The moral is a pretty one, and the Insurrectionists, the Dynamitards, and the Invincibles will not be slow to draw it... Every gaol blown up, every window broken, every shop looted, every corpse found disembowelled means another ten pound note for 'ransom'...

William Morris' *Commonwealth* made a similar point, with less irony (and, incidentally, with more taste): 'in our age of contradictions and absurdities, a fiend-murderer may become a more effective reformer than all the honest propagandists in the world'. Morris himself had, in fact, been involved in an evening of 'honest propaganda', sponsored by the Socialist League, at the International Club, 40 Berner Street, just eight days before Stride's corpse was discovered there. For these Socialist newspapers, nothing but good could ultimately arise from the murders, even if 'four women of the people' had been sacrificed to the cause. It never seemed to occur to them that the image of the East End, as an area where people did not go around murdering one another but where they were dead behind the eyes none the less, had suffered significant damage as a result of the Ripper's experiments in 'slaughterhouse anatomy' (or was it consciousness-raising?). Nor did it occur to them that the 'four women' of the street might not be expendable.[14]

Arthur Morrison, wrote an article on 'Whitechapel' for the *People's Palace Journal* of April 1889, that was much more concerned than the

Social Democrats, the Fabians and the Guild Socialists about the effects of 'graphically-written descriptions of Whitechapel, by people who have never seen the place'. For Morrison, there were two types of description of the East End – one derived from accounts of Jack the Ripper, the other derived from the literature on 'outcast London' as an abyss into which intrepid missionaries might occasionally leap: both failed to take note of the *variety* of life in that sector of London, of the 'ancient industries' which were in decline, of the ways in which those who did *not* live in 'foul slums' existed day-to-day, above all of the human beings who actually managed somehow to survive, and even establish communities, a network of support, in the East End of London.

The first type of account went as follows:

> A horrible black labyrinth…reeking from end to end with the vilest exhalations; its streets, mere kennels of horrid putrefaction; its every wall, its every object, slimy with the indigenous ooze of the place; swarming with human vermin, whose trade is robbery, and whose recreation is murder; the catacombs of London – darker, more tortuous, and more dangerous than those of Rome, and supersaturated with foul life.

The second had a firmer basis in reality, but still could not claim in any way to be representative of the place:

> Black and nasty still, a wilderness of crazy dens into which pallid wastrels crawl to die; where several families lie in each fetid room, and fathers, mothers and children watch each other starve; where bony, blear-eyed wretches, with everything beautiful, brave and worthy crushed out of them, and nothing of the glory and nobleness and jollity of this world within the range of their crippled senses, rasp away their puny lives in the sty of the sweater.

Both descriptions, said Morrison, were written by the kind of man who called Whitechapel 'a shocking place where he once went with a curate'. His own rejection of *both* models of the East End put over by the popular press (and popular novels) was to be reinforced by the publication shortly afterwards of the first volume of Charles Booth's *East London*. Booth, also, had had to fight against the public images of 'outcast London':

> East London lay hidden from view behind a curtain on which were painted terrible pictures...horrors of drunkenness and vice; monsters and demons of inhumanity... Did these pictures truly represent what lay behind, or did they bear to the facts a relation similar to that which the pictures outside a booth at some country fair bear to the performance or show within? This curtain we have tried to lift.

According to Booth's figures only 1.2 per cent of the East End population were in the category of 'loafers and semi-criminals', while well over 60 per cent tried to lead 'decent', 'respectable lives' ('questions of employment' permitting). The rest were not so much 'debased', as living in conditions of almost perpetual poverty, and even so trying to support one another. Neither Jack, nor the 'do-gooders', had presented a true 'picture'.

These three images of the Whitechapel murderer – Dorian Gray, Dr Jekyll, and a political version of the wandering Jew of the penny-dreadfuls – combined with the 'mental sets' with which they were associated by popular writers – decadence, the beast in man, and socialism or racial degeneration – sustained press coverage of the crimes for several months, and enabled editors to slot the Whitechapel events into previously constructed 'angles'. Whichever of the three categories was chosen, it could be linked with a well-defined moral panic, and moral panics were very good for sales. In a sense, the moral panic strategy became a *substitute* for hard copy, since there was so little material available on the actual crimes, and since various steps seem to have been taken to prevent the more exploitable details from getting into print. It also provided three ready-made models of the-sort-of-person-who-might-do-such-things, at a time when the Ripper's motives appeared to go beyond the bounds of a recognisably human nature.

What is surprising is that these explanations are *still* so often accepted by self-styled 'Ripperologists' and their readers, when there is so much evidence, social *and* psychological, to contradict them. The Ripper was much more likely to have been the victim himself of the syndrome that leads some deeply depressed, low self-esteem and highly impressionable men to see a 'fallen woman' as the one last person they can push around than to have been one of the more famous 'other Victorians'; the frustrated victim of powerlessness rather than the possessor of real power. The nowhere man who sits by himself. We now have the language to describe what 'Jack' was up to, and perhaps why he was up to it, but the literature has continued to rely on *Gazette*-like solutions, displacing the only usable evidence there is, in favour of the criminal stereotypes of late-Victorian England – one philistine, one pre-Freudian, one racialist, all of them deeply misogynistic in character. Whoever the Ripper was, he was many worlds away from the 'Dictionary of National Biography'. Moreover the image of the East End as the kind of place where Nancy was regularly murdered by Bill Sikes has also survived into recent books on the Whitechapel murders, although social historians know better.

In 1888, reporters covering the crimes did not have much else to write about, and in any case were bound to exploit the moral panics of the moment as far as they could: this, to some extent, explains the unprecedented interest shown by newspapers catering for such widely different reading publics. True, these were serial murders, and several newspapers were quick to spot the commercial potential of the serial, often inventing fresh 'episodes' of their own to keep up their readers' interest. True, the name 'Jack the Ripper' seems to have struck a distinct chord – hardly surprising, really, since penny-bloods had for years been chronicling the exploits of Gallant Jack, Left-handed Jack, Roving Jack the Pirate Hunter, Jolly Jack Tar, Arab Jack the London Boy, Blind Jack of Knaresborough, Gentleman Jack, Jack Harkaway, Jack the Giant-Killer, Jack Spry, Jack's the Lad, Jack at Eton, Moonlight Jack King of the Road, Sixteen-String Jack the Hero Highwayman, Spring-Heeled Jack the Terror of London, Three-fingered Jack the Terror of the

Antilles, Thrice-Hung Jack, Jack O'Lantern, Jack O'the Cudgel, Jack O'Legs, Jack and Joe the troublesome twins, Slippery Jack, Jack Rann, Jack Junk, Crusoe Jack, and most famous of them all, Jack Sheppard; while newspaper reports of the 'High Rippers', or 'High Rips' – gangs of youths who, like the Hoxton Market and old Nichol Street mobs, went around attacking unaccompanied prostitutes in the East End – had filled many column inches in the early 1880s.

True, the internal squabbles between various branches of the police force (and the resignations which resulted around the time of the Ripper inquiry – James Monro, head of the CID, in August, Sir Charles Warren in November) were always a standby, when material on the Ripper became *too* thin on the ground, or when a newspaper wanted to score points at the expense of those who were hindering inquiries (in the public interest, of course) about the more gory aspects of the story. Accepting all this, we are still left with the fact that the image of the East End in the mental landscape of late-Victorian newspapermen, and the three moral panics with which the crimes were associated, provided the main support for the process of constructing a recognisable 'Jack the Ripper'. And they are still with us. As Michel Foucault has argued, there were some psychological and sexual scenarios which were simply not available in the past, and the usual danger for historians is projecting them back in time. The danger for 'Ripperologists' seems to be the opposite one of keeping alive pre-modern assumptions without realising it.

In this sense, in autumn 1888 Jack was yet another invention of the hardworking Victorian penny-a-liners. Criminologists may write of *Jack l'Éventreur*, or *Giacomo-lo-Squarciatore*, but he only seems to make full sense in an English setting, in the culture which produced the *Mysteries of London*, Sherlock Holmes (who made his first appearance in 1887), and *Dr Jekyll and Mr Hyde*: 'bien sûr, le pays de Sherlock Holmes est plein de malins qui disent "finalement le dernier mot" sur l'Éventreur...'

Thomas Purkess certainly had strong ideas about the commercial potential of the myth, right from the time of the murders: in addition to running a successful publishing house at 286 The Strand, which specialised in 'penny awfuls' about famous crimes and criminals, he owned and edited the *Illustrated Police News*, a penny weekly which was still getting full mileage out of the Ripper crimes in 1892, four years and a total of 184 cover pictures after the last murder was committed. In between advertisements for a reissue of numbers 1 and 2 of his own *Charles Peace, or the Adventures of a Notorious Burglar* 'ready on Monday next, with a free coloured plate, entitled "fooled by a woman"', notices of the forthcoming publication of 'The Missing Fanny – a tale of the Divorce Court' and sensational articles on 'Unavenged murders – number 2, the Murder of Emma Jackson in St Giles', Purkess crammed the *Illustrated Police News* with eye-witness accounts or people who had *heard* eye-witness accounts, new theories about the Ripper's identity and stories about preventative measures every Saturday for year after year. The murders may have lacked the well-tried ingredients of the sensational Victorian crime story, but Purkess was not about to let this affect his coverage. He also rushed out *The Whitechapel Murders or the Mysteries of the East End*, a bizarre part-work in ten fortnightly episodes, after only two of the murders had been committed.[15] On the cover of this, he showed a bearded villain, straight out of the Paragon or the Old Pavilion music hall in the Whitechapel Road, walking away from a very dead prostitute lying prostrate beneath a reward poster which claimed that four murders had occurred already.

To compete with this, Simpkin and Marshall, a rather more respectable publishing house, printed *The Curse Upon Mitre Square, AD 1530-1888*, by John Francis Brewer, an enterprising attempt to show that the murder of Catherine Eddowes in Mitre Square occurred on the exact spot where a demon monk, Brother Martin, had desecrated the high altar of Holy Trinity Church, Aldgate, in 1530, by a scene of bloody murder:

…measure this spot as carefully as you will, and you will find that the piece of ground on which Catherine Eddowes lies is the exact spot where the steps of the high altar of Holy Trinity existed… Is the ghost of Monk Martin still hovering over the scene of his crime? Or is it the vengeance of the Almighty that has cursed this spot? Who is there so bold as to say that there is no Curse Upon Mitre Square?

Both the *Curse* (Gothick-style) and the *Whitechapel Murders* (Newgate-style) were clearly very hastily compiled – well before the real-life serial had progressed beyond the first reel. Neither of them showed the remotest interest in the victims.

By the time the third and fourth murders had been committed, some letter-writers to the newspapers, and even some reporters and editors, were beginning to react against the growth of the Ripper industry, and, specifically, against the more extreme ways in which the events had come to be exploited. There were no complaints about the readiness with which editors jumped at the opportunity to exploit the three main stereotypes of the murderer, of course: these had been around for a long time, and readers would have been surprised if they had occasioned comment. The 'decadent aristocrat' idea had been firmly fixed in the public imagination, and associated with esoteric practices, ever since the Hell Fire Club, and, a bit more recently, the spread of gossip about Lord Byron ('he murdered his mistress, and enjoyed drinking her blood, from a cup made of her cranium…'); the 'demon doctor' idea would have come as no surprise to readers who had heard all about the anatomist who employed the body-snatchers Burke and Hare, or who had enjoyed *Sweeney Todd* the sadistic barber-surgeon; and the suggestion that the Jews might have been at the bottom of it harked right back to such standbys of the penny-a-liners as the Norwich pogrom of 1144 (sparked off by a 'ritualistic' murder) and the King's Road murders of 1771 ('go to Chelsea' being a common slur on passing Jews for many years afterwards), while feeding off common prejudices against the immigrants who were said to be 'polluting' the East End of London. Nor were there any complaints about the profound misogyny which underpinned all three stereotypes of the murderer. So there was no press reaction against the accepted 'explanations' of Jack's behaviour.

Rather, the reaction was against those reporters and editors who were alleged to be hindering the police in their inquiries, who were *enhancing* the Ripper's status as a mythic figure, or who were depraving or corrupting the literate youth (specifically, the literate working-class youth) of England. A correspondent to *The Times* launched into a tirade against the penny crime thrillers which tended to make Dick Turpin, Jack Sheppard or Charley Peace into downmarket versions of Robin Hood: he quoted the case of a youth who had recently been arrested for larceny, and who proceeded to bite the policeman's thumb, shouting 'I am as game as Charley Peace, and I will do as much as him before I die'. On 15 September 1888, *Punch* posed what it considered 'a serious question':

> Is it not within the bounds of probability that to the highly-coloured pictorial advertisements to be seen on almost all the hoardings in London, vividly representing sensational scenes of murder exhibited as 'the great attractions' of certain dramas, the public may be to a certain extent indebted for the horrible crimes in Whitechapel? We say it most seriously – imagine the effect of gigantic pictures of violence and assassination by knife and pistol on the morbid imagination of an unbalanced mind. These hideous picture-posters are a blot on our civilisation and a disgrace to the Drama...

And on 13 October *Punch* continued this campaign for censorship of *Police News*-type illustrations by running a cartoon entitled *Horrible London, or the pandemonium of posters* in which a leering, music-hall Ripper was shown sticking up posters advertising crime thrillers and penny-dreadfuls: one of these was clearly based on the cover of Purkess' *Whitechapel Murders*. On 20 October *Punch* printed a mock-operatic playlet entitled *The Detective's Rescue*, in which the 'Goddess of Lukewarm Public Opinion' – conjured up by Sir Charles Warren, no less

– disperses a crowd of grim 'sensation-mongers' who are asking a 'dismayed detective' exactly what his methods *are*: Warren's position is that 'a Detective is meant to *detect*', and morbid journalists should leave him alone to do just that.

> 'Do you think the detective's so green
> As to let you know all that he's traced?'

In addition to taking a few side-swipes at a 'detective force' that had only been in existence for ten years, one purpose of this campaign seems to have been to separate the 'responsible' treatment of the crimes in the respectable dailies from the exploitative treatment in the working-class press: penny-dreadfuls, the *Illustrated Police* comics and the East End music hall were all associated with the 'sensation-mongers'. The implication was that, if these media were all cleaned up, in other words taken over by the respectable middle classes ('lukewarm public opinion'), then one major 'blot on our civilisation' would have been removed. People like us (readers of *Punch*) were not, of course, entertained by such things. *Punch* had, in fact, been campaigning against 'this poisonous exotic Sensation' ever since 1861 (when developments from 'across the Atlantic' were blamed), but the campaign of autumn 1888 coincided with the first stirrings of the movement to take over the music hall of the East, and make it a suitable place for West Enders to spend an amusing night out: songs like the infamous *Sam Hall* ('They've shut me up in quod, For killing of a sod... Damn your eyes') were not, apparently, considered amusing enough for such a refined audience.

Punch moved up the market, however, when it started another campaign, this time against the publication of all the latest developments in the case as they occurred: such journalistic practice, it was suggested, served only to hamper the movements of the police and especially of the 'defective force'. The specific target of this campaign seems to have been the *Pall Mall Gazette*, under the Liberal editorship of W.T. Stead. As early as 22 September 1888, *Punch* ran a *Detective's Diary à la Mode*, which attempted to show how dangerous it was for the public to expect an instant arrest, or at least instant results from the detective department; and endless 'suggestions' from the press did not help much either.

Monday – Papers full of the latest tragedy. One of them suggested that the assassin was a man who wore a blue coat. Arrested three blue-coat wearers on suspicion.

Tuesday – The blue-coats proved innocent. Released. Evening journal threw out a hint that deed might have been perpetrated by a soldier. Found a small drummer-boy drunk and incapable. Conveyed him to the Station House.

Wednesday – Drummer-boy released. Letter of anonymous correspondent to daily journal declaring that the outrage could only have been committed by a sailor. Decoyed petty officer of Penny Steamboat on shore, and suddenly arrested him.

Thursday – Petty officer allowed to go. Hint thrown out in the correspondence columns that the crime might be traceable to a lunatic. Noticed an old gentleman purchasing a copy of a Rider Haggard novel. Seized him.

Friday – Lunatic despatched to an asylum. Anonymous letter received, denouncing local clergyman as the criminal. Took the reverend gentleman into custody.

Saturday – Eminent ecclesiastic set at liberty with an apology. Ascertain in a periodical that it is thought just possible that the Police may have committed the crime themselves. At the call of duty, finished the week by arresting myself…

This *Detective's Diary* was so full because, as far as the press knew, there was no hard evidence on which to base a charge that would stick, and no agreed expert 'explanation' of the Ripper's actions: the suggestions of that 'evening journal' were thus seen to be without foundation – or worse, actively misleading.

The Lancet was in a stronger position than *Punch* to judge whether or not the police were in possession of hard evidence: after all, when the Coroner asked the gentlemen of the press at an inquest to take heed of Dr Phillips' remarks about the possible misuse of gory details, *The Lancet* alone felt justified in issuing a full account of the Ripper's style in mutilation. As a journal that was read mainly by members of the medical profession (the prime suspects, according to many a reporter), *The Lancet* was able to stand aside from more commercial considerations of crime reporting and criticise 'the press' in general. On 6 October 1888, *The Lancet* lashed out at 'those manuals of instruction in crime – the penny histories of murder and felony which abound on many bookstalls'.

> The ruinous effect of this kind of reading cannot be denied. Tales of silly sentiment, of glaring immorality, of refinement in vice, or romantic passion working out its course in hatred and murder, fill up the pennyworths of garbage which are constantly foisted upon foolish and ignorant purchasers by the gutter purveyors of literature. Youth, untrained in right principle, perhaps overworked, physically and mentally morbid from the want of fresh air and sufficient house room, affords a ground already prepared to receive the tares of this injurious teaching.

This attack on working-class literature (youth, characteristically, seems to have been synonymous with working-class youth) was followed by assorted letters from outraged clerics and retired physicians, and finally by an editorial entitled 'the Growth of Sensationalism', in which 'the press' was attacked for printing what *The Lancet* alone should have been permitted to print. Evidently only card-carrying members of the profession could handle the full story:

> Today, the press takes care to report at inordinate length, and often with objectionable minuteness, the details of the latest murder, divorce or fashionable scandal. The Whitechapel tragedies have afforded a typical case in point – what with gruesome descriptions

of the victims, elaborate conjectures as to the precise mode and motive for the crimes, and interminable theories as to the best means of discovering the criminal, one would think that the thoughts of the entire nation were practically absorbed in the contemplation of revolting wickedness.

There followed an elaboration of the thesis that, in the absence of any substantial evidence about the identity of Jack the Ripper, the exploiters were having to work overtime. Towards the end of this editorial, *The Lancet* gave some suggestions about why so much public interest had been aroused in these crimes, and why the culture industry had been so quick to spot their commercial potential:

> It may be a question how far this craving for excitement is simply the outcome of the overtension of modern industrial civilisation… the modern Englishman lives at such high pressure that simple pleasures may cease to amuse him. If so, the admission is a disquieting one. A return to nature is so much simpler, healthier, and less exhausting – it is important to make this desirable. No benefit can result from a mass exhaustion of emotions.

To reinforce this point, *The Lancet* appended a letter from Lieutenant-Colonel Herbert Everitt of the Church of England Purity Society. (The fact that those who suffered most from 'high pressure' were scarcely in a position to 'return to nature' did not, of course, occur to the editors.)

The Lancet's campaign, however, is an interesting one, coming as it did hot on the heels of an equivalent campaign in the more popular press. If the newspapers' treatment of the Whitechapel murders fed off a series of moral panics that were very much in the news already, that same treatment stimulated yet another moral panic of its own, and the cry to censor the crime-reporting of the working-class press (which might give ignorant people ideas) became louder as the Ripper industry expanded its sphere of operations.[16] *Punch* posed as a middle-of-the-road arbiter of taste – as the spokesperson for what we would now call the silent majority. *The Lancet* posed as the defender of the medical profession's 'right to know', a right which appears to have excluded everyone else. On 3 November, *The Lancet* printed a letter from a Dr G.B. Beale of Tottenham which attributed 'the temporary decline in tone and taste' to 'the Board School system, which has educated to the point of being able to read a vast number who before its institution were unable to do so...' The *British Medical Journal* of 22 September claimed to have found the solution, however: 'all civilising influences tend to improve the brain, especially in young people; and in this way the establishment of evening classes, well-conducted clubs, and athletics will tend to lessen ruffianism'. Meanwhile, the *Illustrated Police News* was content to increase its circulation.

Punch's Detective's Diary was not, in fact, original: it was plagiarised from *Fun* magazine of the previous week, as was the new campaign against lurid posters. *Fun* had also printed *The Crime Cauldron*, 'as brewed by certain papers (with sincere apologies to the author of Macbeth)', the most amusing of all the many attacks on the exploitation of the Ripper tragedies:

Enter three Editors:

Vice seems not to be subdued

Vice and Crime are on the wind.

Round about the cauldron go

In it slips of 'copy' throw.

Headlines of the largest size –

Murderer's letters – all faked lies;

And other spicy bits we've got

To simmer in our charmèd pot.

Bubble, Bubble! Crime and Trouble

Make our circulation double.

Here are gory catalogues

Touching murderer – tracking dogs.

Tales of reeking knives and things,

Which the 'service' hourly brings.

There served up with inquest-trouble

Make our crime-broth boil and bubble.

Etc. Etc.

One ironic result of this campaign was the closing of *Dr Jekyll and Mr Hyde* at the Lyceum. Although the play had been a hit, Richard Mansfield decided to withdraw it from the repertoire after a shortish run – and he withdrew it in style, with a benefit performance for the homeless of the East End. The *Daily Telegraph* was quick to show its admiration for the American actor-manager's grand gesture:

> Mr Richard Mansfield has determined to abandon the 'creepy drama', evidently beloved in America, in favour of wholesome comedy. The murderous Hyde will peer round the drawing-room windows and leap at his victim's throat for the last time… Experience has taught this clever young actor that there is no taste in London just now for horrors on the stage. There is quite sufficient to make us shudder out of doors.

Robert Louis Stevenson himself must have been delighted about Mansfield's decision for he had expressed disapproval of the production from the word go, on the grounds that it dared to interpret the conflict between Jekyll and Hyde in *sexual* terms: 'the harm was in Jekyll because he was a hypocrite', wrote Stevenson, 'not because he was fond of women'.[17] If the audience started imagining that *Dr Jekyll and Mr Hyde* was about *sex*…whatever next? In the film versions, Mr Hyde's crimes were to become synonymous with Jack the Ripper's – with the locale shifting from Soho to Whitechapel, and with the crimes of the novella magnified many times over.

Perhaps because the three powerful Victorian images of the-sort-of-man-who-could-be-the-Whitechapel-murderer have survived into the late-twentieth century – in popular culture, as always someone else's nightmare – the author at the centre of it all, 'Jack the Ripper', remains the elusive figure he always was: a space in the files, an *absence* which has been given a name by 'an enterprising journalist', and a character by successive writers, reporters and members of the reading public. In terms of historical evidence, he does not exist, so, for all sorts of reasons, he has been constantly reinvented. Ever since the autumn of 1888, this space has been used to accommodate the 'beasts', 'monsters' and 'maniacs' of the moment. Each generation has added embellishments to a genre picture which was first created out of the West End's fear of the outcast East, out of a glimpse into the abyss.

The absence in the fog which is 'Jack the Ripper' has proved a stimulus to more creative imaginations as well. For Frank Wedekind and the Expressionists, he provided a suitable come-uppance for Pandora, the girl – or rather the 'female principle' – who released all kinds of dark inhibitions from her box as a punishment for mankind; it was Wedekind, via the film director G.W. Pabst, who popularised some of the obligatory props – the gaslight, the fog, the winding byways of the red-light district, the Salvation Army band on the corner. For Brecht, Jack the Knife was the perfect embodiment of the gangster-as-capitalist, the appropriator of other men's crimes. For the Surrealists, Jack l'Éventreur was one of their satanic majesties, whose activities could be used as material for a college of steel engravings which set out to amuse and shock. An issue of the surrealist journal *Minotaure*, for example, with a cover by Dali and colour reproductions of Picasso's work, included a short play by Maurice Heine entitled *Regards sur l'enfer anthropoclasique*, which, with considerable relish, told the story of a meeting between the Marquis de Sade, the Comte de Mesanges and the Reverend Jack the Ripper.

> THE COUNT *(To JACK)*: Your work is all over very quickly: butcher's work...technically skilful, perhaps, but there's no *art* in that.

JACK: Art is the child of leisure, Monseigneur, and necessity encouraged me to get a move on. The essential precaution against all surprise or interruption was to move quickly; that is to say, to give the subject a speedy, silent and neat despatch. That's what this weapon assured me of – wielded with the left hand, but directed towards the point where a right-handed person would have begun, and whence the blood had to spurt far away from me. As for what you style 'art', it was more convenient for me to practise *that* on the bloodless flesh of a docile corpse. I never neglected to devote short periods of time to it – as circumstances permitted me. Would you like to see proof of this? Do grant me that you see here at least a few artistic touches. (He hands the Comte de Mesanges the photograph reproduced as plate 1).[18]

For Hollywood in the golden age, he could help to turn the expressionist aesthetic into the set of slightly camp visual clichés of horror with which he has been associated ever since, completing the Pabst process. For George Orwell, he was one of the last of the English murderers as old masters, whose work threw into relief the activities of modern-day suburban hacks who had seen too many Hollywood B movies. For film director Michael Powell, he could have been an obsessive *voyeur* who saw life through the lens of a film camera, and who killed his victims with a knife attached to the tripod: Mark (or Jack) could not engage with life, or communicate at all except through this mass medium. More recently, he has been portrayed on the stage as a suitable candidate for a seat in the House of Lords (*The Ruling Class*), in films as part of an elaborate cover-up engineered by All Her Majesty's Men (*Murder by Decree*), on television as an intergalactic impulse which feeds off the fear of beautiful women who walk home alone at night (*Star Trek*), and in music as a singing social worker from Toynbee Hall. The interest generated by those murders of a hundred years ago has been sufficient to support a minor industry – the products of which include books, plays, magazines, television series, advertisements, comics, bubble-gum cards, a board-game and, of course, countless 'splatter movies' where the man with the knife strikes again and again. I recently saw in a crime-novel bookshop in New York a 'Jack the Ripper' board-game where each player becomes a leading 'suspect' and a throw of the dice moves the Duke of Clarence, and chums, around the back streets of Victorian Whitechapel. It was next to a book called 'The Jack the Ripper Walking Tour Murders', the plot of which involves a series of killings during the centenary year of 1888, on sites associated in the public mind with the original murders – Hanbury Street, Madame Tussaud's Chamber of Horrors, Scotland Yard's Black Museum. The murderer turns out to be the East German tenor who sings the part of 'Jack' in a production of Alban Berg's opera 'Lulu'. So the Whitechapel Murders have turned post-modernist.

The institutionalised misogyny – shared by police, doctors, journalists and readers alike – which sustained press coverage of the crimes in autumn 1888, and which treated the 'unfortunate' victims as in some sense expendable, has also helped to sustain outdated 'solutions' to the mystery right up to the present day, 'solutions' which have survived to become deeply embedded in the culture. The latest bibliography lists some 300 titles on the subject, nearly all written by men. One result is that it has become inconceivable that 'Jack the Ripper' could have been the man next door. He must have been some kind of celebrity.

> MR USHER: I wonder if the police have got any sort of line on this necktie murderer.
>
> DOCTOR: Oh, I shouldn't think so. With psychopaths there's usually no linking motive.
>
> MR USHER: Well, let's hope he slips up soon.
>
> DOCTOR: In one way, I rather hope he doesn't. We haven't had a good juicy series of sex murders since Christie, and they're so good for the tourist trade. Foreigners somehow expect the squares of London to be fog wreathed, full of hansom cabs and littered with ripped whores – don't you think…?[19]

Looking back, the *real* story of Jack the Ripper isn't a 'whodunnit' at all: they didn't know then and we don't know now. It's the story of how and why these gruesome events have passed into English heritage. This is the house that Jack built.

(ENDNOTES)

1   This article benefitted greatly from discussions, at various stages in its drafting, with Angela
     Carter, Robert Reiner, Graham Cox and research students in the Department of Cultural
     History, Royal College of Art. It was first published, in an earlier form, in Tomaselli and
     Porter: *Rape – an historical and social enquiry* (Oxford 1986), pp. 174-215.

2   My account of the 'image' of the East End in the late 1880s owes a great deal to three works
     by Peter Keating: *The Working Classes in Victorian Fiction* (New York, 1971), esp. pp. 93-
     124, 167-198 and 223-245; *Working Class Stories of the 1890s* (London, 1971); and *Into
     Unknown England, 1866-1913* (London, 1976). Also to Gareth Stedman-Jones, *Outcast
     London* (Harmondsworth, 1984), esp. pp. 99-151, and 215-314; and Kellow Chesney, *The
     Victorian Underworld* (Harmondsworth, Middlesex, 1974).

3   William Vincent's *The Whitechapel Murders* (in *Police Review*, 16 December 1977 to 14
     April 1978) is particularly useful on the attitude of the various branches of the police to the
     crimes and to the newspapers' coverage of them.

4   Extracts from 'suggestions' in the Home Office files are printed in the books by Donald
     Rumbelow and Stephen Knight, see note 5 below. One of the more bizarre suggestions in
     the files is that the Ripper was a renegade cowboy from Buffalo Bill's Wild West.

5   For a more detailed historical study of the tradition in popular culture from which this
     theme emerged, see my *Vampyre – Lord Ruthven to Count Dracula* (London, 1978), esp. pp.
     14-82. The following account of the Whitechapel murders and their legacy has been pieced
     together from (a) a cross-section of contemporary sources: *The Times* (September 1888–
     January 1889); *Daily Telegraph* (September 1888–January 1889); *Pall Mall Gazette: an
     evening newspaper and review* (September 1888–January 1889)); *The Star* (September 1888–
     January 1989); *Illustrated Police News Law Courts and Weekly Record* (August 1888–January
     1889); *Penny Illustrated Paper and Illustrated Times* (September 1888–January 1889); *The
     Lancet* (September 1888–January 1889); *British Medical Journal* (October 1888–December
     1888); *Punch* (August 1888–January 1889); and *Fun* (August 1888–January 1889); and
     (b) the major secondary sources (in order of appearance): Leonard Matters, *The Mystery
     of Jack the Ripper* (London, 1929), which opts for an insane 'Dr Stanley' as the culprit;
     William Stewart, *Jack the Ripper: a new theory* (London, 1939), which opts for an insane
     woman (probably a midwife) as the culprit; Donald McCormick, *The Identity of Jack
     the Ripper* (London, 1959), which opts for Alexander Pedachenko, a Czarist doctor and
     secret agent; Robin Odell, *Jack the Ripper in Fact and Fiction* (London, 1965), which opts
     for an insane schochet, or Jewish slaughterman; Tom Cullen, *Autumn of Terror: Jack the
     Ripper, his crimes and times* (London, 1965), the most scholarly of the secondary sources
     so far, which, however, cannot resist opting for Montague Druitt, the cricketing barrister,
     as the culprit; Michael Harrison, *Clarence* (London, 1972), which opts for the Duke of
     Clarence and Avondale, KG; Daniel Farson, *Jack the Ripper* (London, 1972), which opts
     for Montague Druitt, with new 'evidence'; Donald Rumbelow, *The Complete Jack the
     Ripper* (London, 1975), which sensibly concludes 'I have always had the feeling that on
     the Day of Judgement, when all things shall be known, when I and other generations of
     Ripperologists ask for Jack the Ripper to step forward and call out his true name, then we
     shall turn and look with blank astonishment at one another…and say "who?"'; Elwyn Jones
     and John Lloyd, *The Ripper File* (London, 1975), which opts for Sir William Gull, the Royal
     Physician, aided by John Netley, a coachman, as the culprits, and suggests that the murders
     were decreed by 'the highest in the land'; Richard Whittington-Egan, *A Casebook on Jack the
     Ripper* (London, 1975), which sifts through all the available evidence, and comes up with
     a revived suspect, Roslyn D'Onston, an insane occultist who was, however, sane enough
     to be author of *The Patristic Gospels* (London, 1904); Stephen Knight, *Jack the Ripper – the
     final solution* (London, 1976), which develops the Gull/Netley thesis and adds the painter

Walter Sickert as a *third* culprit; William Vincent, *The Whitechapel Murders* (in *Police Review*, London, weekly from 16 December 1977 to 14 April 1978), which aims to 'inspire some officers of today to delve into the mystery – come on, have a go'; and Frank Spiering, *Prince Jack* (New York, 1978), which reasserts the 'Clarence' solution. There have been many other (non-book) contributions to the debate, some of which are catalogued in Alexander Kelly, *Jack the Ripper: a bibliography and review of the literature* (London, 1973).

6   Hornung, E.W., *Raffles the Amateur Cracksman* (Nelson Library edition, London, 1909), pp. 34-5 of 'A Costume Piece', and pp. 54-5 of 'Gentlemen and Players'.

7   On 'French naturalism and English working-class fiction', see Paul Keating, *The Working Classes in Victorian Fiction*, (London, 1979) pp. 125-38.

8   The fashion, and the phrase, were launched by Steven Marcus, *The Other Victorians: a study of sexuality and pornography in mid-nineteenth-century England* (London, 1966), a book which has helped to inspire more recent studies of sexual ideology and social structure, but which has too *undifferentiated* an approach to 'Victorian culture' and 'sexual mores'.

9   Greene, Graham, *The Return of A.J. Raffles* (London, 1975). Where popular entertainers are concerned, most of the printed 'solutions' to this hundred-year-old whodunit have been turned into films – a clear indication of their strong *resonance* in contemporary popular culture. The 'insane doctor' thesis has appeared, not only in the five major versions of *Dr Jekyll and Mr Hyde* (of which Rouben Mamoulian's of 1932 is still the most impressive), but also in the British film of *Jack the Ripper* (Robert S. Baker, 1958). The 'Jill the Ripper' thesis has appeared in *Dr Jekyll and Sister Hyde* (Roy Ward Baker, 1971), and *Hands of the Ripper* (Peter Sasdy, 1971). The 'decadent aristocrat' thesis has appeared in *A Study in Terror* (James Hill, 1966, based on Ellery Queen's story which pits Sherlock Holmes against Jack the Ripper, and names 'the Duke of Shires'); and *Murder by Decree* (Bob Clark, 1979, which implicates, but does not name, Gull, Netley and Clarence). Variations on these themes have, of course, appeared in countless 'splatter movies' which ostensibly have nothing to do with the Whitechapel murders: in these, the insane psychiatrist seems to be a favourite contender. An interesting link between the two traditions was made in *Time After Time* (Nicholas Meyer, 1980), which had an 'insane doctor' from Victorian London splattering his way around contemporary Los Angeles, to which he had travelled in H.G. Wells' time machine. All the main 'solutions' have found their way into popular fiction (usually short stories) as well: two representative collections are Allan Barnard (ed.), *The Harlot Killer* (New York, 1953) and Michel Parry (ed.), *Jack the Knife* (Herts, 1975). The most famous short story inspired by Jack the Ripper – Marie Belloc Lowndes' *The Lodger* (1911, later turned into a novel) – has been the source of two classic films, the first directed by Alfred Hitchcock (1926), the second by John Brahm (1944), and two others (1932, 1953). Robert Bloch, the American author of *Psycho* (1960), has written so many versions of the Jack the Ripper story that he has managed to incorporate most of the main 'solutions' at one time or another: his stories include *Yours Truly, Jack the Ripper* (1943, set in contemporary Chicago); *Psycho* (1960); the *Star Trek* episode *Wolf in the Fold* (first screened 22 December 1967, published 1974, concerning an intergalactic non-corporeal Ripper which feeds on frightened women, and lives in the foggy sector of assorted planets); *A Most Unusual Murder* (1976, concerning the perils of researching the subject); and the novel *Night of the Ripper* (New York, 1984), which manages to include among the cast of characters nearly *all* the recent 'suspects'). In Britain, Richard Gordon added to the 'Ripper industry' of the 1970s with *The Private Life of Jack the Ripper* (London, 1980), a 'medical mystery novel' which names 'Dr Bertram Randolph' as the culprit, and reprints, with professional comment, a lot of nasty material from *The Lancet* of 1888. It is significant that although details of the character of 'the Ripper' may vary from story to story and from film to film, in this bizarre sub-genre, the characters of the *victims* remain much the same as the stereotypical 'five little whores' presented in the popular press of autumn 1888. It is as if the murderer will be interesting to readers, while the

victims will not. Perhaps the best comment on this 'Ripper industry' is contained in Marcel Carné's film *Drôle de Drame* (1937): the film treats 'Victorian Limehouse' as the excuse for much surreal satire and the Ripper (Jean-Louis Barrault) is in fact a vegetarian and animal liberationist who kills only meat butchers…

10 On 18 June 1978, *The Sunday Times* reported Sickert's admission under the headline *Jack the Ripper 'solution' was a hoax, man confesses*: Joseph Sickert added 'as an artist I found it easy to paint Jack the Ripper into the story'. Six years later, in 1984, Stephen Knight's *Jack the Ripper – the final solution* was reprinted by the Treasure Press, London, virtually uncorrected. Clearly, this story was *so* good that a little matter of factual inaccuracy could not be allowed to stand in its way. It *had* to be true. And some still believe it.

11 Stevenson, Robert Louis, *The Strange Case of Dr Jekyll and Mr Hyde*, Corgi edn (London, 1964), pp. 51-2 of 'Henry Jekyll's full statement of the case'.

12 This myth may have started life in a citation from the *British Journal of Photography* (17 February 1888), which refers to a story about a French assassin, as recounted by an American journalist. Certainly, the *Journal* makes no mention of the myth in its coverage of autumn 1888.

13 For some key sources, see n. 9. Also Gareth Stedman Jones, *Languages of Class: studies in English working class history 1832-1982* (Cambridge, 1983), pp. 204-35, especially useful on the music halls of the period; and Judith R. Walkowitz, *Prostitution and Victorian Society* (Cambridge, 1982), which, although it deals predominantly with the 1860s, provides an important frame of reference.

14 For a very welcome if all too brief analysis of the coverage of the Whitechapel murders from a feminist perspective, see Judith Walkowitz, 'Jack the Ripper and the Myth of Male Violence', *Feminist Studies*, 8 (1982), pp. 543-74. Although Judith Walkowitz and I have been researching independently for several years – and from somewhat different sources – our conclusions are in some ways congruent.

15 Parts 1-5 are in the John Johnson collection of ephemera, at the Bodleian Library. Parts 6-10 do not seem to have survived.

16 For a study of parallel phenomena, see Geoffrey Pearson, *Hooligan: A History of Respectable Fears* (London, 1983), and Pearson's 'Falling Standards: a short, sharp history of moral decline', in Martin Baker, *The Video Nasties* (London, 1984), pp. 88-103.

17 Cited in S.S. Prawer, *Caligari's Children* (Oxford, 1980), p. 106.

18 Heine, Maurice, *Regards sur l'enfer anthropoclasique* (sic), in *Minotaure* (issue number 8, Paris, 15 June 1936). Heine's play, which occupies five double-column pages, pp. 41-5, includes two post-mortem photographs of Jack the Ripper's victims reprinted from Prof. A. Lacassagne, *Vacher l'Éventreur et les crimes sadiques* (Lyons, 1899); the author's other contributions to *Minotaure* (as occasional member of the editorial committee, with André Breton and Marcel Duchamp) included a study of 'le roman noir' in issue number 5, especially the writings of Horace Walpole, the Marquis de Sade and Monk Lewis, and a study of Lautréamont's *Maldoror* in issue number 12. For general background to *Minotaure*, see Dawn Ades, *Dada and Surrealism Reviewed* (London, 1978), pp. 279-93. Heine may have been reminded of the story of Jack the Ripper by a production of the melodrama *Jack l'Éventreur* (written by André de Lorde and Pierre Chaine) at the Grand-Guignol, which opened on 30 September 1934. Act II of this 'boulevard nasty' set near 'le quartier d'Holborn Square' ends with the murderer disembowelling one of his victims on the stage while screaming, 'Ah! du sang…du sang!'

19 A conversation overheard in the Nell of Old Drury from Anthony Shaffer's script for the film *Frenzy* (Alfred Hitchcock, 1972).

6

Home Counties Transylvania

Introduction

LIKE ANGELA CARTER, *I grew up with the pop Gothic of Hammer Films – a company which found its own voice, its repertory of actors and locations and its brand, in May 1957 when* The Curse of Frankenstein *threw a pot of bright-red paint in the respectable face of mainstream uptight British cinema. She wrote of 'the Hammer Films I enjoyed as a child'. In Angela's case, she recalled that her early experiences of 'the big-screen experience' were often at the Granada Tooting, South London, near her family home in Balham. This gave her a taste for 'anything that flickers'. At the time, the early Hammer films were far from respectable with the film establishment – and indeed the Board of Censors – which of course made them all the more fun to watch. A guilty pleasure. At precisely the time when critical/academic attitudes towards Hammer were beginning to mature – in the mid-1970s – Angela contacted Aida Young, who had produced some of the latter-day Christopher Lee* Draculas, *with a view to possibly collaborating on a Gothic project. I have always thought it was sad that this never happened. The* Company of Wolves *(1984), the only theatrical film adapted from her work to be made in her lifetime, would have benefitted considerably from a dose of Hammer's visual flair, experience and full-bloodedness. In time, the new respectability of Hammer – allied with the fashion for studying the Gothic on university literature courses – inevitably led to projections onto the films of ideas about identity, class and gender which were smart but anachronistic. The experience of watching Hammer films – and Roger Corman's Edgar Allan Poe adaptations – at a tender age, I'm convinced, had a profound impact on the generation of critics and academics who championed 'the Gothic' when they grew up.*

Home Counties Transylvania

SEVERAL YEARS AGO, I received a strange request from England's Heritage Lottery Fund, the body which distributes 'good cause' lottery money to national heritage projects.[1] Would I comment on an application for funding to house in a museum a large collection of artefacts associated with Hammer horror films – mainly 'special effects makeup', the Phil Leakey and Roy Ashton collections – from the late 1950s to the mid 1970s? There was a detailed inventory in the package that included some 'dental appliances with a reservoir of blood, operated by the actor's tongue' from *Dracula* (1958), eye inserts, a 'box of rubber noses and oriental eye pieces', moulds for scars, plaster-cast heads of Christopher Lee and Peter Cushing, prostheses and makeup boxes including the ingredients of Kensington Gore (fake blood), plus assorted pen-and-pencil sketches, pilot-drawings, character designs, production photos, scrapbooks, press cuttings and documents. The main focus of the collection was on films from *The Curse of Frankenstein* (1957) to *The Reptile* (1965). Did they, or did they not, deserve to be considered part of the national heritage? Were they 'national' or an offshore product of Hollywood? What was their 'historical importance'? What was their cultural impact? And their effect on the post-war British film industry? Above all, were the collections – as an archive – worthy of support as significant examples of 'the heritage'? As someone who had written and broadcast on both the Gothic novel *and* horror movies, I seemed in a good position to answer these questions. A follow-up telephone call explained that the Heritage Lottery advisers were in a quandary about how to react to this application. The application was dated December 1997. A decision had to be made by the end of January 1998, because the collection would then be put onto the open market and probably be dispersed.

I did not hesitate. Of course, the material culture of Hammer films deserved a place, preferably a prominent place, in a museum. Why not? Why the hesitation? Where significance and impact were concerned, the five film versions of the *Frankenstein* story made between 1956 and

1972 (with Peter Cushing as the arrogant aristocratic scientist), the six versions of *Dracula* made between 1957 and 1970 (with Christopher Lee as the *grand saigneur*), plus *The Mummy* (1959, with both of them) and *The Devil Rides Out* (1967, with Lee as the good guy, for once) represented for me a key moment in the history of British cinema. It was a moment when a small studio at Bray, just off the main Maidenhead-Windsor road, a gap in the market, a repertory company of directors, designers, musicians, technicians and actors, and a great deal of entrepreneurial flair, created a distinctive product, a distinctively stylish product, which even took the American market by storm and eventually won the Queen's Award to Industry in 1968 (the only film company to be so honoured). At the time of *The Curse of Frankenstein* – Hammer's breakthrough colour film in 1957 – some Madison Avenue financial backers expressed concern that 'just how British [the actors] are by way of accent' might hold back the film's chances on the American market. Hammer replied reassuringly that 'the British cast will be absolutely first class and will have no trace whatsoever of British accent'. Which was very odd, since the very *Britishness* of the project turned out to be part of its appeal. Roger Corman's Edgar Allan Poe cycle, in some ways a spin-off from Hammer, was deliberately to contrast the barnstorming acting style of Vincent Price (school of the Barrymores in their prime) with the beach party delivery of the youngsters. Hammer's repertory company belonged to a more restrained British tradition: costume drama on stage – Peter Cushing learned about the importance of movement and unexpected gesture from watching Laurence Olivier at close quarters – and costume drama in film, which had been heralded by popular Gainsborough Studios historical romances and by post-war Charles Dickens adaptations. So although these films revisited the stories of Hollywood films made some twenty-five years before, they were undoubtedly British – if that was one of the concerns of the Lottery advisers – British, with an important Celtic flavour: Mary Shelley grew up partly in Scotland, Robert Louis Stevenson was born and bred there, Arthur Conan-Doyle had his roots there and Bram Stoker was –

according to which biography you read – 'Anglo-Irish', 'Irish-Protestant' or 'Anglo-Celt'. (My report was written well before 'the Irish Dracula', the interpretation of the novel from various post-colonial perspectives, had become fashionable.)

The stories were also in direct line of descent from the Gothic novels of the eighteenth/ nineteenth centuries, and in the case of the vampires from the public image of Lord Byron himself.[2] *There* was a credential: a direct link with the House of Lords! In this sense, too, they were definitely a part of the national heritage. Just after the arrival of the novel – Eng. Lit.'s first eleven of robust and rational players, which had no doubt been studied by the Lottery advisers at school or university – had come this parallel form of *irrational* fiction. I remember paraphrasing a critic of the time on this, who had written:

> We began to reorder the natural world with seed drills and crop rotation, steam power and longitudinal navigation; we began to drink tea and approve of reticence in public manners; and then we came home in the evenings to wallow in, say, *Vathek* – 1786's big hit, by the creepy William Beckford, with great gross-outs – 'he awoke stung...by wormwood-colour flies, which emitted from their wings a suffocating stench' – and necrophiliac tendencies: 'My taste for dead bodies,' says *Vathek*'s usually lingerie-clad mother, 'and everything like mummy, is decided.' It's a line Barbara Shelley should have delivered in a Hammer film...[3]

This parallel form, this *other*, had been mocked in uneasy ways by members of the Eng. Lit. cricket eleven, partly because it had proved so very successful with the reading public. Bookending the first phase of the Gothic, Henry Fielding introduced book eight of *Tom Jones* (1749) with some jokes about the sorts of authors who resorted to horror and wonders to make their fictions interesting; then Jane Austen famously satirised the craze for Gothic fiction in *Northanger Abbey*.[4] And the authors of the original Gothic novels had not – until surprisingly recently – been admitted into literature's first eleven by the academic community. They had been filed under 'the popular novel' instead, the sort of material Queenie Leavis – rather than her husband F.R. Leavis with his 'great tradition' – wrote about, in her studies of fiction and the reading public. Maybe this was another of the quandaries the advisers found themselves in. Was the post-1960s interest in the Gothic a *lasting* development? The late eighteenth-century debates about the 'legitimate' depiction of horror (best seen out of the corner of the eye) and the 'illegitimate' depiction of gore, had resurfaced in even starker terms when Hammer's *Curse of Frankenstein* and *Dracula* were first released in 1957 and 1958. These debates too went right back to the era when Mrs Radcliffe's *The Mysteries of Udolpho* was thought to be a good example of 'suggestion' or 'obscurity' and M.G. Lewis's *The Monk* was thought to be far too graphic for its own good. Another example of Hammer as heritage. Had the academic community moved substantively beyond these traditional concerns?

Then there was the question of originality. One reason why Hammer films made such a splash at the time of their first release – strongly disliked by the critics and equally strongly liked by the public – was that there had in fact been surprisingly few British horror films made before the late 1950s. Surprisingly, given the importance of the native literary tradition. Boris Karloff and Bela Lugosi had made one or two in the 1930s (not their finest hours), but these did not perform well at the box office and they weren't a patch on the actors' Hollywood products. The Universal cycle of horror films made in Hollywood had been dominated by European talent including British director James Whale; British actors Colin Clive, Boris Karloff and Cedric Hardwicke, and British production designer Charles D. 'Danny' Hall. But that had been in Hollywood, on the Universal backlot, when horror was associated with the old world – German Expressionism, pre-modern superstition, sets left over from First World War dramas – when American stars thought playing the evil guys was bad for their image (they still do) and when the early talkies were kind to theatre-trained British accents. An old-world genre in the new world of talkies. Between 1942 and 1945, the import to Britain of all 'H' certificate films was banned outright by the Central Office of Information and the British Board of Film Censors. The thinking was that there were horrors enough for the public to cope with in real life – a misunderstanding, incidentally, of how horror stories function. Who would risk being hit by a flying bomb while watching *The Boogie Man Will Get You*, about an experimental breed of super-soldiers developed to do battle with the Nazis? Even after the Second World War, and the flood of Hollywood back numbers, a survey of the British film industry commissioned by the reconstruction Political and Economic Planning Group – which studied, by theme, 572 films screened in Britain between 1948 and 1950 – concluded that only 1.9% of the total fell into the 'Supernatural' category (meaning 'beyond the known powers of the laws of nature'), compared with 26.9% in 'Crime' and 19.6% in 'Love' (including 'courtship and married life')[5]. The only categories below 'Supernatural' on the list were 'Pathological' (relating to mental or physical illness) and 'Social Problems'. Another official survey of the narratives of all films released in Britain between 1955 and 1957 showed that 'Horror' represented just over 1% of the total in 1955, 2% in 1956 and just under 5% in 1957. 'Love' showed a steep decline in the same period, as did 'Comedy' and 'Historical'.

So when *The Curse of Frankenstein* opened on May 2 1957 – soon moving to two Leicester Square cinemas simultaneously – it must have seemed, to misquote John Ruskin, like a pot of bright-red paint flung in the face of the film establishment, complete with resurrected dog and eyeballs preserved in jam jars. The garish palette, well-endowed servant girl/mistress, Technicolor gore, the apparent revelling in realistic details and the foregrounding of the up-to-now repressed – all these cast early Hammer horrors into the outer darkness. Most of the serious reviewers concluded that for such material to be justified, it needed either 'poetry and art' on the one hand, or comedic detachment on the other: the best of the Gothic novels – or the James Whale approach. Hammer seemed to have neither. C.A. Lejeune famously began her review in *The Observer*: 'Without hesitation I should rank *The Curse of Frankenstein* among the half-dozen most repulsive films I have encountered, in the course of some 10,000 miles of film reviewing.' To which Campbell Dixon in *The Daily Telegraph* added: '…when the screen gives us severed heads and hands, eyeballs dropped in a wine glass and magnified, and brains dished up on a plate like spaghetti, I can only suggest a new certificate – "S.O." perhaps, for Sadists Only.' Dilys Powell, in *The Sunday Times*, concluded: 'after its early promise of rich absurdity, [the film] drops into the merely disgusting'.[6]

'Repulsive' and 'disgusting' were interesting words to have used in this context, because horror films – like their literary counterparts – had indeed often revelled in being transgressive; in challenging social taboos. There had been the Hollywood version of *Murders in the Rue Morgue* (1932) in which Dr Mirakle (Bela Lugosi) tried to re-enact the literal truth of Darwin's thesis about the descent of man with help from the over-sexed Erik the ape; or, another example, the British Censors cutting the sequence where Karloff's creature plays with the little girl by the lakeside, in *Frankenstein* (1931), and throws her into the water thinking she will float like a flower – a cut that actually *created* the impression that the girl had been abused; or *The Island of Lost Souls* (1933), with its crazy surgical experiments fusing people and beasts and its hint of bestiality, which had been banned outright in Britain. One of the functions of the Gothic was, traditionally, to provide a set of metaphors, of grown-up fairytales, with which to challenge mainstream morality and the tyranny of good taste. It has held up a haunted mirror – like the antique one in Ealing's *Dead of Night* (1945), which reveals how repressed and artificial its *bourgeois* owners are – to the realist, true-to-life mainstream of English literature and cinema.

At that point I rested my case. I had argued in my report that Hammer Films represented an important moment in British cinema history, were distinctively *British*, were descended from the Gothic novel of the eighteenth century and its neo-Gothic followers, had been critically neglected, were original and – like the Gothic novel – were in their own way transgressive. The extreme reactions of the serious newspaper critics revealed the impact they had made. One of the best early books about Hammer (1973) – and the films' connections with Gothic literary themes: the fated man, the beauty of the Medusa, Milton's Satan – had been called *A Heritage of Horror*, by David Pirie.[7] I hoped these arguments would enable the Lottery advisers to support the application. Hammer Films, like them or not, were indeed 'historically important', made a big 'cultural impact' and were significant examples of 'the heritage'.

In retrospect, my defence of Hammer-as-heritage now seems rather too broad-brush, too a-historical in the case it makes ('The Gothic Novel'; 'The Horror Film'; 'Critical Clichés'; 'Horror and Transgression'); not specific or precise enough in its delineation of what 'the heritage' and 'the cultural impact' might mean at any particular time. It has often been said that we get the horrors we deserve – and that what is considered 'horrific' by the consensus changes significantly over time, in tandem with wider social and cultural changes: the same certainly applies to notions of 'the heritage'. In the 1950s, for example, big houses were known as 'stately homes'; by the 1980s they had become 'historic houses', a less socially stratified phrase. And, to be precise, the Heritage Lottery application covered the whole of Hammer's history at Bray up to 1966, and not just the early colour horror films of 1956-1960 (from *The Curse of Frankenstein* to *The Curse of the Werewolf*, say) – with very little on the years at ABPC Elstree (1967-1970) and MGM-EMI Elstree (1970-1975): a ten-year slice of British film history, rather than the four-year slice on which I had concentrated.

So I want in this essay to try and recapture, to pinpoint the moment in May 1958 when Hammer's *Dracula* was first released in Britain, by focusing its cultural impact more than was possible in the confines of my Heritage Lottery report.[8] Just what *was* it that upset the critics so much, and that seemed – in the context of British cinema – so novel at the time. The critics had treated *The Curse of Frankenstein* as unusually 'sick-making' and 'nauseating' and had emphasised more than anything else the Technicolor gore: the two novelties were, apparently, the colour and the emphasis on physical detail. This reaction completely baffled the American distributors, who reacted to *The Curse* as standard teenage drive-in fare. But when *Dracula* was released the following year, it was something else – beyond the fact that the film was the first *Dracula* to be shot in colour – that appalled the critics and even encouraged some of them to ask the Censor to intervene.

A month after *The Curse of Frankenstein* went on general release in Britain – with record box-office figures already being reported – screenwriter Jimmy Sangster was commissioned to begin work on his adaptation of *Dracula*.[9] It was in late June 1957:

> When I wrote *The Curse*, I hadn't read Mary Shelley's *Frankenstein* – but everyone knew the story of a man who makes a monster. I did read Bram Stoker's *Dracula*, twice, and was rather overwhelmed by it actually – turning this 450 page novel into a 90 page script. But I completed my final draft in about a month.

Sangster had been involved with Hammer as a company since the late 1940s, first as a third assistant, then first assistant, then production manager and then scriptwriter. He had worked with director Terence Fisher on 'at least six of the pre-Gothic run-of-the-mill B-movies' made by Hammer. So when he prepared his scripts, it was second nature to him to think about the exact cost of every word where budget and schedule were concerned. 'We had no wolves, no gypsies, no Renfield, no boat, no Whitby – we couldn't afford any of them. Every page was carefully costed.' Sangster delivered the final script in October 1957.

The film was budgeted at £81,412 (£750 for Sangster's fee, £7788 for constructing the sets, £7810 for the artistes' fees, £5000 for producer and director fees).[10] The settings of Bram Stoker's novel (Transylvania to Whitby to London to Transylvania) were reduced to Castle Dracula near Klausenberg, which is a coach-ride from Carlstadt, where the Holmwoods live, via a customs post at Ingolstadt. The main sets were the Castle (entrance hall, dining room recycled from the graveyard set, library/Gothic Room, Harker's bedroom, crypt) and the

Holmwood house (drawing room, cellar). The exterior of the Castle entrance, enhanced by a glass painting of turrets and Alpine peaks, was thought to be so impressive, and such good value for money, that it was soon to be recycled as Baskerville Hall (1958) and as an Indian village in *The Stranglers of Bombay* (1959). In this reduced physical space – with its basic contrast between 'Castle' and 'Holmwood house', desire and domesticity – Sangster turned *Dracula* into a fast-paced, non-stop 82-minute three-act adventure (arrival at the Castle/Lucy and Mina vampirised/the chase) with some comic relief (a dotty undertaker called Marx, a bumbling Customs official, a suspicious innkeeper) to ease the tension. Sangster now calls this kind of comic relief 'the "pass the marmalade" line' – after Peter Cushing's memorably dry request to his betrothed at the breakfast table after one of the gory scenes in *The Curse of Frankenstein*. It works in the same way as the 'Porter at the gate' scene after King Duncan's murder in *Macbeth*.

I showed Jimmy Sangster some of director Terence Fisher's preparatory notes[11] – which had recently been published, in facsimile – on how to transform the novel into filmable material:

p. 3	Insert (Tedious).
p. 4	? Accents for Innkeeper and wife.
p. 6	Coach arrives Ext? Harker hears villagers' dialogue as he goes through them.
	? Foreign Language (Language Dictionary Dialogue).
p. 7	Int. Coach? Accents.
p. 10/11	Calèche and wolves episode.
p. 12	Dracula? White moustache.
p. 16	Geography of House (Hall from Dining Room in relation to 1st entrance).
p. 22/23	No dialogue for 3 girls – Dancers (Mime only and whispers).

What happened, I wondered, to the Transylvanian insert, the calèche, the wolves, and how did the three silent dancing girls – the brides of Dracula – turn into Valerie Gaunt, in only her second film role as Hammer's bad girl, insisting: 'A reason! You ask for a reason! Is it not reason enough that he keeps me locked up in this house, holds me against my will…', just before trying to insert her upper canines into Jonathan Harker's neck?

> Maybe we couldn't afford three girls, though there were three in the novel. Or the coach and the wolves. No one can remember whether we had a coach or not! Jonathan Harker ended up arriving on foot. I think I had a coach scene at the beginning, in my script. And Dracula certainly didn't have a white moustache. He was tall and dark and wore a black cloak and hat. This all reminds me of when I was later asked to write a pirate film for Hammer: "There's just one thing," they said. "We can't afford a ship"!

The solution to the '? Accents for Innkeeper and wife'/'? Foreign Language'/'Int. Coach? Accents' problem was to set the film in a Home Counties Transylvania – peopled with eccentric British character actors such as bumbling Miles Malleson, mummerset-accented George Woodbridge and officious George Benson – and to present the Holmwood household as a haven of Victorian domesticity. The Universal *Dracula* – like its *Frankenstein* – had been set in a strange hybrid of the past and the present. It had featured Eastern European accents. Sangster's *Dracula* was set roughly in the historical era the novel was written (May to December 1885 rather than 1891-7), and turned the story into a period piece – which was to have implications for its presentation of the Count as sexual threat. And it was Home Counties.

Where his 'white moustache' is concerned – and Bram Stoker's celebrated description of Count Dracula as an aged military commander with massive eyebrows and a breath problem – the character was to be a younger, more brisk and sexually active figure, as well as a perfect host, from the early drafts onwards. And his ability to change himself into a bat or wolf had gone, too. Jimmy Sangster redefined the rules of earlier vampire films – and of the novel – in the scene where Van Helsing listens to phonograph recordings of his research notes, and records some of his new discoveries:

> Established that victims consciously detest being dominated by vampirism but are unable to relinquish the practice – similar to addiction to drugs. Death results from loss of blood but unlike normal death no peace manifests itself, for they enter into the fearful state of the un-dead.

Had Jimmy Sangster at that stage seen *Nosferatu* (1922), where the vampiric Count is a folkloric creature with pointy ears, rodent teeth and a bald head, and where his contagion is likened to the plague? 'No.' Or Hollywood's first *Dracula* (1931), where he was played in pre-Freudian style by Bela Lugosi as a hypnotic Hungarian in full evening dress, who comes across like a melodramatic demon king? 'No.' Really? 'No.' In fact, the protracted negotiations with Universal about who owned the film and performing rights to Bram Stoker's *Dracula* – which had been going on since October 1956 – were still inconclusive when Sangster was putting together his draft scripts.[12] This was not because Universal owned the remake rights to the novel, but to protect Hammer from accusations of copying the innovations from the 1931 version and its theatrical source (the Count's cloak and Van Helsing's kit of wooden stakes, for example). Eventually, a deal was struck which gave Universal distribution rights outside the United Kingdom.

Had Van Helsing's new vampire rules also been dictated by budgetary considerations?

> One of my reasons was that [the transformation into a bat and a wolf] had never been done very well. I tried to ground the script to some extent in reality. I thought the idea of being able to change into a wolf or bat made the film seem more like a fairytale than it needed to be.[13]

Hence, the 'addiction to drugs' parallel, which made the dominance/dependence relationship between vampire and victim seem more real, more tangible, to a 1957 audience. As did the new-look Count, who had become a demon lover, a sexual predator. The scenes where these two came together involved Dracula's seduction of Lucy (Carol Marsh) and Mina Holmwood (Melissa Stribling). In the film as released, these were among the most original contributions:[14]

```
LUCY'S BEDROOM, later that same night.

Medium close-up, Lucy in a four-poster bed,
in a low-cut, blue chiffon night-gown, her
hair in plaits. She is agitated.

CUT TO:

The French windows in Lucy's bedroom. One
of them is open.

CUT TO:

Close-up, Lucy is more agitated. She feels
the two puncture marks on her neck.

CUT TO:

Close-up,  swirling  autumn  leaves  just
outside the open window.

CUT TO:

VAN  HELSING'S  STUDY/HOTEL  SUITE.  He  is
looking at Harker's diary while his voice
is heard coming from the phonograph...

CUT TO:

LUCY'S BEDROOM. Extreme close-up, Dracula's
face,  with  key  light  on  his  eyes,  as  he
stands at the French windows. "His eyes are
blazing with hypnotic intensity."
```

CUT TO:

Lucy in bed. She is now very agitated, "waiting".

CUT TO:

Leaves swirling.

CUT TO:

Long shot. In the foreground is Lucy in the four-poster bed. Over her, standing in the open window, is Dracula. He slowly walks forward, coming round the foot of Lucy's bed, finally reaching her. Pulling up his cape, Dracula conceals her from view. The black cape fills the screen.

CUT TO:

The next morning. Mina and Dr Seward come out of Lucy's bedroom...

* * *

VAN HELSING: You must get some garlic flowers, as many as you can, place them by the windows and the door, and by the bedside. They may be taken out during the day but under no circumstances are they to be removed at night, even if she implores you. I cannot impress upon you enough how important it is that you obey my instructions. Do exactly as I say and you may be able to save her. If you don't she will die. I'll be here in the morning.

CUT TO:

LUCY'S BEDROOM, that same night. She is now wearing a white night-dress. The room is full of garlic flowers, with vases of them on either side of her bed. In bed, Lucy is tossing and turning – struggling to reach one of the vases of flowers. Eventually she succeeds in knocking it over. The maidservant Gerda, in a dressing-gown, her hair plaited, enters the room to inquire about the noise. She is flustered.

GERDA: Heavens, child... what is it?

LUCY: Gerda, these flowers, I can't stand them.

GERDA: They do smell strong... but Mrs Holmwood said...

LUCY: Please Gerda, they stifle me.

GERDA: Oh well... I'll take them out.

LUCY: And the windows, you'll open the windows.

GERDA: Yes, Miss, if that's what you want.

Gerda opens the French windows and removes some of the garlic flowers. As she leaves she turns to Lucy.

GERDA: I'll come back for the rest.

Exit Gerda.

CUT TO:

MEDIUM CLOSE-UP, leaves swirling outside the window.

CUT TO:

MEDIUM CLOSE-UP, Lucy in bed, her apprehension and excitement mounting. "She rolls her head in the direction of the French windows. There is something almost like a smile at the corner of her mouth."

CUT TO:

LONG SHOT, Dracula standing in the window.

CUT TO:

The full moon, as clouds pass across its face.

CUT TO:

Lucy in bed, a sheet pulled up over her face. Van Helsing stands near her, Mina and Arthur stand at the foot of the bed and Gerda stands by the door...

VAN HELSING: Mrs Holmwood, did you do as I told you?

ARTHUR: She did. And you can see the result.

* * *

CUT TO:

CLOSE-UP OF Mina standing in the doorway, inside the Holmwoods' house, "looking radiant". She has a fur collar pulled up around her neck, a green coat, and she has a warm twinkle in her eyes that has not been there before. She is looking vibrant and sensual.

MINA: Good morning.

ARTHUR: Mina, you gave me quite a fright. Where have you been at this hour of the morning?

MINA: It was such a lovely day I got up early and went for a walk in the garden. I didn't expect you back so soon.

ARTHUR: I'm afraid I've got to go out again.

MINA: Oh! When will you be back?

ARTHUR: I can't say for sure. Mina, you look very ill, are you all right?

MINA: Arthur darling, don't fuss, I feel perfectly well. Goodbye darling.

✻ ✻ ✻

CUT TO:

VAN HELSING: I know I ask a great deal of you but you mustn't weaken now. We have it within our power to rid the world of this evil, and with God's help we'll succeed.

CUT TO:

EXTERIOR, GARDEN OF THE HOLMWOODS' HOUSE.
NIGHT. Arthur is standing, jiggling a
crucifix in his hand. He looks up at the
window of Mina's bedroom.

CUT TO:

INTERIOR, MINA'S AND ARTHUR'S BEDROOM. Mina
is sitting on the edge of her bed.

CUT TO:

ARTHUR IN THE GARDEN, KEEPING WATCH. He is
not surprisingly very apprehensive. A wolf
howls.

CUT TO:

INTERIOR OF THE HOUSE. HALL. Dracula is
standing in the hall, at the bottom of the
stairs. The camera is high, looking down.
As Dracula slowly ascends the stairs the
camera tracks across the top of the stairs,
finally bringing Dracula into close-up.

CUT TO:

MINA SITTING ON THE EDGE OF THE BED, also
apprehensive – but eager. "Her eyes blaze,
her lips are parted, she gasps for breath."
Dracula enters the room and approaches her.
"Her body begins to shake as if with fever."
Dracula plays his face close to hers and
pushes her back onto the bed. "She moans
quickly. He gently brushes her forehead
with his full lips... then her cheek... then
her neck. Mina stops shuddering, holds her
breath." There is a scream.

```
CUT TO:

CLOSE-UP OF AN OWL HOOTING IN A TREE IN THE
GARDEN.

CUT TO:

ARTHUR, STILL KEEPING WATCH. He takes a deep
breath...
```

Did Jimmy Sangster recall writing these scenes? 'The ones with Lucy, they were definitely me. The scene of Melissa Stribling at the door, smiling, that in the film was mainly Terry Fisher. I just wrote "enter Melissa Stribling". The scene of Melissa Stribling being visited by Dracula in her bedroom, that was partly me, partly Terry.'[15]

On 8 October 1957, the day before Terence Fisher was signed as the director of *Dracula*, the second draft of Jimmy Sangster's screenplay was submitted to the recently appointed new secretary of the British Board of Film Censors, John Nicholls.[16] Five days later, an internal Board memo sounded an ominous note – socially as well as morally:

> 'The uncouth, uneducated, disgusting and vulgar style of Mr Jimmy Sangster cannot quite obscure the remnants of a good horror story, though they do give one the gravest misgivings about treatment…'

The memo continued with serious worries about 'Technicolor blood', 'shots of blood' and 'stake-work', which were summarised by Nicholls in a letter to the Hammer people of 21 October. These worries mirrored the recent concerns of the newspaper critics about *The Curse of Frankenstein*. Sangster's *Dracula* had introduced colour, fangs, red contact lenses, in-shot stakings – and décolletage – for the first time. At this stage, the Board's reservations seemed to be almost entirely about the gore quotient, though there was a first warning about another issue as well:

p. 10, 29, 45 etc. It is important that the women in the film should be decently clad, not seen in transparent night-dresses or with bared breasts, or in unduly suggestive garments. I would add that anything which cross-emphasises the sex aspect of the story is likely, in a horror subject of this kind, to involve cuts in the completed film.

Which was presumably put in to protect the BBFC's back in case subsequent drafts – or the film itself – went beyond the submitted words on the page.

Jimmy Sangster had already crossed swords with the British Board, on *X The Unknown* (1956) and *The Curse of Frankenstein* (1957), but his final shooting script was dated 18 October – so while the Board was busy discussing his second draft, and having problems with it, Hammer was pressing ahead regardless. This was shortly to prove a source of irritation to the Board, and teach the Hammer executives a lesson about clearing up any misunderstandings well in advance of shooting expensive film stock. Filming began on 11 November 1957, partly on the new sound stage at Bray, and wrapped at the end of January 1958; on 5 February a black-and-white print of *Dracula* – minus six scenes and without 'full sound' – was winging its way to the BBFC. That same afternoon, an internal memo noted sniffily that 'the producers have ignored the script letter and also have deviated from the script'. Just as they had feared, in the 21 October letter. By a week later, Hammer had belatedly agreed to make the cuts outlined by the BBFC at the script stage over three months before, and resubmitted a print on 12 February. This time, in addition to the graphic detail of the stakings and the disintegration of Dracula – the Board's original concerns – a new sequence was added to the censors' little list for the first time:

'Reel 8. The whole episode of Dracula and Mina together whenever either of them have sexual pleasure. There must, for instance, be no kissing or fondling.'

Plus 'caution is also required with regard to the music effects, especially "shock" music...'

James Carreras, the managing director of the company, immediately fired back a letter to Nicholls with 'Just a few general observations on "horror pictures"':

> ... The horror audience is a very specialised one and many people who go to 'X for sex' pictures will not go to see a horror film... The specialised audience who will go to see *Dracula* will expect thrills but the cuts that you are asking us to make, in our opinion, are taking every thrill out of the picture, in fact, it is not as horrific as any of the past *Draculas* and we cannot believe that that is your intention.

So the Board decided as a concession to screen the film again on 14 February, and this time one of the BBFC examiners noted:

> ... Reel 8. There is still a strong sex element in this scene. This is due to Mina's anticipating expression in close-up and Dracula's face (and expression) as it hovers over Mina's before he applies himself to her neck. We are very doubtful whether this sex element can be removed... Cut the scene from immediately after Mina gets on the bed to shot of owl screaming...

On 3 April, a colour print – complete with James Bernard's thrashing, orgasmic music; high-volume variations on the three syllables of Dra-cu-la followed by rising scales – was submitted, incorporating further small cuts in the staking of Lucy and the disintegration of the Count. Having watched this print, the Board concluded that it was now prepared to pass everything *except* Reel 8, which 'should be resubmitted':

> '...shot of Dracula's face approaching Mina as she lies on the bed, with her reaction, must go. There should be a cut from where he enters the room to the owl (and the sound of the screams) outside...'

Hammer's good-humoured but firm response to this was to reiterate that they

> ...could not see how [Dracula's] face looks more censorable in colour than it did in black and white: he is wearing no special makeup. There is no blood on his face, he is not wearing contact-lenses – in fact, the rather *pink* look he has makes him look, if anything, a little prettier than he did before!...

In the end, following a face-to-face meeting to resolve the deadlock on 14 April, the Board relented:

> Reel 8. While we consider that, in the approach of Dracula to Mina the sex-element is still too prevalent, in view of the apparent misunderstanding over this [the suggestion that if the scene did not look worse in colour than black and white, it would automatically be passed] and the technical difficulty of effecting further reductions, we are prepared to waive our objection to this scene.

But a brief shot of the disintegrating face of Dracula at the end, with 'his hand pulling down' had to go. On this basis, an 'X' certificate was duly issued a week later. The next Sangster-scripted Hammer horror, *The Revenge of Frankenstein*, would have an even rougher ride – with the BBFC making a point of being crystal clear about its reservations from the outset. When the Board first read the script of *Dracula*, its main concern – as it had been with *The Curse* – was the explicitness of the gore. Then, when the BBFC viewed the black-and-white print of *Dracula*, the bedroom scene involving Dracula and Mina – together with 'the sex aspect of the story' – began more seriously to alarm them, and especially the look on the Count's face and Mina's reaction to it. The 'sex-element is still too prevalent'. But Hammer managed to persuade the board, on a technicality, to leave the scene alone. Why had it taken so long for the censors to notice the full implications of this scene? Jimmy Sangster's view on this is clear:

It is because it wasn't all in the script. [The BBFC memo of 5 February noted that the Hammer had 'deviated from the script']. It was a mixture of my script, Terry's direction, James Bernard's music and Bernard Robinson's sets.'[17]

Terence Fisher, who joined the team after Sangster's first two drafts had been completed, always appreciated the way in which Sangster formatted his scripts: set the scene, present the dialogue, don't be too prescriptive about staging. And it is clear that the staging and cutting of the Lucy and Mina scenes – together with the thrashing music – was what drew particular attention to the 'sex aspect'. Fisher always maintained that this was what he brought to the project: 'I think my greatest contribution to the Dracula myth was to bring out the underlying sexual element in the story...'[18] It was already in the script, but sometimes 'between the lines'.

Where the Lucy bedroom scenes were concerned, he recalled them as versions of the virginal bride waiting eagerly in her powder-blue night-dress for a nocturnal visitor:

It's almost ballet the way she opens the doors, goes back and lies down again, her eyes focused, waiting for him to appear... You know, it's a distortion of the so-called 'true love', and this is the power of evil working from a distance. Dracula could cause himself to appear there right at the moment when he realised that any resistance to him she might have had was gone.

And as for the controversial scenes involving Mina Holmwood, Terence Fisher saw these as being partly about the state of the Holmwoods' marriage:

Dracula preyed upon the sexual frustrations of his women victims. The [Arthur/Mina] marriage was one in which she was not sexually satisfied and that was the weakness as far as Dracula's approach to her was concerned. When she arrived back after having been away all night [in the basement of the Friedrichstrasse undertaker's parlour] she said it all in one close-up at the door...

Fisher remembered advising Melissa Stribling to 'imagine you have had one whale of a sexual night, *the* one of your whole sexual experience. Give me that in your face!' And she certainly did. A confident, sexy, emancipated half-smile, rather than her usual wan detachment. All Arthur can say, in time-honoured fashion, is: 'You look very ill, are you all right?'

So Terence Fisher's direction, plus composer James Bernard's music – brass and woodwind for the climaxes, strings for the lyrical bits – turned the potential on the page into something to frighten the censors. In the process, the director brought his own strong sense of good and evil – as well as of convention and transgression – to Hammer's first *Dracula*. Lucy's 'true love' is contrasted with 'the power of evil'. Remember that old-fashioned 'Love' films were going seriously out of fashion at the time. The physical/sensual side of a marriage provides the demon with his opportunity. The audience is positioned as innocent bystanders, watching a morality play.

> …all right, call it a vampire, call it the power of evil, call it the attraction of the power of evil – the important thing was the attraction of the power of evil. One of the greatest things that the power of evil has is to make its temptation tremendously attractive. There was a very strong sexual influence in *Dracula*, which is important, because two of his victims were women and they were… – apart from the superstition or legend of the power of the mind. You know what I'm trying to get at? It was human. It wasn't impressionistic…it was an attempt to put it into realistic settings, of everybody's personal experiences of what the power of evil is and how they can be controlled by it sexually, emotionally, any other way you can. If you go back to the Bible and the temptation of Jesus on the mountain…

The temptation took the charismatic form of a new-look Count Dracula, with gentlemanly Christopher Frank Carandini Lee (he'd signed on 29 October) in the title role – surprisingly, the first British actor ever to play the part on screen. Frankenstein was British in Hollywood. So were the Mummy and Dr Moreau. But Dracula was either Eastern European or American (from the South). Lee's career as an actor had, by his own admission, been 'moving very slowly' up to that point, despite having acted in over forty films since his debut in 1947. He had come to specialise in portraying 'The Other' in assorted period adventure films – Spanish captains, Arab traders, a Montevidean in *The Battle of the River Plate*, the creature in *The Curse of Frankenstein*, and, most recently, the Marquis St Evrémonde in *A Tale of Two Cities*. 'I'm the tallest actor in the country [6'4"],' he said – in stark contrast with the vertically challenged John Mills and Richard Todd and Richard Attenborough and most of the other stalwarts of British war/adventure films – 'and am not entirely British in appearance.' Here was another solution to the 'accent' problem. He had proved himself a gifted mime, good at playing clipped or sinister aristocratic charm; and he could hiss and blaze convincingly when thwarted. These were essential talents because unlike Count Orlok in *Nosferatu*, he did not depend on grotesque makeup to be plausible; and unlike Bela Lugosi in Universal's *Dracula*, he had no need of hypnotism to get his way with his victims. And he didn't have to transmute into bats or wolves to enhance his charisma. All he had to do was to stand magisterially at a suburban window in a floor-length cloak, the lights on his eyes, and leave his victims – as well as the audience – to do the rest. Lee had only thirteen lines in the film, all of them in the first two reels – which was admittedly thirteen more than he'd had in *The Curse of Frankenstein*. But *Dracula* was to be his breakthrough movie. By Christmas 1958, a newspaper was featuring a cartoon about 'Peter Cushion and Christopher Flea in *Santa Claws*'. An article in *Picturegoer* quoted Lee as saying that his name now meant more in the USA than 'Bogarde, Mills or Hawkins put together'.

Christopher Lee's take on the story in many ways seems to have matched Terence Fisher's: 'a morality play with an admixture of pantomime, fairy story and melodrama…this is black, this is white; this is good, this is bad'. Where the character of the Count was concerned,

Lee tried to emphasise his sadness, 'a tragic quality – the curse of being immortal...the loneliness of evil'. This was to be emphasised more in subsequent Hammer Draculas. But in interviews he was reluctant to be drawn on the character's sexual implications as demon lover, a new take on Beauty and the Beast: 'There is a sexual element in vampirism, I suppose... I've never thought of fangs that way, quite honestly...'[19]

But Sangster and Fisher's project, to bring out the underlying sexual element in the story, was what made Dracula scary again after all those years of retreads and parodies. Executive producer Michael Carreras, grandson of the company's founder, grasped this immediately: 'The greatest difference between our Dracula and anybody else's was the sexual connotation. There was no real horror in it, the women were eager to be nipped by Dracula and I think that gave it a fresh look... [plus] they were the first Gothic horror films to be in colour.'[20] After the black-and-white years, British filmmakers had at last found a roundabout way of telling stories about sex. So this would be the unique selling proposition which would be emblazoned all over the British posters. 'Every night he rises from his coffin-bed to silently seek the soft flesh, the warm blood he needs...' Complete with split infinitive. At the Gaumont, Haymarket, where the film premiered on 20 May 1958, the word 'DRACULA' was lit up in huge neon letters, and beneath them: 'The terrifying lover who died...yet *lived*!' A gigantic cut-out Christopher Lee lunged towards Melissa Stribling's neck – as on the posters – and by some mechanism managed to draw blood from the puncture-holes he'd made in her neck, which seemed to flow vertically down her hair.[21] This, despite James Carreras' assurance to the censors that this would not be an 'X for sex' picture in any way. His son Michael Carreras complained about the publicity issued for *The Horror of Dracula* (as it was called) by Universal's marketing department in New York, which was 'along the lines of the old Dracula pictures with Bela Lugosi' – because it had completely missed the point:

'Our Dracula is handsome and sexy... His victims are young, attractive women. The campaign in London is on horror sex lines and I would be grateful if you would re-examine.'

Out with the old bogeyman flapping his wings in evening dress, and in with Dracula sinking his fangs into Mina Holmwood's neck. His wish was their command.[22]

By emphasising 'the underlying sexual element of the story', Hammer's *Dracula* was certainly to have a profound impact on the academic study of Stoker's *Dracula*, as well as on the future of the vampire film. Before 1958, those commentators who wrote in any depth about *Dracula* – and there were very few of them – tended to place the book firmly in the context of Victorian neo-Gothic sensation literature.[23] A kind of literary curiosity. Queenie Leavis in her *Fiction and the Reading Public* (1939), her 'outline of popular fiction' in the late nineteenth/early twentieth centuries, did not mention *Dracula* at all. Hall Caine yes, Bram Stoker no. Montague Summers, eccentric specialist in large antiquarian tomes about literary and folkloric vampires, with a bibliographical emphasis, acknowledged that 'there is no sensational romance which in modern days has achieved so universal a reputation', but complained that 'Dracula is by no means briefly told', that it contained 'much careless writing' and that it lost its way from 'the rather tedious courtship of Lucy Westenra' onwards. The reason for the novel's immense popularity lay in the choice of subject-matter rather than its treatment. The scant two pages Summers devoted to *Dracula* – in a chapter on 'The Vampire in Literature' (1928) – consisted mainly of plot summary (he particularly liked the Transylvania section) and ended on misspellings of the names Hamilton Deane ('Deans') and Bela Lugosi ('Lugoni'). Peter Penzoldt's *The Supernatural in Fiction* (1952), based on an academic thesis, included Stoker's *Dracula* in the bibliography but had only two brief things to say about the novel in the text: that Hollywood had 'taken it over' and that it was not in fact Bram Stoker 'who introduced the vampire into English literature'. Devendra P. Varma, whose *The Gothic Flame* was first published the year before

Hammer's *Dracula* was released, noted that Stoker had created 'the prince of vampires' through bringing to perfection 'each piece of crude and creaking machinery of Gothic romance'. Varma found in Gothic novels 'the same sinister overtones and the same solemn grandeur' that twelfth-century cathedrals 'evoked in medieval man': *Dracula* was well beneath his intellectual threshold. Mario Praz's *The Romantic Agony*, first issued in 1933 and revised in 1951, sought 'the erotic sensibility' and 'the pathology of Romanticism' in a boisterously thematic approach to the literature of horror from De Sade to D'Annunzio – the Beauty of the Medusa, The Metamorphoses of Satan, The Shadow of De Sade, La Belle Dame Sans Merci, Le Vice Anglais, themes later customised by David Pirie – but was much more concerned with the poetry and prose of the nineteenth-century romantics than with the more conventional neo-horrors of Bram Stoker. *Dracula* is not mentioned once, although Praz's themes have all been applied to the novel – many times – since the 1970s. Summers was upset by Praz's over-emphasis (in his view) on eroticism and called the book 'disjointed gimcrack'. Other earlier studies of tales of terror – by Edith Birkhead (1921) and Michael Sadleir (1927) – were not interested in either eroticism or *Dracula*: their emphasis was on bibliography, and rescuing the early Gothic novels from critical condescension. Sigmund Freud's biographer Ernest Jones devoted a chapter to vampires in his *On the Nightmare* (1931), but omitted to cite *Dracula* in support of his thesis about repressed incestuous desires and the psychology of the living: Stoker's blood transfusion scene would in fact have helped his thesis considerably, but he focused instead on medieval folklore and German Romanticism.[24] The one major exception to this neglect of Bram Stoker was another card-carrying Freudian critic, who wrote partly in response to Ernest Jones. In December 1959 (just after the release of Hammer's *Dracula*, but in some ways harking back to an earlier tradition), the journalist and surrealist writer Maurice Richardson published a half-serious, half-tongue-in-cheek, article about the psychoanalytical implications of ghost stories in general and *Dracula* in particular which he referred to as '...a bisexual oral-and-genital sadomasochistic orgy', a parable of Oedipal conflict (the Count as big daddy), totem and taboo, and the dilution of the sexual drive. The date of publication may be significant, as we'll see.

Today, the study of *Dracula* has changed utterly.[25] The novel is at the centre of the extensive literature around 'new Gothic criticism'. The approach now is to displace the basic function of the genre, which is to scare its readers in pleasurable ways, by solemnly deconstructing the words on the page into the 'unsaid' psychological or socio-political elements which may lie beneath them. Gothic novels have become texts, above all other forms of fiction, where 'the repressed' can return, where 'the abject' can be disguised, and where social anxieties can be buried – waiting for critics from today's more liberated perspectives to dig them up. Since Foucault, it has become a critical cliché to set the category 'Victorian' against all that is 'liberated' and 'modern'. And the key anxieties are to do with gender, sexuality and middle-class respectability in conflict with uncontrollable forces. Chris Baldick and Robert Mighall have concluded from this that it is as if literary criticism itself has become some kind of Gothic project creating its own melodramas.[26] From defensiveness to defiance. As Matthew Sweet has observed:

> Dracula Studies first emerged as a serious discipline in the late 1960s and soon established the parameters of its interest. As Robert Mighall has argued in his book [*A Geography of Victorian Gothic Fiction: Mapping History's Nightmares* (1999)], this kind of Freud-slaked, programmatically anti-Victorian criticism proposed that 'the vampire is monstrous not because it is a supernatural being which threatens to suck the protagonists' blood and damn their souls, but because at some "deeper level" it symbolises an erotic threat.' So, Mighall contends, a book that contains no obvious allusions to sex – apart from one use of the word 'voluptuous' – has been used to prove how much energy the Victorians invested in their programme to police sex into silence.[27]

Sometimes, Mighall concludes in a paraphrase of Freud's famous remark about a cigar, 'sometimes a vampire is only a vampire'. The less the book actually mentions sex, the more it provides evidence for the repression of Victorian society. QED. '[This] serves less to illuminate a body of fiction than to congratulate itself, on behalf of modern progressive opinion, upon its liberation from the dungeons of Victorian sexual repression or social hierarchy.' By setting the story in the drawing-rooms and bedrooms of the Victorian past, vintage autumn 1885, and by using the character of Count Dracula as a catalyst for revealing Victorian hypocrisy and outmoded forms of sexual morality, Jimmy Sangster and team transformed perceptions of *Dracula*. The scholars who first encountered the film and book in the 1960s have themselves now become the critical/academic consensus. As Sweet concludes, 'Lee's performance convinced a generation of scholars that *Dracula* was a book about sex, and not about vampires.'

Actually, the sub-discipline of 'Dracula Studies' emerged in a serious way not in the late 1960s but the early 1970s. The first sustained study of the novel's sexual symbolism was written in 1972, of its psychology of dominance and dependence in the same year; of its menstrual subtext in 1978; my own analysis of the literary genesis of *Dracula* – which reprinted Jones's chapter and parts of Richardson's article for the first time – appeared in 1978; the first detailed study to examine the novel's take on the 'New Woman' emerged in 1982; and its implications for gender studies were first fully explored in 1984. The Oxford World's Classics edition of *Dracula*, with its introduction by A.N. Wilson calling it 'a great story of the second-rate type', completely ignoring the critical reappraisals since the early 1970s, was published in 1983. This approach had become well-nigh unthinkable, where serious scholarship was concerned, by the late 1980s. By then, the point of Bram Stoker's original story had been inverted, with the Count becoming the liberator and his victims the forces of orthodoxy and repression. David Punter wrote of this turnaround amongst the academics: 'The middle class is perfectly imaged in the form of the person sitting rigidly in the darkened chamber while monstrous forces press against the window.'[28] Recognise the scene? It was the one Jimmy Sangster wrote. Subsequent literary and film versions of the vampire – the vampire as addict, the vampire as contagion, the vampire as last romantic, the vampire as embodiment of adolescent growing pains – have all fed off this insight. Van Helsing has become the bad guy, a fundamentalist spoilsport.

But the *precise* cultural significance of the moment of Hammer's *Dracula* in May 1958 is some way away from the subsequent rise of Gothic studies – coinciding with the growing interest in identity and sexual politics – from the early 1970s onwards. In fact, in some ways its significance is the opposite[29] – because in Jimmy Sangster's script and Terence Fisher's direction, the precise context for 'the sexual element' in the story was a defence of family values and true love. We have seen how in *Dracula* the key conflict at the heart of the film is between Dracula and Arthur as the heads of two dramatically opposed households – the Castle and the family home – with Van Helsing as the priest/marriage guidance counsellor who helps to resolve the problems in Arthur's marriage to Mina. Adultery is explicitly associated with letting the evil one in ('everybody's personal experience of what the power of evil is,' according to Terence Fisher; 'Dracula has the power, in a twisted way, to make Lucy and Mina give a sexual reaction'). When the sexual act is not confined to marriage and the home (Mina is married; Lucy is engaged) it must be destroyed, if necessary with the help of a counsellor, a specialist in such things. Arthur cannot at first cope with the thought that the family itself may contain the seeds of Dracula's power. He resents Van Helsing's interference, thinks his wife must be unwell, and represses his and his wife's libido and associates Dracula entirely with outside forces. Nothing to do with him and his marriage. But as Terence Fisher, again, put it: 'Dracula preys on Mina's vulnerabilities, her sexual frustration.' Only when Arthur acknowledges – with Van Helsing's professional guidance – that his wife is an adulteress (is being vampirised), that she has sensual needs that he is not satisfying, that he must in future face up to his own libido (and confront Dracula as the male head of a rival household), only then can the Count be defeated by the forces of good. Meanwhile, Dracula – who has lost his 'bride' (remember Valerie Gaunt?) thanks to Jonathan Harker – desperately seeks another partner in the form of first Lucy (he has seen her framed photo in Harker's bedroom: 'May I ask her name?…Charming') and then, via Lucy, Mina Holmwood. Unlike in the novel, he appears to vampirise one partner or mate of the opposite sex at a time. The stripping-down of the story, in short, turns it into a fairytale about adultery. The women in the film – the bride of Dracula, Lucy and Mina – are receptacles to be possessed by either 'Good' or 'Evil'. Van Helsing has no qualms at all about using them as bait to catch the Count. Dracula does vampirise Jonathan Harker, but that is treated as a revenge-killing rather than a seduction: British cinema was nowhere near ready for any other interpretation.

The celebrated ending of the film shows Dracula in the Gothic Room/ Library of his castle being forced into the light by the power of the crucifix, and disintegrating in the sun's rays; this is intercut with a shot of the crossed hands of Arthur and Mina. As her *stigma* – the burn-mark of the cross – fades, the camera remains on her hands for a few frames, making us aware of her wedding ring. Mina has been received back into the family, and to symbolise this Arthur kisses her hand. Meanwhile, 'the only place [the Count] can make for now is home', as Van Helsing has put it just before the final chase. There's no place like home. I have seen it suggested that the final shot of the film reinforces this message. Dracula has been burned to dust, and all that is left of him is a pile of ashes and *his* ring (wedding ring?). Set into the marble floor beneath him, in the centre of the Gothic Room, is a circular zodiac design with inscriptions in Latin (on an outer ring) and ancient Greek (on an inner ring). The final shot shows the pile of ashes, the ring and a single Greek word. It has been suggested that the word is 'ἑστία', meaning 'home or household or family hearth'.[30] In Greek mythology, the virginal Hestia (Εστία), was the guardian of the domestic hearth fire, which was not allowed to go out unless it had been ritually extinguished, after which it was renewed in a ceremony of purification – just the right place for the undead to die. It is a nice idea – attributing much subtlety to production designer Bernard Robinson[31] – but unfortunately the word is not Ἑστία but ἐστίν, which simply means 'it is', part of an illegible phrase around the inner ring. The accent above the iota, in the design, is written the wrong way round and means nothing. Nevertheless, there's no place like home. Roll the credits.

So in Terence Fisher's words, it is 'the ultimate victory of good over evil'. In May 1958, several years before the Chatterley ban and the Beatles' first LP, exactly two years before the first birth control pill was developed in the USA, the conclusion of Hammer's *Dracula* is that permissiveness (as it was then called) is a serious threat to the stability of the family, which is in turn one of the strongest bulwarks of society. Yes, Terence Fisher's *Dracula* pits inhibition against abandon, repression against desire, convention against the abject – all in the context of Hammer's Eastmancolor version of Victorian domesticity around 1885 – but the film is *not* concluding from all this that liberation is or will be a social good. That thought was not available to mainstream filmmakers in 1958. Subsequent, post-1970s, commentators on *Dracula* have projected the thought backwards because they *want* the film to be agreeing with them. They want today's more liberated perspective to be there – even if 'unsaid' – so they can find it. Actually, and in some ways ironically, Hammer's *Dracula* is far closer in spirit to Bram Stoker's novel than to the post-1970s politics of liberation.

George Orwell, had he lived, could have written a classic essay – along the lines of 'The Art of Donald McGill' (1941) or 'Boys' Weeklies' (1940) – about the cultural significance of Hammer's 1958 *Dracula*. Orwell was a keen observer of British cultural metaphors and what they revealed about underlying social attitudes: *Dracula* would have provided him with excellent material. Which in turn would perhaps have helped the Heritage Lottery to treat Hammer films unproblematically as part of the national heritage. I'm delighted to say that my report helped to persuade them, that the decision was made in time, and that the archive now resides in the National Museum of Photography, Film and Television in Bradford.

(ENDNOTES)

1   Application to the Heritage Lottery Fund, dated 19 December 1997, entitled 'Acquisition of Collection of Artifacts Associated with Hammer Films', plus appendices 1-9 with supplementary information.

2   The citations I gave were to my then-recent *Nightmare – the birth of horror* (BBC Books, London, 1996) and Christopher Frayling: *Vampyres – Lord Byron to Count Dracula* (Faber, London, 1991), esp. pp. 107-144.

3   Vera Rule: *The Refreshing Grapes of Goth* (*The Guardian*, August 5 1996, p.10), previewing *Nightmare – the birth of horror*.

4   For more on this, see my *Introduction* to ed. Martin Myrone and Christopher Frayling: *The Gothic Reader* (Tate Gallery, London, 2006), pp. 12-20, and the *Reader* itself.

5   The findings of the surveys of 1948-1950 and 1955-1957 are reproduced in David Pirie: *Hammer – a cinema case study* (British Film Institute, London, 1980), pp. 6-7 and part three document 43.

6   Newspaper reviews photographically reproduced in Pirie op. cit. part four document 46.

7   Revised in 2008 as David Pirie: *A New Heritage of Horror* (I.B. Tauris, London, 2008).

8   This account of the genesis of Hammer's *Dracula* (1958) owes much to Denis Meikle: *A History of Horrors* (Scarecrow, Maryland, 1996), pp. 56-64; Marcus Hearn and Alan Barnes: *The Hammer Story* (Titan, London, 1997), pp. 30-33; David Pirie: *A New Heritage of Horror*, pp. 95-112; Wayne Kinsey: *Hammer Films – The Bray Studios Years* (Reynolds and Hearn, London), pp. 91-113; David Pirie: *Hammer – a cinema case study*, pp. 51-62, and part six documents; and ed. Richard Klemensen: *Hammer – yesterday, today and tomorrow* (Little Shoppe of Horrors number 4, Iowa, April 1978), pp. 23-118.

9   Interview with scriptwriter Jimmy Sangster at the Royal College of Art, November 2007.

10   Production budget for *Dracula* from Pirie: *Hammer – a cinema case study*, part six documents 71 and 72.

11   Terence Fisher's preparatory notes are reproduced in ed. Richard Klemensen: *Terence Fisher – Hammer's master of Gothic Horror* (Little Shoppe of Horrors 19, Iowa, September 2007), pp. 52-54.

12   See Pirie: *Hammer – a cinema case study*, part six document 68 dated October 31st 1956.

13   My interview with Jimmy Sangster; see also Meikle, op. cit., and Kinsey, op. cit.

14   Dialogue and stage directions are my transcriptions from the film itself, checked against Jimmy Sangster's final draft shooting script.

15   Interview with Jimmy Sangster, November 2007.

16   The correspondence with the British Board of Film Censors is quoted in detail in Wayne Kinsey, op. cit., pp. 94-96 and 110-113.

17   Interview with Jimmy Sangster, November 2007.

18   Terence Fisher's quotes are from Kinsey, op. cit., pp. 100-101; Pirie: *Hammer – a cinema case study*, p. 56; *Cinefantastique* (Oak Park, Illinois, vol. 4 no. 3), issue *The Films of Terence Fisher*, pp. 19-28; *Little Shoppe of Horrors* 19, pp. 13-16, 36-51, 63-75; *Fandom's Film Gallery* issue 1 (Deurne, Belgium, 1975); ed. Allen Eyles, Robert Adkinson and Nicholas Fry: *The House of Horror* (Lorimer, London, 1973), pp. 12-15.

19 Christopher Lee's quotes are from Pirie: *Hammer – a cinema case study*, p. 56; Eyles et al: *The House of Horror*, p. 15-19; Kinsey, op. cit., p. 104; and *Fandom's Film Gallery* issue 1.

20 Pirie, op. cit., p. 56.

21 Kinsey, op. cit., p. 126.

22 Matthew Sweet: *Flesh and Blood* (*The Guardian Review*, 27 October 2007, p. 14).

23 See Queenie Leavis: *Fiction and the Reading Public* (Chatto & Windus, London, 1939); Montague Summers: *The Vampire – his kith and kin* (Kegan Paul, London, 1928) pp. 333-337; Peter Penzoldt: *The Supernatural in Fiction* (Peter Nevill, London, 1952), pp. 37-40; Devendra P. Varma: *The Gothic Flame* (Russell, New York), pp. 160, 205; Mario Praz: *The Romantic Agony* (Oxford University Press, 1970).

24 For the relevant extract from Ernest Jones: *On the Nightmare*, see Christopher Frayling: *Vampyres – Lord Byron to Count Dracula* (Faber, London, 1991), pp. 398-417; and for the extract from Maurice Richardson's essay see Christopher Frayling, op. cit., pp. 418-422.

25 On the new critical landscape surrounding Bram Stoker's *Dracula*, see especially William Hughes: *Bram Stoker: Dracula – a reader's guide to essential criticism* (Palgrave Macmillan, Hampshire, 2009).

26 See Chris Baldick and Robert Mighall: *Gothic Criticism* (in ed. David Punter: *A Companion to the Gothic*, Blackwell, Oxford, 2012), pp. 209-228 and co-ed. Christopher Frayling: *The Gothic Reader* introduction.

27 Matthew Sweet, op. cit.

28 Baldick and Mighall, op. cit., p. 225, citing David Punter's *The Literature of Terror* ((Longman, Harlow, vol. 2), pp. 201-202.

29 This reading of Hammer's *Dracula* was originally inspired by discussions with Fern Presant – then a postgraduate student in the School of Film and Television – at the Royal College of Art in 1980.

30 See, for example, Henry Liddell and Robert Scott: *A Greek-English Lexicon*, part one, 1846, p. 556. The word appears in Homer, Aeschylus and Heroditus.

31 On Bernard Robinson's sets, see especially Kinsey, op. cit., pp. 98-100; and ed. Kinsey, *The House that Hammer Built*, issue 11, volume 2:3 (1999), pp. 137-176.

7

Disney and the Beast

Introduction

SEVERAL OF THE STORIES *in* The Bloody Chamber – *including* The Courtship of Mr Lyon, The Tiger's Bride *and even* The Bloody Chamber *itself – are at some level elaborate re-imaginings of the* Beauty and the Beast *story, the mid-eighteenth-century version written for well-behaved young girls by Jeanne-Marie Leprince de Beaumont* and *its ancient, Classical originals. Madame de Beaumont's tale has an unusual setting in a middle-class mercantile family – rather than among princes or peasants. Jean Cocteau's film (1946) was one of Angela Carter's desert island movies, and when she became ill I supplied her with a videotape of it, together with another one of William Dieterle and Max Reinhardt's* A Midsummer Night's Dream *(1935) based on a spectacular theatrical production at the Hollywood Bowl the year before – complete with Mendelssohn's music made more lush by Erich Wolfgang Korngold. She could now enjoy both films at home with her family in Clapham. The Hollywood version of* Dream *plays a key role in her last novel* Wise Children *(1991): as she summarised it, a big-budget film production of the play 'starts off as Hollywood art and is rapidly subverted':*

> *'They've built one of the great stage sets of all time which is the wood. "Wood" is the Anglo-Saxon word for "mad". Hollywood – the wood that makes you mad… It's where you take leave of your senses.'*

The Walt Disney animated Beauty and the Beast, *from a screenplay by Linda Woolverton – the first Disney animated feature to be written by a woman – was released in November 1991, three months before Angela's death. In retrospect, this film seems part of Hollywood's belated realisation that the age-old public domain stories could fruitfully and profitably be revisited with resourceful, gutsy heroines at their centre this time round, heroines who read books, who have learned to 'run with the tigers'. The Disney version also owed a great deal – uncredited – to the Cocteau film, especially the scenes set in the magic castle. What would Angela Carter have made of it? Would she perhaps have agreed with Marina Warner who wrote, 'admitting to enjoying a fairytale cartoon from the same studio that made* Snow White *and* Cinderella*…goes against the grain'…*

Disney and the Beast

AT THE BEGINNING of Jean Cocteau's celebrated live-action version of *La belle et la bête* (1946), the artist stands up and writes a message to his audience on a blackboard: 'Children believe what we tell them, they have complete faith in us, they believe that a rose plucked from a garden can bring drama to a family. I ask of *you* a little of this childlike simplicity, and to bring us luck let me speak four truly magical words, childhood's "open sesame": *once upon a time*.'

Cocteau evidently assumed that his audience would be adult, that it would enjoy a self-consciously poetic version of a well-known story and that it had read the classics – for his film was full of esoteric references to the classical origin of this fairytale. He also seems to have assumed that the audience would be predominantly male: the focus of *La belle et la bête* is mainly in the transformation of Jean Marais from backcombed lion with fangs dressed in glitter into poetic prince who acts in the traditionally rhetorical style of La Comédie Française. La Belle, needless to say, is a bashful blonde whose role it is to drift around the enchanted palace as if on a cloud, inspiring the Beast (and the artist) to greater and more arty things. Cocteau's message on the blackboard was a challenge to his Surrealist pals: his film will not over-intellectualise; it will be a plea for directness and 'childlike simplicity'. These are what are needed after the devastation of war.

1946 was also the year in which a French critic wrote of Walt Disney's animated films – and in particular of *Snow White and the Seven Dwarfs* (1937) – the immortal phrase '*perfection technique au service du crétinisme'*. Too much engineering, not enough imagination. Cocteau's film, by contrast, may have had technological imperfections, but it was self-evidently the work of an *artist* – albeit one who was aiming for the qualities of a fairytale.

After an initial honeymoon period of critical support and respect for Disney's animation work, this kind of severe judgment was beginning to spread: James Agee had written in 1943 that 'Disney's famous cuteness, however richly it may mirror national infantilism, is hard on my stomach'; educators were beginning to worry about the 'Disneyfication' of the rich heritage of fairytales; and learned articles began to appear that contrasted the *closed* atmosphere of the films (nostalgia; regression; small-town morality; barnyard jokes) with the wide-ranging creative and imaginative possibilities of the originals. In *Pinocchio* (1940), *Dumbo* (1941) and *Bambi* (1942), little animals had begun to step forward (respectively, a cricket with a carpetbag and voice like Ed Wynn; a uniformed mouse with a large ego and shrewd business sense; and a cutesy-pie little bunny called Thumper) to hammer home the stories' moral message. And above all, fairy-stories that had been around since Classical Greece and Rome were in the process of becoming *Walt Disney's Pied Piper* (1933), *Walt Disney's Tortoise and the Hare* (1935), *Walt Disney's Country Cousin* (1936), *Walt Disney's Ugly Duckling* (1939) and, of course, *Walt Disney's Snow White*. Disney is said to have replied to the criticism that the original stories weren't quite like his versions – 'Well, they are now.' He was right: Disney's *Snow White* is far better known, as a global text, than the tale on which it was based, the much darker, more sadistic version called *Snowdrop* translated from the Brothers Grimm and published in 1823.

A few years ago, I talked to the animator Zack Schwarz, who helped on the Rackham-inspired backgrounds for *Snow White*, before co-ordinating the *Sorcerer's Apprentice* sequence in *Fantasia* (1940), about how 'Uncle Walt' used to conduct the story conferences where such decisions were made. Apparently, he would spend much of the time acting out all the characters, complete with voices. During one of these conferences, the question of Snow White's personal relationship with the dwarfs came up. In the original story, they are presented as wrinkled little old men who are wise, crafty and possibly libidinous, and who spend their lives digging for gold and precious jewels that the less vertically challenged humans have overlooked. 'The problem,' said Schwarz, 'was how these little men would *relate* to Snow White. Disney's daughter had said to her father, "Please don't do a story about dwarfs – there's something so *nasty* about them," and we obviously had to get away from any kind of sexual reference. So in the end we turned Snow White into the dwarfs' mom, who teaches them how to wash up, make their bed, have good manners at table, wash behind the ears and so on, and we turned the dwarfs into her children.' She also teaches them about the division of labour (or as Walt put it, 'the swing-shift').

At another conference, the vexed question of how the wicked stepmother would get her just desserts was the main topic. In the Grimm version, the queen does much more terrible things, such as eating what she believes to be Snow White's heart, and she certainly pays for it: 'At the wedding feast, when the queen's crime was exposed, slippers of iron were heated in a fire until red hot, and they were brought in with tongs, and the queen was forced to put on the red-hot slippers, and to dance until she dropped down dead.' That was the punishment for old hags who themselves punish their pubescent stepdaughters.

This, in the bowdlerised English-language version of 1823, turned into: 'And when she saw that Snowdrop was the prince's bride, she choked with passion, and fell ill and died.' And in Disney's version it becomes a chase through the forest, followed by the wicked crone falling to her death in a thunderstorm. Even so, the child psychologist Dr Benjamin Spock used to say that 'Nelson Rockefeller told my wife a long time ago that they had to re-upholster the seats in Radio City Music Hall because they were wet so often by frightened schoolchildren' after watching this sequence. And it became the most talked-about aspect of the film.

One recurring topic at the Snow White conferences, recalled Schwarz, was the problem of animating 'human' characters – and the problems of introducing *motivation* (of a kind which would make sense to a post-Freudian audience) into traditional tales where actions and behaviour were much more important than character. Disney was aware that the story would have to be retold to fit the dreams and expectations of a mid-1930s American audience, and a lot of the changes emerged from the process of discussing exactly how. As Schwarz put it to me, 'Forget about the "for-all-time" quality, forget about fixed archetypes; these stories had to work.'

Between *Snow White* and *Beauty and the Beast*, the studio has – surprisingly – produced only three full-length animated versions of fairytales: two based on Charles Perrault, *Cinderella* (1950) and *Sleeping Beauty* (1959), and one based on Hans Christian Andersen, *The Little Mermaid* (1989) – which outgrossed all the others, hence *Beauty*. It made countless shorts based on fairytales, but these didn't make their way into the cultural bloodstream nearly so effectively. Where *Cinderella* and *Sleeping Beauty* were concerned, many critics felt that the technical innovations of *Snow White* had long since turned into visual clichés and that 1950s Disney was still imitating 1930s Disney: his interpretation of the stories had, quite simply, not moved sufficiently with the times, and they no longer *worked*.

With this critical heritage to live down to, and with Disney's 'classic' features by now firmly embedded within the vocabulary of postmodernist film-making – the Gremlins going to watch *Snow White*, Uncle Walt himself in *The Twilight Zone*, Spielberg's mothership taking off to the strains of *When You Wish Upon a Star*, Robert Stack watching *Dumbo* in Spielberg's *1941* – the question is, how does the Disney Studio cope with *Beauty and the Beast* – how does it 'make the story work' – in the early 1990s?

Well, in the event, Walt Disney Pictures' *Beauty and the Beast* – the first of the studio's fairytale features ever to have been written by a woman, Linda Woolverton, who has a master's degree in the significance of theatre for children – comes as a very pleasant surprise. Belle, far from being the iconic blonde with both feet planted in the air of Cocteau's version, is a gutsy, down-to-earth brunette with strong views about the limitations of French provincial life in the eighteenth century. And – a postmodernist reference? – she particularly enjoys reading the fairytales of Charles Perrault, such as *Cinderella*. Her only animal friends are the local sheep, who observe her reading habits with blank expressions on their faces. The Beast – a mixture of Picasso's Minotaur and a fierce American buffalo with Jean Marais-style fangs – is genuinely beastly to begin with, although he doesn't ever upset the greener members of the audience by going hunting at night and returning with his jaws and paws covered in blood as in the Cocteau version; his blue eyes are the mirror of his soul – and the first clue, for Belle, that he has hidden depths. Most interesting of all, the scriptwriter and first-time directors Gary Trousdale and Kirk Wise have adapted two aspects of the Cocteau version, and taken them a lot further.

The first is the enchanted castle. With its human arms holding candlesticks, its corridor of billowing curtains, its talking furniture and fusion of classicism and surrealism, this was the most memorable and influential aspect of *La belle et la bête*: the Disney version has cracked the problem of how to make the castle sequences interesting by introducing a talking candlestick called Lumière, a camp speaking-clock called Cogsworth, a cockney teapot called Mrs Potts (based, says Angela Lansbury who provides the voice, on Mrs Bridges in *Upstairs, Downstairs*) and a set-piece dance number (which could have been called Busby Berkeley's *Knives and Forks of 1992*) by all the palace's kitchen utensils.

The second, and more interesting, inheritance from Cocteau is the character of Gaston (Avenant in the 1946 version), who is a shadow version of the Beast. Gaston is a macho village lout; he's built like Arnie Schwarzenegger, goes around shooting birds – 'No beast alive gets past you; no girl either,' says his sidekick, Le Four – and has three buxom bimbos (parodies of the three white bunny rabbits who hero-worship Max Hare in Disney's 1935 *The Tortoise and the Hare*) forever swooning at his feet. He spends the entire movie chasing after Belle, who is far too sensible to fall for his beastly charms. In the Cocteau version, we were supposed to believe that Belle was in love with the obnoxious Avenant, so in this respect Disney has actually improved on Cocteau. Finally, instead of being a merchant, Belle's father, Maurice, becomes an inventor who looks like Albert Einstein; and the visualisation of Madame Le Prince de Beaumont's sinister forest, 'with wolves, whom they heard howling all around them', comes straight out of countless remakes of *Dracula*.

The author and critic Marina Warner has recently written: 'Liking a Disney film doesn't come easily: admitting to enjoying a fairytale cartoon from the same studio that made *Snow White* and *Cinderella* that held up simpering, gutless, niminy-piminy idiots as paragons and introduced children everywhere to expect malignancy from older women goes against the grain, like accepting all of a sudden that… the Pope has become a feminist.' This judgment may be a bit severe on Disney's previous films but, as far as *Beauty and the Beast* goes, it is right on target. The film *works*, and the original is adaptable enough to take it.

It is pitched at grown-ups as well as children, it assumes an understanding of the conventions of fairytales (and of Cocteau's film) and in the end not everyone lives happily ever after. Uncle Walt once said, 'the word "culture" has a faintly un-American feel to it.' What would *he* have thought of all this? Maybe the studio has at last outgrown his shadow, and stopped asking that question.

8

Nothing But a Hound Dog

Introduction

The collection The Bloody Chamber *contains a variety of carnivorous creatures. In Bath, Angela Carter lived just up the road from Walcot – gateway to 'alternative Bath' – which she wrote was full of 'occultists, neo-Platonists, natural lifers, macrobiotics, people who make perfumed candles, kite-flyers, do you believe in fairies?' She was intrigued by picture-books about mysterious phenomena – some written by local authors – and why people were so drawn to them: in some ways, they were, she thought, successors to orally-transmitted fables, 'old-fashioned popular culture'. One of these phenomena was the occasional appearance of 'black dogs', or of creatures resembling black dogs, on Dartmoor and Bodmin Moor. As usual, there were spoilsports who insisted on rational explanations, like Sherlock Holmes at the end of* The Hound of the Baskervilles, *when he concludes that the hound was actually purchased from a pet shop in the Fulham Road.*

In the mid-1970s, Angela Carter was referred to by Radio Times *as 'herself a novelist based in the West Country', a regional and therefore marginal figure, which was how metropolitan critics tended to view 'provincial' novelists in those days. Before moving to Bath, I worked for a time at Exeter University, where the resident Fellow in Folklore Studies was an authority on West Country black dog legends and 'entrances to the other world' especially on and around Dartmoor. We sometimes explored the moor together, looking for where sightings were reported to have happened and for big holes in the ground. And she introduced me to a genial vicar who had tried to exorcise an Accident Black Spot on a remote rural road near Widecombe...*

Nothing But a Hound Dog

I HAVE ALWAYS ASSOCIATED *The Hound of the Baskervilles* in my mind's eye with Sir Edwin Landseer's painting *Dignity and Impudence* (1839)), which was on exhibition in London's National Gallery during Arthur Conan Doyle's lifetime and which now hangs – periodically – in the Victorian Gallery of Tate Britain at Millbank. It was in fact one of Queen Victoria's favourite paintings, by her favourite artist. She even entrusted Landseer with the prized commission to paint a portrait of the royal dogs, not corgis in those days but spaniels and greyhounds. *Dignity and Impudence* shows a large, slightly supercilious-looking, unperturbed bloodhound on the left of the picture, with his paw extending over the entrance, next to a tiny, eager-looking white Scottish West Highland White terrier who looks as though he is about to spring out and start barking at any moment – a bit like a Scots version of Toto – both framed by the entrance to a wooden kennel in a parody of seventeenth-century Dutch domestic paintings. In the Dutch versions, the figure tends to be framed by a window, with a hand extending over the edge to help the illusion. Here it is the bloodhound's paw. Landseer deliberately gave the two dogs almost human qualities. An engraving of this, Landseer's most popular and reproduced work, was on the library wall of the small school in the Sussex countryside, where I first read *The Hound of the Baskervilles* (in a run of the *Strand Magazine*, at the age of ten). Although Landseer's bloodhound was actually called Grafton and the terrier Scratch – the dogs belonged to the man who commissioned the picture – in my imagination they were for ever Sherlock Holmes and Dr Watson, precursors in canine form of the immortal partnership. A pure-blooded, well-trained hunting hound on the one hand; and a terrier who is the type to bound up to his master and expect a pat on the head – only to be disappointed. Rather like Watson. The dogs were also more than a little grotesque and scary, another reason they stuck in my mind. Alfred Hitchcock featured *Dignity and Impudence* on the wall of the house where Marnie (Tippi Hedren) first sees red, at the gory climax of his film *Marnie* (1964).

In real life, Grafton was once locked by mistake in a stable with another dog. The following morning, the bloodhound and the other dog were found exhausted in opposite corners of the stable, badly wounded, the walls spattered with blood. Grafton was expected to die, but in the end recovered. His owner said he would shoot him if he ever did anything like that again. The strange thing was that while the two dogs were fighting, they did not wake anyone up – the curious incident of the dogs in the night-time.

History has unfortunately not recorded Conan Doyle's verdict on *Dignity and Impudence*. But we know he liked well-crafted paintings, gundogs and 'that gracious lady' Queen Victoria, so Landseer almost certainly appealed to his taste. We also know that Conan Doyle's attitude to more modern art was dismissive – to say the least – as his private journal was later to reveal: 'a wave of [artistic] insanity is breaking out in various forms in various places. If it stops where it is, it will only be a curious phenomenon… One should put one's shoulder to the door and keep out the insanity all one can'. So he probably liked the dogs very much indeed.

The 'curious phenomenon' of modern art was, of course, to become much more than that – one reason why Landseer's *Dignity and Impudence* has spent so much of its recent life buried in the basement of Tate Britain – but the Hound of the Baskervilles has remained for me Sherlock Holmes's greatest adversary, greater still than Moriarty. Here is Watson's thrilling description of the beast in chapter 14:

> A hound it was, an enormous coal-black hound, but not such a hound as mortal eyes have ever seen. Fire burst from its open mouth, its eyes glowed with a smouldering glare, its muzzle and hackles and dewlap were outlined in flickering flame. Never in the delirious dream of a disordered brain could anything more savage, more appalling, more hellish, be conceived than that dark form and savage face which broke upon us out of the wall of fog.

This description has created problems, well-known in the business, for the production designers of film versions of *The Hound* – eighteen major versions at the last count, which makes it the most filmed of all crime novels. The dilemma is not only how to find a dog which can do what the director wants, it is also to find one which can live up to Watson's description. Solutions have included Great Danes with big masks on their heads for close-ups; Great Danes with enhanced teeth; children dressed up as Holmes and Sir Henry confronting apparently gigantic creatures on pint-sized sets (this one was seriously contemplated by Hammer Films in 1959); animated silhouettes; luminous flames scratched on the negative, frame by frame, and, latterly, dogs tinted by computer in post-production with a green phosphorescent halo. In the very first adaptation, made in Denmark in 1903 as *The Grey Dame*, they perhaps sensibly dispensed with the hound altogether. She became The Grey Dame rather than the Great Dane.

I experienced such difficulties first-hand when I made a television programme about the writing of *The Hound of the Baskervilles* in 1996, as part of my series *Nightmare – the birth of horror*, co-produced by the BBC and A&E. One of the ideas behind this programme was to examine the relative claims of various black dog legends, or folktales, to be the origin of *The Hound of the Baskervilles*. I'd discussed them at length with a wonderful woman called Theo Brown, a Fellow in Folklore Studies at Exeter University, who'd spent her life studying Black Dogs and Entrances to the Other World, all over Dartmoor. Her favourite black dog story was of the ghostly Hound of Moretonhampstead, who hung around a ditch opposite a pub looking for spilt beer. Theo's thesis was that black dog legends, especially the commemorative kind, were usually about supporters of King Charles I snapping at the heels of the Parliamentarians. The dogs tended to be of the Stuart persuasion, like their masters. The main contenders for the coveted title 'origin of the Hound' were Black Shuck of Norfolk – a particularly nasty specimen (Shuck or Scucca meaning 'the demon' in Anglo-Saxon), which was the size of a calf and easily recognisable by his saucer-shaped eyes weeping red fire; or the phantom boar-hound of Hergest pronounced Hargest Ridge on the Welsh borders, complete with clanking chains – which made an appearance in the neighbourhood whenever there was about to be a death in the Baskerville-Vaughan family; or a whole pack of spectral Whisht hounds, which were said by some to have hunted the squire Richard Cabel or Cable to his doom at Buckfastleigh on the edge of Dartmoor in the 1670s and which made a come-back every Midsummer's Eve. We thought it would add to the drama of the programme to close each of these sequences – filmed in Cromer, Hergest and Buckfastleigh Churchyard – with a repeated shot of a huge black hound, complete with slavering jaws, lunging towards the camera, in slow motion, and apparently sinking his teeth into it. The camera, I mean. Fade to black, and on to the next location. Well, since Ross and Mangles in the Fulham Road was unaccountably closed at the time, we contacted a company called Animal Actors, or something like that, who promised the biggest mastiff we'd ever seen – with acting experience to boot. In for a penny, in for a hound, so one sunny afternoon in June 1995 I found myself waiting with the film crew in Holland Park Gardens, West London, for the arrival of a gigantic beast who answered, when he felt like it, to the name of Cracker. It had turned into a sweltering day and Cracker, complete with his two well-built minders, arrived in a small caravan with a speckled band round the side bearing the name of the company. To get him to sink his fangs into the lens, we had hired – at considerable expense – an endoscopic camera which is normally used for medical purposes I won't go into – a camera which looked like a floppy pipe-cleaner, appropriately enough, with a lens on the end the size of an orange pip. Around this pipe-cleaner, we had wrapped a dried pig's ear – Cracker's favourite dish, we'd been informed. And Cracker hadn't been fed for twenty-four hours. Everything bode well for the tooth-prints of a gigantic hound. Well, as I say, it was very hot and instead of lunging for the camera, the hapless mastiff – despite his acting experience – wagged his tail, slobbered a bit and sensibly ambled away into the shade. Then, the two minders had the bright idea of running him towards the camera – each clutching an all-but-invisible lead – and letting go at the last minute. Cracker dutifully ran with them – in a lazy sort of way – then just as he reached the pig's ear, sniffed the end of the camera, slobbered some more, started panting and again lolloped away in the opposite direction.

By now, quite a crowd had gathered, intrigued by what must have seemed a very strange spectacle, and the police arrived. At this point, I had a stroke of inspiration. I remembered that our family fox terrier used sometimes to confuse the water coming out of a hose for a stick – and would try to bite the stream of water in mid-air. What if Cracker could be persuaded to bite the water – with the endoscopic camera placed almost inside his mouth. Maybe *that* would do the trick. No one had a hose on them, but one of the film crew did have a bottle of Perrier water, which he reluctantly surrendered for the good of the production. I stood pouring the Perrier, just out of shot, and, yes, Cracker did open his jaws in a languid sort of way – largely because he was very thirsty, and then he sort of grimaced because he didn't like the bubbles – but we'd run out of mineral water before anything very exciting had registered on film. Just as we were packing up the equipment, Cracker – obstinate to the last – began to tuck into his pig's ear, which he'd managed to detach from the camera while we were looking the other way. All *we* had was a few frames of a mastiff guzzling Perrier water and making a funny face. This proved to be one final problem too many, so we gave up on the idea.

I want to share with you an important new piece of evidence about Arthur Conan Doyle (not yet Sir Arthur) and the actual process of writing of *The Hound of the Baskervilles* – a piece of evidence which has never been made public before, and which finally proves beyond any shadow of a doubt the exact order of events which occurred in the first year of the twentieth century, resulting in the novel which is for many the greatest of all the Sherlock Holmes stories.

As we know, the seeds of the novel were first sown in spring 1901, when Doyle was enjoying a brief but much-needed golfing holiday with his young journalist friend Bertram or Bertie Fletcher Robinson at the

Royal Links Hotel in Cromer, a cliff-top hotel on the north coast of Norfolk, with eighty rooms, a billiard-table, and an eighteen-hole golf-course attached. Doyle had in fact stayed there before, with his wife and son, on 17-20 September 1897, in happier times. And this is where my new piece of evidence first enters the case. It is a small self-registering pocket diary for 1901, in a leather binding, complete with numerous manuscript entries in Doyle's handwriting and two of his visiting cards tucked into a flap at the front. John Dickson Carr, in his authorised *Life of Sir Arthur Conan Doyle* published in 1949 and based on privileged access to the family archives, claimed that the four-day visit to Cromer happened 'in March [of 1901]'. Richard Lancelyn Green later carefully pieced together Conan Doyle's movements that spring, and especially the various dinner parties he attended – with Winston Churchill among others – and also found the author's account book with a payment of £6.0.0 to the Royal Links Hotel, Cromer, on 30 April. So, as Richard said, it *looked* as though Doyle stayed there in April rather than March. Well, the diary reveals that he originally intended to stay there on the weekend of 21/22 April, but then changed his mind and went with Robinson on Friday 26, Saturday 27, Sunday 28 and Monday 29 April. Then he returned to London and the Athenaeum Club (to which he had recently been elected, on 8 March 1901) for a dinner with Churchill, Anthony Hope, James Barrie, Edmund Gosse and others on Tuesday 30 April.

So it was on the afternoon of Sunday 28 April – as we can now be sure – when the breeze from the North Sea was blowing too strongly for the two friends to play a round of golf on Lighthouse Hills, that Conan Doyle and Fletcher Robinson had their celebrated conversation about dogs, indoors at the Royal Links Hotel.

On Sunday 28 April – the letter itself is undated, as usual – Conan Doyle wrote in the heat of the moment to his mother Mary, from the hotel:

> A line to you, dear old Mammie, to say that I have had much good out of my 2 days here, where I have slept soundly at last. All goes

well in every way. On Tuesday I give a dinner at the Athenaeum Club... [And then on the second page] Fletcher Robinson came here with me and we are going to do a small book together 'The Hound of the Baskervilles' – a real Creeper.

Also from the Royal Links, he gave advance notice to the editor of the *Strand*, using exactly the same words:

I have the idea of a real creeper for the 'Strand'. It would run, I think, to not less than 40,000 words. It is just the sort of thing that would suit you, full of surprises, and breaking naturally into good lengths for serial purposes. It would be called 'The Hound of the Baskervilles'. Let me have [the illustrator Sidney] Paget if you take it.

We can now say for sure that the seeds of *The Hound* were sown on 28 April 1901.

Neither Fletcher Robinson nor Conan Doyle thought of *The Hound of the Baskervilles* as a Sherlock Holmes novel, at this early stage. It was a real creeper, a horror novel, a shaggy dog story, quite short at 'not less than 40,000 words' maybe with Dr Mortimer as the central character, a character loosely based on Fletcher Robinson himself. But by 25 May, just under a month after the Cromer holiday, the magazine *Tit-Bits*, a more down-market weekly sister publication to the *Strand* – was confidently announcing under the heading 'The Revival of Sherlock Holmes' that 'presently [Mr Conan Doyle] will give us an important story to appear in 'The Strand', in which the great Sherlock Holmes is the principal character... It will be published as a serial of from 30,000 to 50,000 words [it had grown longer], and the plot is one of the most interesting and striking that have [*sic*] ever been put before us'. Earlier in the same month Conan Doyle wrote again in another undated letter to the editor of the *Strand*:

The price I quoted [in the Royal Links letter] has for years been my serial price not only with you but with other journals. Now it is evident that this is a very special occasion since as far as I can judge the revival of Holmes would attract a great deal of attention. If put up to open competition I could get very particular terms for this story… Holmes is at a premium in America just now.

The directors of the *Strand*, sensible fellows, did not hesitate. So this was to be, as the novel's subtitle was to put it, 'Another Adventure of Sherlock Holmes'. The arrival of the great detective on the scene after the main 'scheme of events' had already been planned was materially to affect the final shape of the novel. He's not in most of it – just six out of fifteen chapters – the second-longest hiatus in the whole series. It has been said of *The Hound* that the story dominates Holmes, rather than Holmes dominating the story. It should more accurately have been subtitled 'Another Adventure of Dr Watson'.

So Doyle started writing *The Hound* shortly after his return from Cromer – based on the chain of events, the plot and some of the incidental details he'd discussed with Robinson at the hotel. Then, some time around the second week of May, he decided that a masterful central figure would be needed, to influence the whole course of events – and that he had a very masterful central figure in stock, albeit one who had apparently exited the scene in *The Final Problem*, December 1893. The first manuscript instalments of *The Hound* reached *The Strand* in mid-May, less than a fortnight after he started writing, and illustrator Sidney Paget's accounts reveal that he had completed the first seven drawings including the frontispiece during that same month of May 1901. And this, at a time when – as the pocket diary reveals – Doyle went to at least five dinner parties at the Athenaeum, the Author's Club, Gray's Inn and private houses, played three long cricket matches (the teams, scores and bowling averages are duly noted), went to a matinée and showed a party of American and colonial visitors, members of the Atlantic Union, around the Temple on a Saturday afternoon. Oh, and he spent his forty-first birthday evening, on 22 May, at dinner with the surgeon and urologist Sir Henry Thompson.

Doyle had heard about Dartmoor, its natural history and folklore, from Fletcher Robinson who seems to have gleaned some of his material from the published works of the Revd Sabine Baring-Gould – who lived at Lewtrenchard on the edge of the moor, and whose output also included the hymn 'Onward, Christian Soldiers', the cleaned-up version of the folk song 'Widdecombe Fair', *The Book of Werewolves* and some now rather unreadable novels. They don't make vicars like that any more. Doyle had also visited Tavistock as a young man and used it as the setting for *Silver Blaze* in 1892 – the one with the famous line about the curious incident of the dog in the night-time – though the scenery and atmosphere in that story were pretty thin on the ground, and Doyle had been criticised for getting some of the details wrong. But in May 1901 he felt he had enough material for the early chapters of the novel – the opening in Baker Street, the manuscript of the curse, the arrival of Sir Henry Baskerville, the visit to the Northumberland Hotel, Watson's departure for Dartmoor in chapter six – but he needed to go to Dartmoor in person to soak up local colour and check details. Again, the diary is helpful here. It reveals that Conan Doyle had attended The Hunterian Oration at the Royal College of Surgeons at 8 p.m on 14 February 1901, where a Dr Macnamara FRS gave a lecture on 'Craniology' in which he gave this description of Neolithic Man: 'They had long dolichocephalic skulls, with slightly projecting supra-orbital ridges, well-formed noses and a fairly developed frontal region.' Clearly, Conan Doyle was taking notes because the words are almost the same as Dr Mortimer's of Sherlock Holmes in chapter one of *The Hound*: 'I had hardly expected so dolicho-cephalic a skull or such well-marked supra-orbital development… It is not my intention to be fulsome, but I confess that I covet your skull'. Why Holmes should have the skull of a Neolithic Man is never explained. But it was a detail which found its way into the book.

Maybe Conan Doyle had progressed further than chapter six before he reached Dartmoor and again he made mistakes. Despite what Doyle put down on paper – in the chapter where Stapleton introduces Watson to the flora and fauna of the place – wild orchids do not flower on Dartmoor or anywhere else in mid-October, any more than bitterns, even then almost extinct, mate in the autumn; and whatever the moor is, it isn't at all 'barren' – Dartmoor has a fascinating and varied eco-system if you look closely at the plants, the wildlife, the groups of stacks, boulders and clefts, the rocky outcrops, the soggy ground and the streams. Some of Watson's and Stapleton's descriptions of this 'vast, barren and mysterious place', with its darkened sky, its mists and bogs and granite silhouettes – much vaster than the actual thing – could fit almost any Gothic wasteland.

So it was as much a literary as a real-life construct. Was *this* chapter written before Doyle went to Dartmoor? It could have been. And it certainly wasn't checked with Fletcher Robinson, who grew up in Ipplepen on the edge of the moor, and was educated at Newton Abbot College. *He* would have known about the boom of the bittern, which is pretty memorable – it sounds like a flat car battery when the ignition key is turned. John Dickson Carr dated Doyle's Dartmoor visit to the beginning of April 1901 – following his supposed visit to Cromer in March. 'The postmark,' he wrote, 'was April 2nd 1901… It was the first baying of *The Hound of the Baskervilles*.' Carr seems to have assumed that the author had to go to Dartmoor for a recce, before committing pen to paper and beginning *The Hound*. But that wasn't the way Conan Doyle worked at all. He wrote very fast indeed, decisively and with a minimum of revisions. His second wife Jean was later to recall, 'I have known him write a Sherlock Holmes story in a room full of people talking…he would write in a train or anywhere.' And Doyle himself confessed to his editor at *The Strand*, 'a story always comes to me as an organic thing and I never recast it without the life going out of it.' In the case of *The Hound*, this meant that one or two drafting errors found their way into the *Strand* version. It also meant that things that were on the author's mind *before* the Dartmoor visit surfaced in the early part of his story: the topography around his home in Hindhead, Surrey; articles in recent issues of the *Strand* magazine; memories and names from the Boer War in South Africa and other military engagements; conversations with Robinson.

Again, Richard Lancelyn Green questioned John Dickson Carr's dating, by carefully compiling the dates of Conan Doyle's cricket matches around the West Country at the time – but no one can have been absolutely certain until now. As the self-registering pocket diary shows, Conan Doyle went on his brief tour of Dartmoor on Friday 31 May, Saturday 1 and Sunday 2 June – then off to Sherborne School in Dorset on 3-4 June playing cricket for the Incogniti, where he was stumped off a leg ball for eleven runs and the match was a draw. He wrote the letter 'D' in his diary against the weekend dates. Fletcher Robinson later said that 'one of the most interesting weeks that I ever spent was with Doyle on Dartmoor.' But it appears that it wasn't a week; just three days. Others have speculated, following Harry Baskerville's lead, that the two men first went to Park Hill House, the home of Robinson's parents in Ipplepen, for a few days, before visiting the moor proper. This does not seem to be the case. By the time Doyle reached D on 31 May, for his short visit, he had already written just under half the novel – that is, 25,000 words or thereabouts out of a total of 59,452 words. If he wrote it in sequence, which seems likely, that included the arrival at Baskerville Hall *and* part of the Stapleton chapter. Intriguingly, for Wednesday 20 May, just before Dartmoor, Doyle has 'MCC v Richmond Town' in the diary – but with a line through it. Was he playing cricket in South London two days before leaving for Dartmoor?

Arthur Conan Doyle and Fletcher Robinson seem to have travelled down together from London on Friday 31 May, they stayed at the Rowe's Duchy Hotel, Princetown, just down the road from Dartmoor prison, and they explored the moor together on Saturday 1 June. The hotel building was said in its publicity to have been constructed by French prisoners-of-war in Napoleonic times (which must have struck a chord with Conan Doyle, whose first Brigadier Gerard stories had been written in 1894-5), but this was – sadly – a legend. It was originally built in 1785, four years before the French Revolution. The nearby prison had a thousand inmates, and civil guards policed its perimeter.

From this hotel, Conan Doyle wrote a famous letter on headed notepaper to his mother. It was postmarked not 2 April 1901 as Dickson Carr claimed, but Sunday 2 June 1901 – which is to say, just over a month after Conan Doyle had the original idea, and around three weeks after he decided to turn it into a Sherlock Holmes story.

> Dearest of Mams, Here I am in the highest town in England. Robinson and I are exploring the Moor over our Sherlock Holmes book. I think it will work out splendidly – indeed I have already done nearly half of it. Holmes is at his very best, and it is a highly dramatic idea – which I owe to Robinson. We did 14 miles over the Moor and we are now pleasantly weary. It is a great place, very sad and wild, dotted with dwellings of prehistoric man, strange monoliths and huts and graves.

That is the extract from the letter that is usually quoted. But there was more, and it is very interesting.

> In those old days there was evidently a population of very many thousands here and now you may walk all day and never see one human being. Everywhere there are gutted tin mines. Tomorrow [Sunday] we drive 6 miles to Ipplepen where R's parents live. Then on Monday Sherborne for cricket, 2 days at Bath, 2 days at Cheltenham. Home on Monday the 10th. That is my programme. My work will proceed all the better…

Conan Doyle did indeed play cricket on the Incogniti School Tour – with E.W. Hornung on his team – against Sherborne School, as we've seen, the first of three matches, then another for the Incogniti against Lansdown Cricket Club at Coombe Park Bath on Wednesday 5 and Thursday 6 – where in delightful weather he scored two caught at the wicket in the first innings, four played on in the second – followed by yet another match against Cheltenham College at Cheltenham on Friday 7 and Saturday 8 – where he was bowled for thirty-eight, and caught for thirteen 'a short one'. This Incogniti School Tour was arranged by his friend Captain Philip Trevor. On 6th of that month, there was a payment in his account book to Robinson of £3.0.0. The total paid to Fletcher Robinson in the latter half of 1901 was some £500.0.

Up until recently, the first half of Conan Doyle's letter to his mother was the only primary evidence of Doyle's visit to Dartmoor. But an article has turned up, from the *Sunday Magazine* for 26 November 1905, which tells the story from Fletcher Robinson's point of view as well. In the article, Robinson describes their stay at the comfortable old-fashioned inn 'near the famous convict prison of Princetown' in much more detail, including a visit to the smoking room from the prison governor, the deputy governor, the chaplain and the doctor, who left a note at the hotel rather sweetly explaining they had 'come to call on Mr Sherlock Holmes' though they hadn't had the nerve to mention the fact. Little did they know that Conan Doyle was even then writing the detective's greatest adventure.

Fletcher Robinson wrote, in his rather stilted style:

> One morning [it must have been Saturday 1 June] I took Doyle to see the mighty bog…which figured so prominently in *The Hound* [Aaron Rowe, the hotel landlord, was to say he accompanied them as well]… From the bog, we tramped eastward to the stone fort of Grimspound, which the savages of the Stone Age in Britain…raised with enormous labour to act as a haven of refuge from the marauding tribes to the South. The good preservation in which the Grimspound fort still remains is marvellous [it had been partially restored in the early 1890s]… It was one of the loneliest spots in Great Britain…

This must have been the '14 miles over the Moor' mentioned by Conan Doyle in the letter to his mother: from Princetown to Fox Tor Mire (the 'mighty bog' with nearby tin mine which became Grimpen Mire in the novel), eastward to the stone huts of Grimspound (the hiding-place of Sherlock Holmes: the name came from the Norse god Grim, better known as Odin) and back to the hotel again; on foot it is actually nearer twenty-one miles than fourteen. I've done it. From Conan Doyle's brief account, it is not clear whether they walked all the way or not: a day-long ride in the Robinsons' carriage, plus hiking for the inaccessible parts of the journey would also – presumably – have made him 'pleasantly weary' at the age of forty-one, even if he was a more than competent cricketer in good physical condition. Some of Robinson's reminiscences come almost verbatim from *A Book of Dartmoor*, published the previous year, by our old friend the Revd Sabine Baring-Gould.

Conan Doyle, as well, almost certainly read *A Book of Dartmoor*: perhaps he even read it *on* Dartmoor. The book's descriptions of the 'fog, dense as cotton wool', the quaking bogs and Neolithic stone huts, escaped convicts stumbling around the moor and legends dating from the time of the great Rebellion, closely resemble the equivalents in the novel. As does the overall atmosphere of a primeval wilderness, a never-land of mist, legend and antiquity.

A Book of Dartmoor was in fact a plea for a certain kind of conservation, and a polemic in support of the efforts of the new Dartmoor Preservation Society to control 'wanton trippers', over-zealous restorers, enclosing farmers, tin-miners and the military authorities who since the Boer War had been turning the place into a shooting range. Baring-Gould's Dartmoor is not a living, working landscape. It is a place which should always remain 'uncontaminated by the hand of man'.

In other words, a place just like Conan Doyle's perception of the moor as 'very sad and wild, dotted with…strange monoliths and huts and graves'. There is some evidence that Conan Doyle *was* reading Baring-Gould while he was visiting Dartmoor – or shortly before – in the second half of that letter to his mother. Remember he wrote, 'In those old days there was evidently a population of very many thousands here and now you may walk all day and never see one human being.' Well, since 1895 Baring-Gould had been involved in a heated controversy about how many people *did* live on Dartmoor in prehistoric times. His position was that 'tens of thousands of [ancient] habitations have been destroyed', and that the neolithic population was much greater than other archaeologists realised. This was hotly disputed by one Richard Hansford Worth in the columns of the *Transactions of the Devonshire Association*. And the controversy was carried over into *A Book of Dartmoor*. Doyle may have read this chapter the night before he wrote to his mother.

Anyway, on Sunday 2 June – it must have been – Conan Doyle and Fletcher Robinson were then driven by horse-drawn coach to Park Hill House, Ipplepen, over near Newton Abbott – where the coachman and groom was Young Henry (or Harry) Baskerville. The local vicar, the Revd Robert Cooke, another vicar, always claimed that he, too, guided Doyle and Mr Robinson on 'the details of the background', and that he 'had helped to write a very well-known book'. Doyle appears to have stayed the night at Park Hill House, then off on the Monday to Sherborne for cricket.

By a fortnight later, on Monday 17 June, he was returning the proofs of the second instalment *The Problem/Sir Henry Baskerville* to the editor of the *Strand* – from Morley's Hotel, off Trafalgar Square – and complaining that his copy of the preceding instalment had not been returned: the 'matter is complex', he wrote, and it was hard to hold all the threads of the story in his head. But the third instalment was nearly finished. So he was still tightening up his draft, finishing the story off and making final corrections in mid-June. *And* he was playing a lot of cricket: for the MCC, the Author's Eleven (captained by E W Hornung), the Gentlemen of the MCC and Dr Conan Doyle's eleven at Grayshott and Haslemere. By the end of June, he had corrected the first five instalments – up to *The Light Upon the Moor* – and was saying again from Morley's Hotel that he hoped that 50,000 words would not after all be the upper limit for the serial: if a few thousand extra were needed, he trusted he would be paid for them at the agreed higher rate. He was to overshoot the 50,000 by nearly 10,000 words.

'I write under some difficulty,' he reiterated, 'through not having any of the proofs, so I cannot refer back.'

One of the attractions of Morley's Hotel, we now know, was that Jean Leckie would sometimes take rooms at the nearby Golden Cross Hotel. Then, the final reference he made to the writing of *The Hound*, on 17 July: Doyle wrote from the Esplanade Hotel in Southsea – where he was having a holiday from 15-20 July – correcting an early detail and saying he had now finished the proofs of the sixth and seventh instalments. He also took the opportunity to play two cricket matches in Southsea, against RMA and USCC, again noted to the pocket diary. So the plot of *The Hound* was hatched on 28 April. By the second week of May, Sherlock Holmes had entered the scene. The Dartmoor visit was at the end of May, by which time half the book was written. Half the book in one month. Then, between the long trek on Saturday 1 June and a fortnight later on the 17th, Doyle was ready to correct the proofs. So to all intents and purposes, *The Hound of the Baskervilles* was conceived, researched and written in about six or seven weeks flat; then corrected and proofread in another four. No wonder John Dickson Carr thought the visit to Dartmoor *had* to be at the beginning of April, and Cromer in March: that gave an extra two months' writing time, which Conan Doyle did not in fact need. And then there were all those cricket matches, dinners and dinner parties... Just reading about them in the pocket diary is an exhausting experience.

The Hound of the Baskervilles first appeared in the *Strand Magazine* in August 1901, in the same issue as featured H.G. Wells's *The First Man in the Moon*, and in book form the following March. It soon became by far the most successful of all the Sherlock Holmes stories. Since then, as we've seen, it has also become the most filmed of all crime novels – because it is the best loved, the most popular beyond detective story readers and one of the most horrific. It started Holmes movie cycles in 1914 (when the first major film version was made) and 1939 (the Hollywood Basil Rathbone version); the attempt in 1959 by Hammer to start a new cycle was not so successful. But at the most recent count, Sherlock Holmes has appeared in over 211 films, more than any other fictional or historical character (Count Dracula comes in at a mere 159, Frankenstein way behind both). In Billy Wilder's affectionate *The Private Life of Sherlock Holmes* (1970), the book has even reached the Russian impresario Rogozhin, who refers to it as 'Beeg dog from Baskerville'. To which Holmes replies that it possibly seems to suffer in translation.

The combination of well-tried elements (breakfast at 221b Baker Street, a stunning display of Holmes's methods when a client leaves a piece of his property behind, then the introduction of the main mystery), the combination of these with a surprising setting and plot proved to be the winning one: the arrogant certainties of science and reason are confronted by the legends of the superstitious past, and by passions lying just below the surface, so that even Sherlock Holmes begins to have his doubts.

But above all, it is the image of Dartmoor – at the centre of the story – that has continued to capture readers' and moviegoers' imaginations, one of the great fantasy landscapes in all literature, up there with the Brontes' Yorkshire Moors, Dickens's London, Thomas Hardy's Wessex, R.D. Blackmore's Bodmin and Zane Gray's Purple Sage. An image of Dartmoor based on a flying visit which lasted all of two days. Most commentaries on Sherlock Holmes – aided and abetted by publicity for holidays in Devon – say that the landscape of Dartmoor inspired Conan Doyle to write his best-known novel. It didn't. His best-known novel inspired him to take a look at Dartmoor. And Dartmoor has since been inspired by *The Hound*.

At last, one hundred years on, *The Hound of the Baskervilles* has been promoted from the ghetto of Penguin Crime/Mystery to where it rightfully belongs in the pantheon of Penguin Classics, and I'm delighted to have had something to do with that. Okay, in the real world you can't tell from his footprints whether a dog is a Hound, a Great Dane, a St Bernard or even a large Alsatian. But that – I hope you will agree – is beside the point. The point is that it is a great line. 'Mr Holmes, they were the footprints of a gigantic hound.'

* * *

Postscript: At Christmas 1901 Conan Doyle sent out a card to all his friends and acquaintances with a picture of 'Derby the Devil' on it – a large prize bulldog which had been given to the family by Jerome K. Jerome in 1897, as thanks for a generous loan of money. So the year which since Easter had involved one devilish dog ended with another. And Conan Doyle wrote in the back of his pocket diary two New Year's resolutions:

1. To go abroad
2. To cultivate more friends.

So there would be even more dinner-parties in 1902...

9

Peter and the Wolf – the true story

Introduction

ANGELA CARTER'S *version of* Peter and the Wolf *is contained in her collection* Black Venus *(1985), known in the United States as* Saints and Strangers. *The story was first published in the journal* Firebrand 1 *(1982). It concerns a seven-year-old goatherd who encounters and captures in the mountains one spring day a naked wolf 'going on all fours, but hairless as regards the body although hair goes around its head'. This creature is really a little girl fostered by the wolves, the child of grandmother's dead daughter. Her wolf-relatives descend on the village in a pack and rescue her. Later, when he is fourteen and planning to study for the priesthood at the local seminary, Peter – teasingly known by locals as 'Saint Peter' – meets the wolf-child again, with 'her marvellous and private grace'. In an epiphany, he realises that 'there was nothing to be afraid of' – 'He experienced the vertigo of freedom' – and he walks off, emboldened, into 'a different story'.*

Sergei Prokofiev's Peter and the Wolf – *first performed in April 1936, during Stalin's unofficial Year of the Child – has been universalised as the way of introducing children to the sounds of the instrument of the orchestra. There are some 400 recordings of the piece in the West – these days, 25 available at any one time, usually with celebrity voices; but only a very few recordings in Russia, for various historical reasons.* Peter's *origins in Stalin's Soviet Union have been quietly forgotten. Suzie Templeton's animated film, released in December 2006, the most significant version since the 1940s, is a post-Carter reinterpretation of this much-loved 'symphonic fairytale'. The she-wolf is treated with sympathy; the huntsman is a beast; Peter comes of age with the realisation that there is nothing noble about imprisoning a wild forest-creature in a zoo.*

Peter and the Wolf – the true story

I FIRST ENCOUNTERED Suzie Templeton's work when she was assembling her graduation film *Dog* in the Animation Department of London's Royal College of Art in 2001. *Dog* is a very bleak, sad little piece of stop-frame animation – about a red-haired boy and his father, and their dog; it is set in the messy bedroom and grubby kitchen of a terrace house, where the dog is very poorly indeed. He is thin, mangy, submissive and visibly scared. One day a senior civil servant from the government's Department for Education came on an official visit to the studios of the RCA and we thought it a good idea to show him Suzie Templeton's completed *Dog*, as part of his walkabout. Halfway through, this senior Whitehall man muttered 'the dog's going to be all right, isn't he?' Well, not only does the dog die in the story, he's put out of his misery by the little boy's father in a particularly unpleasant way. 'It was very peaceful,' says the father. 'Like Mum?' says the little boy. The end. The lights came up and the official had red rims round his eyes. I thought – hell, we'll have our government grant taken away from us! We should perhaps have chosen something with a happy ending, or a few more laughs.

It was as a direct result of *Dog* – which deservedly won a BAFTA award – that Suzie Templeton was given the commission by BreakThru Films together with conductor Mark Stephenson to make *Peter and the Wolf*. It took five years to develop and complete, filmed at the Se-Ma-For studio in Łódź, Poland. Suzie Templeton tells me she did little else for that five years – it was a full-time commitment, including research trips to Moscow, rural Russia and a wolf sanctuary; conversations with 'young children in Russia – also old men and hunters: I couldn't even imagine the film if I couldn't imagine the place it was coming from'. Production designer Marek Skrobecki and team were selected after a viewing of the short *Icthys* featuring a man in a bowler hat in a small boat, and a giant fish. Polish animators made the models, the 'hyper-realistic' sets – a miniaturised world – and the digital effects. *Dog* was based on Templeton's own idea – *Peter*, of course, is based on a pre-existing work with a very precise shape to it, Sergei Prokofiev's famous words and music for *Peter and the Wolf*, which made things even more complicated. It is one of the most often recorded classical works in the repertoire – nearly 400 versions at the last count, reportedly beaten only by *The Four Seasons* – and the narration has been recorded by just about every distinct celebrity voice in the business – often, these days, with the narrative and the music being recorded separately and over-dubbed, leading to an irritating clash of acoustics, but useful for multiple pre-existing versions. The first-ever voices were the baritone Richard Hale (1939, on Victor – he was later to be the blind soothsayer in the 1953 *Julius Caesar*), Frank Luther (1940, on Decca) and Basil Rathbone (1941, on Columbia – by then best known for playing Sherlock Holmes): until the end of the Second World War, and the Walt Disney version, these were the only recordings. Among the more bizarre versions are Eleanor Roosevelt, Dame Edna Everage and Mikhail Gorbachev (2003, Introduction only). There have been very few recorded versions in Russian, as we shall see. As Suzie Templeton discovered, '*Peter* doesn't play nearly such a big part in Russian childhood memories. Every single English person I spoke to had that record when they were a child. But the Russians were much more vague about it…'

So, everybody in the West knows *Peter and the Wolf* from their childhood. Or do they? Behind its story is another, less well-known one – of a composer choosing to work in the Soviet Union, Stalin's Soviet Union on the cusp of the purges, and of a much-loved, cuddly, cheerful children's classic which started life as an uplifting tale written for 'the little citizens of the workers' and peasants' state'…

Sergei Prokofiev composed the story and music of *How Pioneer Petia Captured the Wolf* – as it was then called – in four days flat, then orchestrated it the following week, in April 1936, for the Central Children's Theatre in Moscow, as a young person's introduction to the instruments of the symphony orchestra. It was, he said, 'a present not only to the children of Moscow but also to my own sons'. There was no back and forth with musicians in the composition: he wrote it, without a superfluous bar, very quickly. In his *Memoir* Prokofiev is offhand about the piece: 'there was a need for music for children' – and that's all he had to say about it. He first visited the Children's Theatre, unexpectedly, with his wife Lina Ivanovna and two sons, in June of the previous year, to see a children's opera about a fisherman and a goldfish loosely inspired by a Pushkin story. The story of *Peter* was, he recalled elsewhere, partly based on memories dating from his own childhood growing up on a remote rural estate in the Donetsk region of the Eastern Ukraine; and he called it 'a symphonic fairytale'. It's tempting to imagine him listening in wonder to Russian folktales told by a wholesome, ruddy-faced peasant nurse in an embroidered apron. In fact, his childhood was full of serious study, he had a private tutor, and it's likely that his first encounter with fairytales was in much more refined eighteenth-century French versions. Prokofiev's mother – who strongly encouraged his studies – was very learned, with aristocratic pretensions; his father was more steeped in old Russian roots. Originally, the story of *Peter* was written for him in verse, but he didn't like the result at all – he called the poetess Nina Sakonskyaya an 'interfering incompetent' and added that she'd made the words get in the way of the music – so he started again with his own libretto. Each of the characters was to be associated with a particular musical instrument. Peter – string quartet; Grandfather – bassoon; Bird – flute; Duck – oboe; Cat – clarinet playing staccato in a low register; Wolf – 3 French horns; Hunters – kettledrums and bass drum. The main themes of the story would be: you can't be a hero if you don't take risks for the greater good; you need teamwork to achieve big things; if at first you don't succeed – try and try again; don't be frightened of a technological solution; and challenge the wisdom of your elders. Young Pioneer Petia is, in short, an active and resourceful member of the Vladimir Ilyich Lenin All-Union Pioneer Organisation, for children aged 10-15. Its motto – not 'be prepared', but 'always prepared'. As Catriona Kelly, Professor of Russian at Oxford University and a specialist in Soviet childhood, has pointed out, since 1932 and the tenth anniversary of the founding of the Young Pioneers, fairytales had been 'restored to favour'. In the mid-1920s they had been frowned upon – as encouraging unworldly fantasies, not materialist enough. Prokofiev's first draft, dated 'April 1936', is kept in the State Archive of Literature and Art in Moscow:

1.   Early one morning, Young Pioneer Petia went for a walk. He opened the wicket-gate and walked out into the big green meadow, because he'd decided to do some surveillance there.

2.   On a branch of a tall tree sat a little bird, Petia's friend. 'All quiet on the meadow front,' chirped the bird happily...

The draft continues:

7.   ... Just then Grandfather came out. He was upset because Petia had gone through the gate and out into the meadow by himself. 'It's a dangerous place. What would happen if a wolf came out of the forest?'

8.   But Petia started arguing with his grandfather and said that Young Pioneers are not at all frightened of wolves. Then Grandfather took Petia by the hand and led him back inside.

9.   No sooner had Petia gone home, than a huge grey wolf came out of the forest...

It concludes:

15.   ... Meanwhile Young Pioneer Petia made a lasso out of the rope, and carefully letting it down, looped it around the wolf's tail – and pulled with all his might. Feeling himself caught, the wolf began to jump wildly trying to get loose. But Petia tied the other end of the rope to the

tree, and the wolf's jumping about only made the rope around his tail tighter and tighter.

[Folio 2]   Just then, three hunters came out of the forest, following the wolf's footprints and shooting at him as they approached.

16.   But Petia, sitting in the tree, said 'Don't shoot! The little bird and I have already caught the wolf. All you have to do is to take him away to the zoo.'

17.   And now, they made a grand procession: Petia at the head of the procession, after him the hunters leading the wolf followed by the Grandfather with the cat, and the bird flying overhead.

18.   And if you listened very carefully, you could hear the duck quacking inside the wolf's stomach, because the wolf in his hurry had swallowed him alive.

So off they go, in their parade or 'grand procession', to the zoo – perhaps a reference to the tenth anniversary of the elaborate modernisation of Moscow Zoo in the mid-1920s, which had just been celebrated.

The Moscow State Children's Theatre became, in early 1936, the *Central* Children's Theatre – with a pan-Soviet reach – and was relocated to smarter new premises next to the Bolshoi. It remained under the sponsorship of the Committee on Arts Affairs. Prokofiev made a return visit for its inaugural concert. This 'theatre for the little citizens of a workers' and peasants' state' was run by a tough-minded and energetic artistic director the 33-year-old Natalia Sats, who commissioned *How Pioneer Petia Captured the Wolf*. In her theatre, she had said in a lecture in 1934:

We do not shun fairytales and dreams, but we want the dreams to picture a new world that can and must be created. We want seven-league boots and magic carpets to be transformed into automobiles and planes... [The children of the future] will perform fairytale deeds in the real world.

So there would be warm-up sessions for the children on preparations for defence, and the importance of surveillance, woodcrafts, the need to question the accepted wisdom of grown-ups, and on the class struggle, followed by fairytales featuring inspirational heroes and easy-to-follow stories about loyalty, steadfastness and ingenuity. Natalia Sats referred to her audience of Young Pioneers as 'my activists'. Audience participation was encouraged. The year of spring 1935 to spring 1936, the year of *Peter's* first performances, has been called Stalin's unofficial 'year of the child', with images of intrepid young citizens all over the propaganda posters, the First Congress on children's literature, and numerous articles in *Pravda* and *Izvestia* about the contrast between growing up in Nazi Germany and in the enlightened Soviet Union. But Natalia Sats also understood that 'fairytale deeds in the real world' had to be presented in ways which would appeal emotionally to children: it would be counter-productive simply to harangue from the stage. When she commissioned Prokofiev, she was well aware that the resulting piece had to be on message as well. After all, she was part of the inner circle of the Stalinist establishment. As Simon Morrison, Professor of Music at Princeton and author of *The People's Artist – Prokofiev's Soviet Years* (2009), has said:

> There was this split in the composition... Sats knew that her task was to make a lesson – about right-thinking youth challenging the representatives of the old world; the idea of taming nature on the one hand, and taming anonymous external threats on the other; the idea that we are in paradise and there is a dark shadow just beyond the fence – we need to be on our guard against it. What is beyond the fence is the external enemy, which is really what reinforced the Stalinist regime – and which we see played over and over again.

On the other hand, Sats was also aware that Prokofiev was uniquely placed to create a piece that would be *child-centred*. Morrison continues:

> There were no classes in the Soviet Union except children –
> that was the one privileged class. And so there were plenty of
> opportunities for Prokofiev to write music for children, and
> when Sats approached him, she knew full well that here was a
> composer who throughout his career had been interested in music
> for children and youth – this was to some degree his mindset. The
> spoilt child from the provinces who was indulged and who indulged
> his fantasies…

Natalia Sats met Prokofiev in the Metropole Hotel Moscow, to discuss the idea of a 'fairytale to tell children about the instruments of the orchestra'. It would have narration – 'never done before' – and it was she who initially recommended the poetess – who 'adored Prokofiev's music' – to write the words in verse. But 'sparks flew from Prokofiev's eyes', and Sats quickly learned that he had a lot of temperament: 'the balance between words and music' was all wrong. But they soon settled into a pattern of work, and discovered that they were in synch about the project. Prokofiev wrote the words and music; Sats made suggestions about instruments and the characters. She later said she was apprehensive about seeming too clichéd in her ideas; but that Prokofiev was always receptive. The very first performance of *Pioneer Petia* took place in Natalia Sats' office at the Theatre on 15 April 1936, with Prokofiev at the piano and 'Auntie Natasha' narrating, in front of ten selected 'activists'. This was the pre-score version. They loved it and asked for the final processional march to be repeated three times. The second performance – this time of the fully scored version – was at a matinée concert of the Moscow Philharmonia. This was not a success. The third performance, and the most celebrated, was on 5 May 1936 at the Central Children's Theatre, as a contribution to a Festival of Soviet Art, with Sats narrating and the children in the audience all sitting in serried ranks wearing their red neckerchiefs and white shirts with badges of rank sewn on them – and with a large red banner decorating the auditorium.

1936 was certainly turning into a confusing year for Soviet composers. Shostakovich had been slammed by *Pravda* for his opera *Lady Macbeth of the Mtsensk District*, after Comrade Stalin had walked out of it, and there was much talk in Moscow of purging 'hostile influences on Soviet art' and eradicating bourgeois, anti-democratic Modernism. Perhaps the safest thing a composer could do was to write for children – the time-honoured resort to fairytales and metaphor at times of repression. Can *Peter and the Wolf* be read as an allegory – in any but the most generalised terms? Prokofiev called it an answer to 'the need for music for children [which] could be clearly felt', rather than any *overt* political statement. I have heard it seriously suggested recently that the wolf was 'a saboteur', the duck a vacillating member of the bourgeoisie, and the hunters the secret police. I've also heard that the wolf was meant to be Comrade Stalin himself! Musicologists like their Soviet musical heroes to have been quietly subversive in the dark days of Stalin. In this case, not at all likely. Far too literal. As we have seen, the subtexts were more diffuse – about 'the dark shadow beyond the fence'. There were plenty of more obviously didactic works performed at Sats' Theatre, and this was not one of them. 'Auntie Natasha' would simply introduce each of the instruments, then – as Natalia Sats – narrate the story, 'to keep the children interested – discovering the instrumental sounds without concentrating on the instruments themselves'. Suzie Templeton's *Peter and the Wolf*, by contrast, opts to tell the story entirely through pictures rather than words. As she told a group of students at the RCA, 'from the very beginning I realised this film could not have a narrator; the work of leading the visual imagination is now done by the animation; this way, the pictures are not just illustrative'.

Since it was originally written, *Peter and the Wolf* has inevitably attracted several animators, who always seem to like animating animals and moving them to music, which is so much easier than directing them live – a point made by the Soviet film-maker and theorist Sergei

Eisenstein in his celebrated essay on Walt Disney. Eisenstein had visited the Disney studio in autumn 1930, where he had his photograph taken shaking hands with Mickey Mouse: 'from Mickey Mouse to Willie the Whale', he wrote after viewing the Disney portmanteau film *Make Mine Music*, '...no one else has managed to make the movement of a drawing's outline conform to the melody'. For Eisenstein, Disney's particular skill was superimposing the 'drawing' of a melody over a graphic drawing. Not surprising then, that the most important animated version of *Peter and the Wolf* was by Disney and that Chuck Jones created a version too – albeit in his twilight years. The Disney version is fascinating – animated by some of the people who'd recently made *Pinocchio*, *Bambi* and *The Three Caballeros*, and directed by Clyde Geronimi, who had specialised in Pluto shorts during the Second World War, as well as directing the chilling anti-war *Education For Death* and parts of *Victory Through Air Power*. Ward Kimball was responsible for the cat, Eric Larson the duck. It, too, is of its moment, because it has the main title in Russian and a joke about the wolf in Russian when the bird writes the word волк – meaning 'volk' or grey Russian wolf – in the snow, to warn the hunters; it seems to celebrate the alliance at the end of the Second World War between the Soviet Union and America, Stalin and Roosevelt, which had already begun to fall apart by summer 1946 when the film was released. And it gives the animals names – Sasha the bird, Sonia the duck, Ivan the cat – and the dancing, bearded hunters with their blunderbusses are called Vladimir, Misha and Yasha. The prolix narration, spoken by Sterling Holloway in a high falsetto voice – midway between adult and child – engages closely with the characters and even intervenes in the story at key moments. There is a happy ending. Sasha the bird finds his lost playmate Sonia the duck hiding in a tree – despite appearances she hasn't been eaten by the wolf after all. 'Oh this is a most wonderful, wonderful day', says Sterling Holloway. This was not how the story originally ended. Holloway's was the earliest post-war recording.

Disney's *Peter and the Wolf* was part of the first feature to be completed by the studio after the war – *Make Mine Music* (originally called *Swing Street*) in which it was the seventh segment out of ten. The tenth was *The Whale Who Wanted to Sing at the Met* (or, as it was later known when re-released as a free-standing short, *Willie the Operatic Whale*), the one which Eisenstein appreciated so much. The idea of animating *Peter* had been on the stocks for some time, in the wake of *Fantasia*; Disney originally planned to vary the programme content of his 'concert film' in later releases, with new versions circulating every year. Another possible entry was extracts from Wagner's *Ring* cycle with Grumpy and Dopey as the Nibelungen. How did Walt Disney come to be animating a symphonic fairytale about a Soviet Young Pioneer? In January 1938, Prokofiev travelled to the United States – where, as he said in his application to the Committee on Arts Affairs: 'I shall have the opportunity to make favourable reference to the success of Soviet music.' In Boston, he conducted the American première of *Peter and the Wolf* – a performance which he treated as a rebuke to the Boston musical establishment for having failed to appreciate his more complex full-length works. In Denver, after other concerts Prokofiev saw Disney's *Snow White and the Seven Dwarfs* two nights running. Then he arrived on 26 February for a three-week stay in Los Angeles, at the invitation of the artists' agent Rudolph Polk, who hoped to arrange for Prokofiev to become a Hollywood film composer. It was Polk who took the composer to meet Disney, at his studio, on 28 February with the aim of selling *Peter* 'for one of his animated cartoons'. Also present was the composer Leigh Harline. *Pinocchio* and *Fantasia* were in preparation. Disney expert Brian Sibley takes up the story:

> It's interesting that Prokofiev had so recently seen *Snow White*, and I think what engaged him so much was the fact that the story was told through music. So he was fascinated to see "le papa de Mickey Mouse" as he called him, and hoped to find out what made the man tick.

Prokofiev gave a personal performance of *Peter* on the studio's old upright piano, while Polk translated and narrated it – 'one of the studio's most exciting adventures' which Disney re-enacted, complete with a lookalike playing Prokofiev, as a curtain-raiser to the cartoon version in a mid-1950s episode of *Disneyland* on television. Walt looked on, dressed in a tight knitted jumper, entranced. According to him, Prokofiev introduced the piece by saying, 'I've composed this with the hope that I'd get to see you and that you would make a cartoon with my music': in other words, that *Peter* was written specially for Disney. Which, if he *did* say it 'in the flush of the moment', was very far from the truth. The story does date from the period when Walt Disney famously observed to Leopold Stokowski of the centaurs and centaurettes in *Fantasia*, 'I think this thing will *make* Beethoven'. On the plus side, it has been suggested that the character of the duck in Prokofiev's libretto *may* have been inspired by Donald, who had made his first appearance in 1934 in *The Wise Little Hen*. Animated cartoons were very popular with multilingual Soviet audiences at the time. So there could have been a connection – if not a direct one.

Prokofiev then visited Paramount Studios, as Simon Morrison relates:

> He was swept up into this world of being fêted. Paramount talked of recruiting him to write musical comedies, and a lot of promises were made to him, and suggestions about the potential he could have as a Hollywood composer. His wife Lina loved this to the point where she fatefully rented an apartment – signed a lease there. [This was later used in evidence against her, after the couple had split up in 1941, and after Lina was arrested in 1948.] But they couldn't stay because their own children were stuck back in Moscow going to school – and were effectively hostages… And that was the grim reality. The discussions about *Peter and the Wolf* were part of a mix of selling this piece on the one hand – and of several other overtures he received in Los Angeles. There was so much sadness built into this moment of his career.

Sadness, after the happy ending supplied by Walt Disney, who bought the rights to *Peter* – via Rudolph Polk – for 1500 dollars a while later. In March 1938, Prokofiev returned from his final trip abroad to Moscow.

Where Disney's version was concerned, after the contract had been signed in February 1941, the earliest concepts for *Peter and the Wolf* – backgrounds and characters – were much more 'Russian' than the final cut: colourful folk crafts for the backgrounds, Peter with the close-cropped hair and uniform of a Young Pioneer on a Soviet propaganda poster, a wooden rifle rather than a pop-gun, a grungy-looking wolf with tufts of hair sticking out of its bald skin. Later, Peter would have long fair hair, a red nose and a cute ill-fitting uniform. Walt Disney's attitude to Russian culture at this time is interesting. He was evidently flattered by Sergei Eisenstein's visit and enthusiasm (they corresponded for some time after 1930) and to judge by the *Disneyland* re-enactment, was thrilled to meet 'the great Russian composer'. Awestruck, even. Animator Ollie Johnston recollected that the *Peter* idea was indeed originally developed for *Fantasia II* in the early 1940s, and revived in 1944. Disney's attitude to Soviet culture, and to the Red Menace, was soon to change. Sterling Holloway's over-explanatory commentary in *Peter* suggests that Disney was far from confident about whether the original would be fully understood by an American audience. The words were embellished and the music pruned and re-scored to match the visual action, Mickey Mouse-style. Holloway (who subsequently recorded his narration twice) treated the text as if it was a radio drama, and often spoke over the music. Prokofiev intended them to be separate, and in discussion with Natalia Sats explicitly said that the sounds 'are not sound imitations as in an animated cartoon, but real musical expressions of the life of these images'.

Back in Moscow, Prokofiev was experiencing a new darkness on the cultural scene, as Simon Morrison explains:

> 'It was not quite yet the period of the great purges, when people disappeared in the apartment building where he lived – that

was about to happen. But there was a really strong sense that artists needed to perform to this nascent ideal platform – which involved educating children in a certain way, and conforming to what became known as "Socialist Realism".'

The previous August, August 1937, Natalia Sats had been arrested, interrogated in the Lubyanka and sentenced to five years in a Siberian work camp as 'the wife of a traitor of the motherland' – she was married to the now-disgraced Commissar of Trade – a wife who had also consorted with artistic counter-revolutionaries. Her two children became wards of the state. The year of the twentieth anniversary of the Revolution also saw the Committee on Arts Affairs seriously tightening its grip, and a new artistic manifesto published in *Pravda*: soon, all art would be expected to toe the party line. Prokofiev defended himself in print – 'Yes, I have been to the West, but this does not mean I have become a "Westerner"', he wrote, and added that he had always been interested in melody and folk tunes and making his work accessible. But his political music became, of necessity, more and more doctrinaire, and he began a series of compositions in which he tried to curry favour with the regime. His return to Moscow had been far from triumphal… which eventually led to serious depression. He died following a cerebral haemorrhage, at the age of 61, on the evening of 5 May 1953 – about fifty minutes before Joseph Stalin also died. Prokofiev's obituary did not appear in the Soviet press until thirteen days later, long after his passing had been announced and discussed in the West. While tearful throngs queued up in Red Square to catch a glimpse of Stalin lying in state, musicians in Moscow were weeping more privately. It looked as though they were weeping for Stalin… Where subsequent powers-that-be were concerned, it was only in 1981, on the ninetieth anniversary of the composer's birth, that the Central Committee finally agreed to honour his music at a major festival.

Meanwhile, over in the West, Pioneer Petia had long since emigrated and was starting his new life – as a children's favourite. Michael Biel, a retired College professor of broadcasting, has a vast collection of spoken-word recordings – including '300 out of about 400, in over a dozen languages' versions of *Peter and the Wolf*, starting in 1939 with the Richard Hale version, the first.

> When they were recording a 1995 orchestral version, the Russian musicians had to learn the piece: they knew the title but were unfamiliar with the music… They don't know *Peter and the Wolf* like we do in the United States. There have only ever been four recordings in the Russian language: the first with Vera Maretskaya in 1947 (never reissued), the second with Nikolai Litvinov (1957), the third with Natalia Sats (as late as 1970) and the fourth with K.M Rumyanova (1980), though there have been un-narrated, orchestral versions. There have been no recordings, so far as I know, in any of the other Soviet languages…

In Russia, he adds, the piece tends to be profiled as 'for puppet shows and children's ballets' and kids' theatre – for live performance in a didactic context. Not for grown-up performances or recordings, but for jamborees. In the West, it has since the late 1930s been universalised as *the* introduction to the instruments of the orchestra, a very different musical legacy. Maybe, for some listeners with long memories of Soviet Young Pioneer days, there is a whiff of tainted goods about the piece as well. Maybe. In the West, Peter long ago shed his red neckerchief and badge and entered the memories of successive generations of music-loving children and their well-intentioned parents.

While the Disney Studio was busy working on *Peter and the Wolf*, for *Make Mine Music*, over in England Benjamin Britten was composing *The Young Person's Guide to the Orchestra* – originally written, also with spoken narration, for the film documentary *The Instruments of the Orchestra*. Disney claimed that *Peter* was written specially for him to film – but the Britten piece certainly *was* written for a film, though today most recordings and performances dispense with the words *and* the film. A main theme and variations introduce listeners to each of the four sections of the orchestra – strings, woodwind, brass, percussion –

and then to each individual instrument. 'First', begins the narrator, 'you will hear a theme by the great English composer, Henry Purcell, played by the whole orchestra…' Then the theme is played, in various forms, six times. *The Instruments of the Orchestra* was part of the postwar celebration of the resurgence of beleaguered British culture: its first performances coincided with the popular exhibition *Britain Can Make It* at the Victoria and Albert Museum (wittily subtitled by some visitors, fed up with rationing, 'but Britain can't have it'), the foundation of the Arts Council in August 1946 and the origins of the BBC Third Programme. The title of the piece was intended to be a parody of old-fashioned, dusty school textbooks.

Like the Prokofiev, it uses narration plus musical sound to put over its message – though this time not with a story and characters. Meanwhile, also in 1946, back at Warners in Hollywood Chuck Jones – who had been an animator since the mid-1930s and a director since 1937 – was beginning to find his own voice, and his fast and furious style of using it. He had introduced Pepé le Pew the year before, and in 1949 was to take Bugs Bunny to the opera for the first (but not the last) time in *Long Haired Hare*. The second major animated version of *Peter and the Wolf*, pre-Suzie Templeton, is by Jones. Or rather, it is partly by Jones. Produced in 1995 for television (it won an Emmy that year for 'outstanding primetime children's program'). George Daugherty's *Peter and the Wolf* combines live action – single mother Annie (Kirstie Alley) and her son Peter (Ross Malinger) visit grandfather (Lloyd Bridges) in the old country which may be Switzerland and may be meant to be Russia – with an animated retelling of the story. Chuck Jones gets a variety of credits: 'animated characters designed and created by…', 'executive consultant…', 'animated characters copyright Chuck Jones', but the animated sections of the film were in fact made by Cosgrove Hall in Manchester, England, and directed by Jean Flynn. If only *Peter and the Wolf* had been reworked in the manic, slapstick style of Jones's classic shorts for Warners: Daffy Duck, Road Runner and Sylvester could perhaps have hunted Wile E. Coyote, with Elmer Fudd as the grumpy grandfather or maybe as one of the hunters. Instead, despite a few characteristic moments – the 'deliriously dizzy duck', the scaredy ginger-cat lunging for the bird, falling into the pond and then shaking its paws in time with the music (an idea reworked in Templeton's version) and the hunters as bearded gnomes resembling Inspector Clouseau only with deerstalkers, blunderbusses and yellow wellies – this version is both dull and sentimental, and the animation is as one-dimensional as the characterisations. 'I love you, Peter, I really do,' says the grandfather at the end, while in the bird's nest 'six new babies hatched amid all the excitement', the duck falls safely out of the wolf's mouth and we are told that 'the wolf will be safe at the zoo'. At the moment when the wolf eats the duck, the film reverts to live action with young Peter saying on behalf of the presumed audience who might find the violence too red in tooth and claw, 'I don't like it. It's too sad' – which is a clue as to which way the ending would then go. *Peter and the Wolf* ends with Ross Malinger putting on a yellow peaked cap and buttoned tunic to walk into the animation. And so the cycle begins again. Early 1950s Chuck Jones would have made so much more of the story.

Suzie Templeton's version is, as expected from the director of *Dog*, much darker than this. It is a whole world away from post-war Walt Disney and twilight Chuck Jones. Peter is clumsy and unhappy, with a face resembling the poster of *Angela's Ashes*. He's a boy with attitude, a hero for today rather than a Young Pioneer, and he plays against his sweet, happy musical theme: as Templeton has recalled,

> The first thing I did on this project was to draw a picture of Peter – and that stayed right to the end. It was the picture of a troubled boy, with his own cares and troubles. I also wanted Peter to be a hero in *our* eyes – in 1936, those heroic deeds had a very different context. To catch a wild animal now, and put it into a zoo, is not really what we think is heroic any more. A hero is someone who stands for a strong ethical position of his own – and that's what I wanted for Peter.

The bird is greasy and grungy rather than fluffy and has a broken wing: not a songbird as in the original libretto but a stubborn crow. The duck is no longer a standard farmyard duck but a long-necked, white, Indian Running Duck, who is rather stupid and resembles a skittle. The grandfather is angry most of the time. The cat is overweight – a lap-cat who dreams of himself as a hunter, rather like a Russian version of Garfield. The wolf is female this time: originally, there was to have been an epilogue of her with her cubs. And one of the hunters has become the macho bad guy, a modern Muscovite and militiaman with a gun. Instead of Prokofiev's bright and breezy opening of the published libretto – 'early one morning, Peter opened the gate and walked out into the big green meadow…' – this version of *Peter and the Wolf* opens with a long visual introduction without music, which sets a threatening tone: the run-down and fortified farm at the edge of the forest, the dangerous town where Peter gets thrown into a skip and has a rifle poked in his face. Instead of being set in the past – like most fairytales, once upon a time – it's set in today's Russia mixing new with old, cars with circuses, Western products with old Russia. And as for the ending it, too, is very different from Prokofiev's. The original story went: 'And if you listened very carefully, you could hear the duck quacking inside the wolf's stomach, because the wolf in his hurry had swallowed her alive.' The wolf is taken off in processional triumph to the zoo. Well, Suzie Templeton ends the story with the wolf being set free – limping off into the forest – and the trigger-happy hunter being trapped in the net instead. Earlier shots of a butcher's shop, stuffed animals, a poster for a dancing bear have prepared us for this animal rights twist. The spirit of the duck survives, she is saying, at Peter's greatest moment of understanding. The story has been about the irrational fear of the beast and about a young boy discovering his own identity.

But the score is unchanged – though without the narrator the musical cues come in at very different moments in the story and often for different purposes. This version of *Peter and the Wolf* is a mixture of stop-frame model animation and computer-generated imagery, using the great expertise of the Polish animators at Se-Ma-For, a studio which as it happens was founded in the year of *Make Mine Music*. There were two main sets of puppets – one (scale 1:5) for action scenes and bigger ones for intimate scenes and close-ups. The forest set alone was 22 metres by 16 metres, with 360° coverage. Computers were then used to blot out the metal rigs which held the puppets, and in a couple of scenes to paint in the balloons; they originally tried models but the models looked too solid. So the balloons were computer-generated. But this is not a CGI film: it is definitely a work of puppet animation. It sometimes took a whole day to film one and a half seconds of finished footage. Apart from the general revisionist take on Prokofiev's story, the most memorable moments in Templeton's film include the close-up, which lasts some thirty seconds, of Peter's face when the 'wolf' theme is heard for the first time; Peter's touchingly close relationship with the duck and the bird – he's more comfortable with creatures than humans, it seems, and it is the bird's example which gives him courage; the expression on the cat's face when it discovers it is trapped up a tree after a branch has broken under its very considerable weight; the grandfather's elderly hands – somehow, the latex has been made to look skin-like, taut and blotchy; the wolf's eyes, as it dawns on her that instead of trying to get away from Peter, she should turn on him; and that ending. Which gives the old folktale a fresh emotional punch.

Suzie Templeton's *Peter and the Wolf* was premièred with live orchestra in September 2006 at the Royal Albert Hall, London; then shown on Channel 4 on Christmas Eve and again with live orchestra in Exeter Cathedral in February 2007. It deservedly won an Academy Award for best short animation.

But in the end, it is as a piece of 'words *and* music' – by far the best-known of Prokofiev's many works, at least in the West – that *Peter* has firmly established itself in the classical repertory. The composer subtitled the piece 'a symphonic fairytale', and seems to have regarded it as a simplified symphony with a narrative – rather than as a children's story with musical illustrations. Simon Morrison summarises the long-term musical legacy of *Peter and the Wolf*:

> It is brilliant at several levels. When you think about how quickly he
> composed it, in four days followed by orchestration the following

week. Quite miraculous! The characterisations of animal behaviour are perfect. He took the animals as not simply about the animals – but as references to other works in the canon. The music of the bird comes from the "Bluebird" pas de deux in *The Sleeping Beauty*; the wolf music harks back to the "Wolf's Glen" scene in *Der Freischütz*; the grandfather is an old *opera buffa* relic. So the piece is coded all the way through. It is about Prokofiev's imagination – but the score is about Peter's imagination as well: whether or not these events are real or not, and the music tells us this; maybe those events are just a dream the boy had. The theme associated with Peter is one that passes through different keys – and each of the keys it travels through ends up being attached to one of those creatures. Peter's theme is the entire tonal range encapsulated – and then we have all those keys attached to the duck and the bird and so forth. So it's all his own cosmos. Kids immediately get it…

And so did Natalia Sats, in April 1936. Even when the piece was still called *How Pioneer Petia Captured the Wolf*.

THANKS TO

David Nice, Prokofiev's biographer, who helped in the early stages of this essay; to Professor Catriona Kelly for her insights into Soviet childhood and to Professor Simon Morrison for his knowledge of the composer's Soviet years; to Michael Biel, for sharing his astonishing record collection; to Brian Sibley, for his account of Prokofiev's meeting with Walt Disney; to Suzie Templeton, for her film and her reminiscences about it. Also very useful were the issue of the *Three Oranges Journal*, number 12 November 2006, and *Sketches from My Life* by Natalia Sats (Raduga, Moscow, 1985). The translation of Prokofiev's manuscript was made for BBC Radio 4 'Archive Hour' (Christmas, 2014), produced by Nick Jones. Grateful thanks to Nick, as well.

10

We Live in Gothic Times…

Introduction

ANGELA CARTER *wrote in 1974 that in Gothic fiction, 'characters and events are exaggerated beyond reality, to become symbols, ideas, passions…style will tend to become ornate and unnatural – and thus operate against the perennial human desire to believe the word as fact…[the Gothic] retains a singular moral function – that of provoking unease'. The Gothic should be relocated, and was just beginning to be relocated, in critical circles, she was glad to note, in relation to realism in literature and the visual arts and at the same time associated more precisely with the realms of imagination and desire. Why do we tend to expel from our lives so much that is magical, suggestive, strange and fantastical? Why separate the fantastical and the shadowy from 'real life'? Why not break down the conventional barriers between them? 'I've got absolutely nothing against realism. But there's realism and realism. The questions that I ask myself I think are very much to do with reality.' To do with the negotiations we have to make, the images we have to deconstruct, to find any sort of reality for ourselves. But this was not Gothic for Gothic's sake – it was Gothic as literary device towards a small-p political end, which remained remarkably consistent throughout Carter's professional life. Since the mid-1970s, this set of literary strategies has become more and more fashionable – and increasingly difficult to separate from the defensive/aggressive self-image of some academics in literature departments – to the point where it has long since become received wisdom, the new orthodoxy. Shortly before she died, Angela Carter said that 'the fin in this particular siècle is beginning rather earlier than usual'. This essay, on the rise – and spread – of 'the new Gothic', was originally written for a critical anthology to accompany the* Gothic Nightmares *exhibition at Tate Britain.*

We Live in Gothic Times…

AT THE TIME when Angela Carter was writing *The Bloody Chamber*, in the mid- to late-1970s, prejudice against Gothic fiction from within the academic literary establishment was firmly entrenched – which, to Angela, was part of the fun. The Gothic was thought to be a form of fiction that was deliberately sensationalist; with heroes, heroines and villains who were merely puppets – acting out dramas which had no serious connection with the facts or morals of everyday life – in narratives which were disjointed and irrational; an ephemeral fad with formulaic conventions (antiquated castles, hidden secrets, hauntings, aristocratic villains, put-upon maidens, eighteenth-century heroes and heroines projected back into historical environments) which only deserved to survive as a cult, at best a symptom of nasty consumerism at the end of the eighteenth century and since. Edmund Burke wrote approvingly of 'the terrible sublime' as an antidote to mental lethargy and boredom. Horace Walpole, seven years later, agreed that 'Terror, the author's principal engine, prevents the story from ever languishing'. So this was sensationalism for sensationalism's sake, best read or viewed late at night when the critical faculties were half-asleep. Jane Austen's novels, by contrast, could be read in daylight.

She had famously satirised the craze for Gothic fiction – which had peaked in England during the 1790s – in *Northanger Abbey*, published posthumously a few months before *Frankenstein* at Christmas 1817, though mainly written in the late 1790s, a time when 35 per cent of *all* the novels being published in England were Gothics. In the genteel surroundings of Bath's recently rebuilt Pump Room round the corner from 5, Abbey Churchyard where Mary Shelley had stayed, her two heroines had discussed the latest bloodcurdling romances with all the breathless excitement of today's seventeen year olds texting each other about the latest schlock-horror downloads:

> 'I will read you their names directly; here they are in my pocket book, *Castle of Wolfenbach*, *Clermont*, *Mysterious Warnings*,

Necromancer of the Black Forest, Midnight Bell, Orphan of the Rhine and *Horrid Mysteries…*'

'But are they all *horrid*? Are you sure they are all horrid?'

These titles were not made up: they had all recently been published in the wake of Ann Radcliffe's huge success with the reading public from *A Sicilian Romance* (1790) onwards. Six of them had German connections, and German tales of terror, often with plots hinging on secret societies or conspiracies, were indeed popular during the later stages of the French Revolution; one of them – Regina Roche's *Clermont* (1798) – had been panned as a tired remix of Mrs Radcliffe's early work. *Northanger Abbey* remains a witty commentary on what young female readers saw in Gothic novels, at a time when real terrors were happening just across the Channel – the literary equivalent of James Gillray's celebrated etching of February 1802 *Tales of Wonder!*, which showed three young girls deeply absorbed in a Gothic collection late at night, while a hatchet-faced governess looks on. Jane Austen's judgement of Gothics was to have a very long shelf-life.

In the mid-1970s, with a few honourable exceptions, the commentators who had written in any depth about Gothic novels tended to be eccentric bibliophiles and collectors (Montague Summers' *Gothic Bibliography* (1940), running to 621 pages, was often displayed in antiquarian bookshops although a number of entries did not in fact exist), or veteran art critics with long memories who still reckoned that the Gothics had in some sense been precursors of the dream-language of Surrealism, and who spoke darkly of 'the castle question'. I can remember talking with a fellow research student (who was preparing a doctorate on medieval architecture, as it happens), who seemed a little queasy about the titles of the books I was ordering in the old round Reading Room of the British Museum. The titles resembled Jane Austen's must-read list, only they were all vampire stories. 'Admit it,' said the research student, 'you're writing about horror literature for the money, aren't you?' There couldn't possibly be any other reason. Thirty years after *The Bloody Chamber* and my preparations for *The*

Vampyre, literary-critical attitudes towards Gothic novels, and to the Gothic as aesthetic, have changed utterly, as have their cultural contexts. The International Gothic Association website now lists some fifty-three courses on the subject at undergraduate and postgraduate levels, at forty-four universities around the globe – mainly in Britain and especially the USA, but also in Australia, Bulgaria, China, France, Germany and Taiwan. At the same time, as themes within the wider culture, the Gothic, horror and fantasy have never been so widespread and deep-rooted – at least not since England in the 1790s. 'We are,' as Angela Carter put it, now living 'in Gothic times.' The sublime – in Burke's sense – has become one of the dominant aesthetics of the age. Burke defined the sublime, for him the most satisfying aesthetic experience of all, as a confrontation between the viewer or reader and extreme phenomena which triggers the emotion of terror; a strange and all-embracing mix of desire and loathing, pain and pleasure. In his list of reliable stimuli he included ruined temples, dark landscapes, howling wildernesses, gloomy forests, vicious animals, raging storms, gaping chasms and rough seas – a list that could almost be a menu for the horror novels and paintings that were shortly to come, a Burke's peerage of terror. Were he writing today, his list might still include some awe-inspiring natural phenomena – travel to dangerous places, extreme sports in remote settings, the pleasure of ruins, encountering a big animal in the wild – but even these have become in some ways predictable and mundane through endless mechanical reproduction. We experience these things, mediated through the photographs we have seen of them. So Burke's list would perhaps be just as likely to include phenomena from within the culture as well as from within 'nature': in no particular order, celluloid slashers, gross special effects, rollercoaster 'event movies', the shift from late-night B movies to mainstream spectaculars, violent rap lyrics, bestselling doorstep horror novels where the devil inhabits the central-heating unit, further up the scale writings by Angela Carter, Toni Morrison, Margaret Atwood and Joyce Carol Oates, Damien Hirst's dead cows in formaldehyde which left the artist 'feeling like Dr Frankenstein', the Chapman brothers reworking Goya's *Disasters of War*, the neo-conceptual *Sensation!* generation for whom a well-stocked mind seems to consist of a large collection of horror videos and some xeroxed extracts from Jean Baudrillard, the fashion designs of Alexander McQueen 'dealing with a dark side of my personality' – with 'something kind of Edgar Allan Poe, something kind of deep and melancholic about my collections', multimedia retreads of nineteenth-century Gothics, computer games, themed restaurants and clubs, the Goth subculture, plus of course that dizzying expansion of academic interest. The Gothic has shuffled back to centre stage, this time round revelling in its own clichés – which maybe would disqualify the contemporary genre from Burke's list of sublime stimuli after all, except for that very first confrontation when – as Burke put it – 'the mind is so utterly filled with its object, that it cannot entertain any other'. When the mind is literally blown.

It is astonishing how resilient the old stories have proved to be. Even in Alfred Hitchcock's film *Psycho* (1960), the prototype for all subsequent slasher movies, there is still the castle on the hill in the form of a clapboard gingerbread Gothic Californian mansion. So 'the castle question' continues to intrigue us, even when there is a motel down the path and showers in every suite. The associated Dracula myth has proved so flexible that in Francis Ford Coppola's lush, big-budget remake (1992), Van Helsing becomes the fundamentalist bad guy and the Count becomes the last romantic. Charles Dickens wisely wrote of ghosts in *A Christmas Tree* (1850) that 'it is worthy of remark [that they are] reducible to a very few general types and classes; for, ghosts walk in a beaten track'. The same could certainly be said of contemporary 'new Gothic' novels and films. Which incidentally shows that the foundations of the genre – in literary and visual form – are of much more than antiquarian interest. Some people reckon, as writer Geoffrey O'Brien has observed, that these 'types and classes' are:

> ...are crucial to a genre that seems to define itself by constantly
> recapitulating everything it has been... To watch many horror

movies is in some sense to watch the same movie over and over: they are drawn to their past in the same way that their characters are compelled to go back to the ancestral crypt... The rest is ornament and variations on a theme, a matter of more masks or bigger masks or more convincingly detailed masks.

This super-movie has survived many variations in the twentieth century, since the Surrealists first saw the Gothic as 'fathoming the secret depths of history': the Expressionism of the 1920s in Weimar Germany and the camp Expressionism of Hollywood in the early 1930s; the drive-in triple features of the 1950s; the rise of Hammer Films, where British cinema discovered sex and the gore was presented for the first time in seaside postcard colours; the Italian pop surrealism of the 1960s; the psycho killers and seriously dysfunctional families of the 1970s and 1980s; the shift from margin to mainstream in the 1990s; above all, the change from pre-Second World War horror (where normal society was where the heroes and heroines lived) to post-Seventies horror (where the horror has become a form of liberation, and normality has itself become strange).

Throughout all this history, the more masks and bigger masks and more detailed masks have taken on a life of their own. And as a result the atmosphere surrounding horror films (and popular horror paperbacks) from the beginning has been that of a carnival sideshow – not quite respectable, a glimpse of another world where transgressive things happen, often a bit tacky (let's face it) and above all an experience which does not quite live up to the poster, the promotional gimmicks and the slightly strange showman standing outside the tent. As cultural historian David J. Skal has pointed out, the culture of horror has always had as much to do with carnival-style promotional gimmicks as with the films themselves – just like Dr Caligari standing outside his sideshow at Holstenwall Fair, and inviting the hapless students to see the somnambulist Cesare with a lot of hype and a life-sized poster which looks as though it was painted by Edvard Munch. Even in the eighteenth century, Gothic novels challenged – sometimes deliberately

– the high ground of culture, and were later to problematise high/low distinctions. The carnival gimmicks used by horror movies seldom use the same campaign tactics as what used to be called mainstream Hollywood films: the names of the stars, the quality of the production, the timeliness of the story. Instead they blare out a warning or a challenge usually in the colour yellow: 'Warning! The Monster demands a mate!'; 'When the Screen Screams You'll Scream Too…'; 'You'll wish it were only a nightmare' and my personal favourite (from Robert Aldrich's *Whatever Happened to Baby Jane?*), 'Sister, sister / oh so fair / why is there blood / all over your hair?' These are tales of terror, and unashamed of it. The promotional gimmicks are the modern-day equivalent of all those playful prefaces – starting with Horace Walpole's for *Otranto* – with their counterfeit origins, lost manuscripts, false archaisms and bogus translations. Realist novels did not require these playful gimmicks: their high moral purpose could surely speak for itself.

Stephen King tells the story of film producers Samuel Z. Arkoff and James H. Nicholson, who were the kings of AIP drive-in movies between 1954 and 1968. Their pre-production style was simple and effective. They would think up a catchy title, trawl interest in it, then produce an even more catchy poster, trawl interest in that, and only then – if there was enough take-up – would they begin to think about actually making a film. Title first, poster second, film third. Producer William Castle, in the late 1950s, added a few carnival refinements of his own: the offer of medical treatment, for those who found the horror too much; insuring audiences with Lloyds of London if any of them should die during *Macabre*; some cinema seats wired to produce mild electric shocks for *The Tingler*. His autobiography was called *Step Right Up! I'm Gonna Scare the Pants Off America*.

Astonishingly, some of the visuals used in these campaigns and movies came indirectly – often very indirectly – from the world of visual art. The monster played by Karloff in James Whale's *Frankenstein* (1931) became not a new Adam, but a thing of scars and stitches and skewers – probably based by makeup designer Jack Pierce on a memorable image of mad aristocrats entitled *The Chinchillas* from Goya's series of prints *Caprichos/Caprices* (1799). The monster's female victim – being carried or lying in terror on a bed – in *Frankenstein* and progeny as often as not derived from Fuseli's painting *The Nightmare*. The bride of Frankenstein has a hairdo based on the ancient bust of Nefertiti, which had recently attracted publicity when exhibited in Berlin. Skull Island in *King Kong* is from Böcklin's *Isle of the Dead*. Norman Bates' Gothic mansion deliberately echoes Edward Hopper's *House by the Railroad*. The *Alien* design is blood-kin to Francis Bacon's *Figures at the base of a Crucifixion*. Edvard Munch's *Scream* is everywhere, as is the gnarled dying oak tree and waxing moon from Caspar David Friedrich's *Two Men Contemplating the Moon*. The shadow of Friedrich lies over most of *Nosferatu*. And so on. Much of the art has come from Northern Europe in the late eighteenth and nineteenth centuries, a set of references carried by émigré production designers and art directors who fled to Hollywood.

In the end, the patter of the carnival barker seems to boil down to this: he assumes we want to be terrified; he assumes we want to see, from the relative safety of our cinema seat, the horror that normally would not dare to speak its name; he assumes – like Edmund Burke – that we enjoy 'desire with loathing strangely mixed' or 'the tempestuous loveliness of terror', as Coleridge and Shelley put it. Charles Dickens' fat boy in *The Pickwick Papers* expressed the thing more bluntly: 'I wants to make your flesh creep.' We believe these old, old stories and we don't believe them, both at the same time. We approach them as we do the carnival magician in *The Wizard of Oz*, even when we have realised he is the charlatan behind the curtain.

Much of the recent critical debate about Gothic novels – and horror cinema – has tended to mask or perhaps exorcise this basic function of the genre – which is to scare its readers and viewers in enjoyable ways – by solemnly deconstructing the words on the page or the images on the screen into the psychological or socio-political elements which may lie beneath them; in other words, by reading what is between the lines rather than what is on them. As Jerrold E. Hogle has recently written, in his *Introduction* to the *Cambridge Companion to Gothic Fiction* (2002):

> No other form of writing or theatre is as insistent as Gothic on juxtaposing potential revolution and possible reaction – about gender, sexuality, race, class, the colonisers versus the colonised, the physical versus the metaphysical, and abnormal versus normal psychology – and leaving both extremes sharply before us and far less resolved than the conventional endings in most of these works claim them to be.

The eccentric bibliomania of the pioneering commentators, and the old-style literary history which paralleled it, even the careful speculations by Angela Carter on the 'singular moral function' of the Gothic and her own practice as a novelist, have made way for an embattled kind of defiance of the literary establishment (whatever that may now be) with its great tradition and Enlightenment ideas and preference for the realist tradition, the non-magical kind. The specific enemy is Augustan/neo-classical writers and critics; the more general enemy is most literary critics pre-1985. This defiance chimes with the diffuse 'postmodernism' which has been in the ether at the same time – postmodernism with its hall of mirrors, its fascination with simulacra, forgeries and the artificial, its suspicion of 'natural' appearances and its emphasis on intertextuality rather than authorial intention; the twilight of the real has proved spookily appropriate to the Gothic. It all seemed so promising, when Angela Carter first wrote about it. Maybe today's defiance is also, in part, a defensiveness – like aspects of Film Studies in the same years, which began by explaining visual images but soon preferred to explain them away, as if the commentators were scared of enjoying themselves. Where the Gothic novel is concerned, the key intellectual context is identity politics in the late twentieth century – gender, race, post-colonialism – and the key entry points have been Freud's essay on *The Uncanny* (1919), about how familiar desires and fears particularly scare us when they reappear in unfamiliar guises, and Julia Kristeva's *Powers of Horror* (1980), about how the repressed is 'abjected' or discarded onto the Other and how 'the abject' can challenge the deepest roots of our identity. Also influential have been essays by Roland Barthes and Umberto Eco, on 'open texts' which break the flow and emphasise the arbitrariness of the sign and 'closed texts' which simply contribute to the flow and present the word as fact: many Gothic novels may *seem* closed but are *really* open.

So Gothic novels have become texts, above all other forms of fiction, where 'the repressed' can return, where 'the abject' can be disguised, and where social and political anxieties can be displaced – waiting for critics from today's more liberated perspectives to disinter them. There have been debates about definitions of 'the Gothic' – should the term apply, strictly speaking, only to the period between 1764 (*The Castle of Otranto*) and 1816 (*Frankenstein*) or maybe 1820 (Maturin's *Melmoth the Wanderer*), or should it have much broader application to the heirs of the Gothic in Victorian, twentieth- and twenty-first-century popular culture? John Ruskin famously wrote, in his *Seven Lamps of Architecture*, 'I use the word Gothic in the most extended sense as broadly opposed to classical – that it admits a richness of record altogether unlimited'. Many today would agree. Including curator Martin Myrone, who has observed:

> ...the term Gothic is also widely employed in relation to modern and contemporary literature in the English language and otherwise, cinema, art, and cultural criticism. It may be taken to refer to certain structural tendencies to distortion, the grotesque, and uncanny, rather than a definable, limited genre. As the scholarly industry around the Gothic has proliferated, so Gothicisms have multiplied, so that we might now consider a vast array of historical, generic and geographical versions of the Gothic...

Also there have been debates between those who prefer to emphasise psychoanalytical approaches (as applied to authors *and* readers) and those who are more interested in the redescription of immediate historical contexts – such as the rise of consumerism in the late eighteenth century with its ephemeral choices and shifting fashions, the expansion of the reading public, the commercialisation of publishing, the complex impact of the French Revolution, the politics of gender, all of them presenting a new challenge to fixed social hierarchies. The context of gender has led – at its best – to a welcome reappraisal of the work of Ann Radcliffe from the points of view of women's property rights and family structures in a patriarchal age. It has also led to the less welcome concept of something called 'female Gothic', which apparently empowered its authors through more subtle and sublimated forms of horror than the grosser male version; and to the absorption of *Frankenstein* into the Gothic web where it does not really belong. Psychoanalytical approaches have found Bram Stoker's *Dracula* (1897) to be particularly fertile territory, the site of every imaginable middle-class anxiety about politics, race, gender and especially sexuality with the Count turning into an all-purpose Other. Today, no one seems to be certain whether *Dracula* is in the end about repression or empowerment: it all depends on whether you are on the side of 'the crew of light' or the vampires. As Chris Baldick and Robert Mighall have wisely written, about such approaches to literary deconstruction:

> From psychoanalysis, such Gothic Criticism has taken the model of middle-class respectability divided against itself, deeply driven by and in conflict with uncontrollable forces; from post-structuralism it has taken the model of "violent hierarchies", in which the dominant constructs its identity by the constant suppression of the subordinate; and from neo-Marxist theory it has taken a model of the "political unconscious", the unsaid of a given historical period, which modern criticism is called upon to articulate, finding in the past "subversive" validations of the desires and agendas of the present...

This judgment is harsh, but it certainly fits some of the more extreme contributions to the burgeoning sub-discipline of Gothic Studies. Baldick and Mighall conclude that it is as if literary criticism itself has become a Gothic project creating its own melodramas through which to confront villains within the crumbling hierarchies of the academy. One welcome side-effect of this general reappraisal of the Gothic has been in publishing reissues of important or obscure texts and documents in useful critical editions; and critical debates in the form of substantial anthologies of articles by leading scholars in the field, such as the Oxford and Cambridge *Companions*.

Horace Walpole, in April 1765, wrote of the 'liberty to expatiate through the boundless realms of invention' which his 'Gothic Story' had made possible. The Gothic – as a critical, literary and visual subject – has certainly contained legions. For much of the nineteenth century and much of the twentieth, the Gothic was waiting in the wings. Now it is centre stage. The last time I visited William Beckford's Tower, up Lansdown Hill in Bath, I was greeted by the sight of an Italian film-crew shooting a soft-porn Satanist sequence for a horror movie in the graveyard where the author of *Vathek* is buried. At least, that's what they *said* they were doing. *The History of Caleph Vathek*, the Oriental tale of 1786 – admittedly an exercise in sensual indulgence in the first place, with a barrage of bizarre images and perverse sensations – has certainly travelled a long way since the late eighteenth century. From oriental-erotic fantasy by a man who two years earlier had been driven out of British high society after revelations of a homosexual romance – to oriental-erotic horror fantasy featuring scantily clad starlets with large breasts, intended for the Euro-exploitation circuit. *Vathek* has had quite a journey. Or has it? The film-makers still felt compelled to return to the ancestral crypt…

Index

www.ingramcontent.com/pod-product-compliance
Ingram Content Group UK Ltd.
Pitfield, Milton Keynes, MK11 3LW, UK
UKHW031105020325
455687UK00007B/75